LIB'

This
an

Managing to Change?

The Future of Work Series

Series Editor: **Peter Nolan,** Director of the ESRC Future of Work Programme and the Montague Burton Professor of Industrial Relations at Leeds University Business School in the UK.

Few subjects could be judged more vital to current policy and academic debates than the prospects for work and employment. *The Future of Work* series provides the much needed evidence and theoretical advances to enhance our understanding of the critical developments most likely to impact on people's working lives.

Titles include:

Michael White, Stephen Hill, Colin Mills and Deborah Smeaton
MANAGING TO CHANGE?
British Workplaces and the Future of Work

The Future of Work Series
Series Standing Order ISBN 1-4039-1477-X

You can receive future titles in this series as they are published by placing a standing order. Please contact your bookseller or, in case of difficulty, write to us at the address below with your name and address, the title of the series and one of the ISBNs quoted above.

Customer Services Department, Macmillan Distribution Ltd, Houndmills, Basingstoke, Hampshire RG21 6XS, England

Managing to Change?

British Workplaces and the Future of Work

Michael White, Stephen Hill, Colin Mills and
Deborah Smeaton

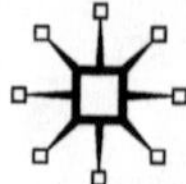

First published 2004 by
PALGRAVE MACMILLAN
Houndmills, Basingstoke, Hampshire RG21 6XS and
175 Fifth Avenue, New York, N. Y. 10010
Companies and representatives throughout the world

PALGRAVE MACMILLAN is the global academic imprint of the Palgrave Macmillan division of St. Martin's Press, LLC and of Palgrave Macmillan Ltd. Macmillan® is a registered trademark in the United States, United Kingdom and other countries. Palgrave is a registered trademark in the European Union and other countries.

ISBN 1-4039-3805-9

This book is printed on paper suitable for recycling and made from fully managed and sustained forest sources.

A catalogue record for this book is available from the British Library.

Library of Congress Cataloging-in-Publication Data
Managing to change? : British workplaces and the future of work / Michael White ... [et al.].
p. cm. – (The future of work)
Includes bibliographical references and index.
ISBN 1-4039-3805-9 (cloth)
1. Labor market–Great Britain. 2. Organizational change–Great Britain. 3. Industrial organization–Great Britain. 4. Personnel management–Great Britain. 5. Globalization–Economic aspects–Great Britain. 6. Employees–Effect of technological innovations on–Great Britain. I. Title: British workplaces and the future of work. II. White, Michael Reginald Maurice, 1938– III. Future of work (Series)

HD5765.A6M36 2004
658.3–dc22 2003070731

10 9 8 7 6 5
13 12 11 10 09 08 07 06 05

Printed and bound in Great Britain by
Antony Rowe Ltd, Chippenham and Eastbourne

Contents

List of Tables and Charts

Tables

Charts

Foreword

Launched six years ago, against the backdrop of heightened speculation about the prospects for paid employment and the shifting boundaries between paid and unpaid work, the ESRC Future of Work Programme has supported the research of more than one hundred researchers at twenty-two UK universities. The research has made important incursions into policy debates about the future of unionism in the workplace, the impact of the National Minimum Wage, the changing occupational structure of the labour force, and the position of women and ethnic minorities in UK labour markets.

The management of workplace change has been a dominant theme of many projects. Are flexible working practices increasing and what forms do they take? Is the traditional career in terminal decline, as many advocates of portfolio working have asserted in the past? Has there been a technological revolution in UK workplaces? Are employers accommodating the new work-life balance aspirations of their employees? Do they have more or less control of the conduct of their employees than in the past?

These, and other, important issues are addressed in this new book by Michael White, Colin Mills, Deborah Smeaton and Stephen Hill. Based on the most authoritative and up-to-date analysis of management practices, their research brings forward systematic, nationally representative evidence and tackles the key issues that have dominated academic and policy debates for the past decade. The analysis which they present overturns many of the current conventional wisdoms about the changing world of work in the UK.

The first in a major new Series on the Future of Work by Palgrave Macmillan, this book provides compelling evidence of the value of systematic research rather than the speculation and futurology that once dominated this vitally important subject. It is sure to have a major impact on the character of contemporary policy debate.

Professor Peter Nolan
Director, ESRC Future of Work Programme

Acknowledgements

The research used as the basis for this book was funded by the Economic and Social Research Council under its Future of Work Research Programme, Phase II, with additional support from The Work Foundation. The Change in Employer Practices Survey 2002 was carried out to the research team's design by IFF Research Ltd., under the direction of Mark Winterbotham. The authors are most grateful to the interviewers at IFF and to the 2000 managers who contributed workplace information to the survey. Special thanks are owed to members of our User Advisory Group, drawn from practitioners in business, professional and representative organisations, for the many valuable ideas they contributed. Thanks also to Patrick McGovern, who was part of the original research team, for his ideas and comments, to Alex Bryson for suggestions concerning Chapter 10, and to Peter Nolan, Director of the Future of Work Research Programme, for his support throughout. Preliminary results were presented to seminars at the Cardiff Business School and the Policy Studies Institute, and at an ESRC International Conference on Skills, Innovation and Performance (April 2003), and we thank the participants for their comments. As always, responsibility for the contents and conclusions of this book rests solely with the authors.

Glossary of Abbreviations

ACAS	Advisory Conciliation and Arbitration Service
CBI	Confederation of British Industry
CIPD	Chartered Institute of Personnel and Development
DTI	Department of Trade and Industry
EPOS	Electronic point-of-sale (equipment)
ESRC	Economic and Social Research Council
ET	Employment Tribunal
ETR	Electronic time recording (system)
HPWS	High performance work system
HR	Human resources
HRM	Human resource management
ICON	(Directive on) Information and Consultation
ICT	Information and communications technology
NES	New Earnings Survey
NVQ	National Vocational Qualification
OPRA	Occupational Pensions Regulatory Authority
PLC	Public Limited Company
TUC	Trades Union Congress
WTR	Working Time Regulations

1
Profiling Change at Work

Human beings, with their capacity for hope and dread, crave to look into the future. In ancient societies, this need was met by the utterances of oracles, and the auguries of priests or soothsayers. In the Middle Ages, public prayer and private magic were the comforts for uncertainty. But as reason and knowledge became pillars of society, the craving took a new turn: the age of Newton was also the age of astrology, regarded then as a science second to none.[1] It is not surprising that towards the end of the twentieth century, and the beginning of the twenty-first, the desire to know or guess the future should reassert itself as strongly as ever. This has been a time of momentous change, in politics, technology, lifestyles, and not least in the business world and the world of work. *Where is all this leading? What lies ahead? What must we do to cope?* We yearn for answers to these questions yet our science and our technology remain silent. To satisfy the yearning, a group of imaginative thinkers has emerged, gurus and futurologists, pioneering a novel kind of literature which has found a large and appreciative audience.[2]

This book is concerned with the same three questions highlighted above. Its focus is upon the changes unfolding at present in British workplaces, and upon the recent trends that underlie them. But it approaches these changes and trends by a wholly different route from that of the gurus and futurologists. Our portrayal of current change is based on up-to-date evidence, drawn from managers, owing little to imagination or speculation but everything to experience. From these sources it is possible, we believe, to see the direction of change – *not* in the long-term, but in the *immediate* future. The new century's first decade is taking shape now in the detailed decisions being taken and the plans being laid in a million workplaces large and small. These decisions and plans will affect every working person, and their families, over the next 5–10 years. Understanding this process of choice and change is the task of this book.

The value of imaginative futurology is perhaps not in whether it turns out to be right or wrong but in stimulating readers' imagination and shaking their complacency. In contrast, getting it right – or as right as possible – is crucial for our own evidence-based approach. Our aim is not only to engage with readers' thought processes, but particularly with those thoughts *which lead to action*. It is to stimulate thinking about the practical challenges, now and in the near future, which need to be tackled by employers and trade unions, by managers and employees, and by government policy-makers. For this, *reliable* knowledge is essential.

Our effort would of course be pointless if current changes and trends were already well-known or self-evident. But they are not. What is stated as fact in the business press, or assumed by academics, is often grossly different from what we find in our evidence. Moreover, some of the major changes which are currently spreading across industry have largely been ignored until now. This is not to point a finger of blame at anyone. Change in the workplace is rapid, complex and varied, and without systematic information it is impossible to get a reliable view of what is going on. That is where this book is meant to make its contribution.

Competitiveness

Why focus on change? In part because Britain was for decades characterised as a nation that was loath to change its ways of working, and this was seen as a prime reason for its dismal decline relative to other leading countries. This was not just a populist view or a media cliché, but was put forward by deep thinkers both from within Britain and from outside. Past diagnoses of this unwillingness to change – the 'British disease' – have included the rigidity of over-complex institutions,[3] the underqualification of management and employees,[4] and an excessive attachment, among the business class, to fine culture and country living.[5]

Most recently, Professor Michael Porter, the corporate strategy expert, was engaged by the British government to provide an assessment of the nation's competitive strengths and weaknesses. The resulting report[6] in many ways makes comforting reading. For instance, it concludes that Britain has more than held its own in recent international competition, points out the advantages of a stable economy and an efficient labour market with low unemployment, and emphasises the great contribution made by an exceptionally hard-working British populace. Yet the Porter report baulks at endorsing British management. Instead, it points to the 'slow adoption of modern management practices' (page 40) as a probable weakness. If this is so, then the British disease has yet to find its full cure. Our evidence relates directly to this issue, since it gauges the adoption and extension of management practices in all kinds of workplace.

People

But why do we focus on the management *of people* – or human resource management (HRM), as it is now usually called? To this question there are two main answers. The first follows on from the issue of competitiveness. It has been strongly argued by business strategists that people constitute the most important competitive advantage for an organisation, especially in a world awash with information and patrolled by international predators, so that the imitation rate of products and services is greatly increased.[7] It is the abilities of people, and the way those abilities are brought together, encouraged and applied, that offer the best chance of competitive success. The management of people, and the introduction of new-to-the-firm HRM practices, thus directly connect with the competitiveness debate.

The second answer is that people are deeply affected, for better or worse, by the way employers treat them, by the practices governing their work, and by the changes in those practices which they must try to adapt to. This applies in an obvious way to any employee, but it applies in an additional way to managers, whose largest task is often to manage people, and who carry the biggest responsibility for implementing change. What to Professor Porter or other business analysts are 'modern management practices' can mean, for individual employees (including or especially managers), the gain or loss of a job, the progress or collapse of a career, greater job satisfaction or intolerable strain. Our inquiry, therefore, bears directly on some of the most important aspects of personal well-being for both managers and other employees.

Ideas of change

Our primary information on current changes in the management of people has been collected through a national survey of managers. This will be sketched at a later point in this chapter (more detail is also provided in Appendix 1). Since time is strictly rationed in a management interview, designing the survey involved carefully focused selection of the key themes and issues. Equally, if we are to make sense of the mass of details provided by a large survey, we need a framework of ideas about the types of change taking place and about the important drivers of change.

In this section, we display the ideas which guided both the design of the survey and the way this book has been organised and presented. We stress, though, that these are the preliminary or *ex ante* ideas, not the end results of the inquiry. Along the way, we may well need to modify these ideas, subtracting, adding, altering the priorities, adapting the interpretations. This, then, is where we started from and how we structured our approach.

A background of long-term change

Our inquiry into change at the workplace begins with the judgement, which we believe is widely shared by people in Britain, that there has been massive long-term change in the structure of the economy, industries and jobs impinging on every working person. For example,

- Britain, like other industrial nations, has changed in the space of one generation from being a manufacturing nation to one where most employment is in services.[8]
- In the same time-scale, manual work has shrunk from providing the majority of jobs to providing less than one job in three.[9]
- Along with this, management and professional jobs have steadily increased until they provide almost 40 per cent of current employment.
- In the early 1970s, half the workforce had no educational qualification whatever.[10] But in the early 2000s, the government's plan is for half the population to go to university.
- Over the post-war period, the proportion of jobs held by women has shifted from one-third to nearly one-half.
- In 1979, one in four women employees resumed paid work within (roughly) a year of having a baby. By the mid-90s, the proportion rose to two in three.[11]
- In 1980, seven in ten employees (inclusive of managers) had their pay set by collective bargaining between employers and trade unions, while by 1998 the proportion was only four in ten, the majority of whom were in the public sector.[12]

These background changes have many implications for the design of an inquiry about change at the workplace. For instance, the survey needs to cover small workplaces, which typify much of the service sector, as well as the larger ones which are more dominant in manufacturing or the public sector. Questions need to be asked about the types of working arrangements, rewards and controls that are applied to white-collar and professional employees, rather than being (as in most past research) preoccupied with manual jobs. Issues about working hours and work-life balance must be given a prominent place in a world of working mothers and two-earner families. And management-employee relations can no longer be equated with relations between employers and unions: they are affected by a whole raft of management practices many of which have been developed and applied in non-union workplaces.

The background of change which we have just sketched is mostly of a gradual kind and covers the entire second half of the twentieth century. But there are several types of change which have come more rapidly to the forefront in the last decade or so. We consider four to be most important:

intensifying competition, accelerating technology, a more proactive business and management ethos, and renewed external regulation.

An ultra-competitive world

The pressures of change have come most persistently from increasing competition. Of course, market economies have always been based on competition, but this competition was for long kept within bounds through government protection or industry and inter-firm agreements.[13] Now the once-cosy front parlour of domestic business deals has been breached and opened to the competitive winds. From the 1980s, international trade and finance expanded at an accelerating rate bringing more overseas goods and services to Britain. British companies of course were also engaging in more overseas activities of their own. Between 1990 and the end of 2002, Britain's trade with the world more than doubled, and more than half of this trade was with the highly sophisticated and productive countries of the European Union.[14] Over the same period, total GDP (the usual measure of the economy's size) increased by 87 per cent, so international trade continues to outstrip overall growth.

The competitive pressures were initially felt most sharply in manufacturing but also progressively extended to services: the symbolic arrival of the McDonalds franchise in the 1970s was followed by a wide-ranging American and European entry into British retailing, hotels, and banking. During the 1980s, the USA itself removed controls and protections from many service industries, including banking, telecommunications, and air transport, and this deregulation had knock-on effects in Europe, forcing such industries to become more open to competition.

One of the most visible results of more intense competition, both in the USA and Europe, was business rationalisation. 'Downsizing' (cutting employee numbers) and 'delayering' (removing whole tiers of management or supervision) entered the English language along with the phrase 'lean production'.[15] The metaphor was one of stripping away the fat, to leave a fitter, meaner organisation. Many business giants who were unable to keep up the diet, died. Others were swallowed up in the endless series of takeovers and mergers, often the prelude to still more downsizing. In Britain, the Thatcher government spread the slash-and-burn treatment to the public sector through privatisation, and by progressively squeezing central and local government spending. Between 1979 and 1996, employment in the public sector fell by nearly one-third.[16]

Yet Britain appears to have survived this competitive pressure in good shape. In the late 1990s, companies operating in the UK for a time were the most profitable in the world. Although this crown subsequently slipped, UK business remains among the profit leaders[17] and growth in profits, at an average around six per cent per annum, has outstripped economic growth over the past decade. Although the picture has been much less rosy in manufacturing, the financial sector has taken over as the engine of the economy and profitability has remained on average high across the service industries, which now provide the great bulk of employment. So, if competition has provided an extreme pressure for change, it is one which Britain seems to have met with reasonable success.

But was this business success bought at employees' cost? Just how lean and mean did businesses get? Clearly a great deal of change was necessary to meet the rise in competition, but were employees winners or losers from that change process? For many commentators, increasing competition was *all bad*: it meant fewer jobs – perhaps eventually no jobs – and it also meant worse jobs.[18] Did British competitiveness result, as this would imply, in more insecurity for employees, fewer prospects, a stripping-away of pensions and fringe benefits, longer hours, more pressure?

These questions provide one of the main themes of the book.

- In Chapter Two we ask about the employment of temporary, casual and agency staff – groups with less security and fewer prospects – and about the use of freelance, self-employed, sub-contracted and 'outsourced' services, all of which reduce the workplace's regular workforce.
- We also ask whether downsizing and delayering continue to be widespread and where they are most often found.
- At various points in later chapters, we probe whether cuts in the workforce affect the organisation's ability or willingness to train, develop and motivate its managers and employees.

From the management viewpoint, labour *flexibility* – the usual label for this whole group of practices – helps to cope with competitive pressures by cutting costs. The unpopularity of the policies has given flexibility a bad name. Yet there are other ways of getting flexibility which meet with more public approval. For example, employees themselves can be made more flexible, or adaptable, through training, varied tasks and jobs, multi-skilling, and team-working – what we call 'intelligent flexibility' because it relies on the intelligence and adaptability of the individual.

- Chapter Three explores the growing use of intelligent flexibility, and related management practices, to arrive at a more balanced view of the flexibility issue.

Flexibility is not the only response to competition. To meet relentless pressures on costs, business and public sector organisations alike must continually find new methods of cost reduction and cost control. Two such developments that are rapidly impinging on managers and other employees are reviewed in the book.

- Organisations are attempting to cut their space requirements and hence their premises costs: the main developments are covered in Chapter Five, including the growth of teleworking, hot-desking and working from home.
- Chapter Six examines the main ways in which organisations are extending or intensifying controls over individual or team performance.

Both these topics also have a new technology dimension which is considered in the section immediately below.

New technology and the shift to 'knowledge work'

While increased competitive pressures initially work themselves out in terms of cost-cutting, subtler forces of change, to do with knowledge and technology, may be equally important for competition now and in the near future. We say 'may be' because there are heated debates about these changes and their implications. Yet, as noted earlier, there can be no doubt that levels of qualification have risen hugely in the workforce, and that there has been a swing from semi-skilled to managerial and professional jobs. Moreover, in the past decade there has been a striking surge in the use, at work, of information and communications technology (ICT), associated with the advent of the Internet and of networked communication systems. The question is how these changes are linked, and how the two together are changing management practice and the jobs and work which people do.

At the technology end, some of the changes involved are fairly obvious. To purchase anything from a theatre ticket to a week-end break to a life insurance policy now involves a telephone transaction with a call-centre, where the friendly voice (if you are lucky enough to get through to it) is just the front for a computer system. Down at the local supermarket check-out, nowadays, every transaction is processed electronically. At the same time the purchases are being automatically logged into a computer database which aids a multitude of behind-the-scenes tasks and provides an inexhaustible supply of information for management's planning and control.

Technology's tentacles reach into unexpected quarters.[19] Virtually every job advertised in the fast-growing world of creative media specifies the requirement for a high level of computer skills. Up-market hairdressers are showing their clients how different styles would look on them, through 'virtual reality' images. The door-calling occupations, from meter-readers to market research interviewers, come with laptops in place of clip-boards.

Knowledge as an aspect of change in the workplace is more abstract than technology, and less easy to get a handle on. It was that doyen of management gurus, Peter Drucker, who already in the 1960s coined the idea of knowledge workers. For him, the shift to knowledge work (typically, the work done by professionals) and to competition on the basis of knowledge is the most important change of the era,[20] heralding a post-industrial age. In the industrial age, businesses competed through their ownership of products, plant and equipment. In the post-industrial age, competition is based on knowledge which is held by key employees who can walk away with it at any time. The point was brought home to the business world in the late 90s when Internet software company Netscape was bought for around $10bn., its real assets consisting mainly of its 2000 staff.[21] Many large companies have responded to the idea of competition via knowledge by launching 'knowledge capture' and 'knowledge management' programmes[22] to preserve the asset value of their own expertise.

The idea of knowledge work, which as we have seen is not a new one, has certainly been given a fresh lease of life by the advent of the Internet, and by other high-profile new technologies, such as advanced materials, biotechnology and the Genome Project. These, it is said, open up huge opportunities for business innovation and create an insatiable demand for creative and technical talent.[23] But just how large is the proportion of employment which involves, or is likely to involve, knowledge work? Robert Reich, former advisor to President Clinton, has estimated that 25 per cent of the US workforce already consists of what he calls 'creative workers' even after excluding public sector jobs, many of which require high levels of qualification.[24] Timothy Bresnahan,[25] who has carried out detailed case studies on the application of ICT, estimates that about one in five working people are now high-level users of technology, which fits reasonably well with Reich's estimate. But Bresnahan considers that the most significant contribution of ICT is to facilitate innovation in the routine administrative and customer service functions which now form such a huge slice of business and employment. All the people caught up in the innovative restructuring of business and public services may be considered, in a sense, knowledge workers. But their knowledge depends less on qualifications than on know-how gained at the front line of implementing organisational change. If the pace of innovation with ICT is rapid enough, the *majority* of employees can be regarded as knowledge workers.

All this is 'in principle' but how *in practice* are these types of change affecting employees and their jobs? This is where differences in the current predictions are sharpest. New technology and especially ICT has been portrayed by some as a job-eating dragon, leaving in its wake a society ravaged by insecurity, where only the smartest and most powerful can prosper.[26] Even professionals, it has been argued, are undermined by the rapidly changing knowledge base and by employers' increasing tendency to seek the best available talent in the job market. As a result, lifetime jobs and corporate careers have come, or are coming, to an end. Even the most cautious analysts admit that, while many more creative or high-level jobs are being created by new technology or the hunger for applied knowledge, some jobs are continuing to be down-graded or down-skilled by technology – as has always been the case.[27]

A jobs scenario with a more positive tone owes its birth to the British management guru Charles Handy,[28] although many others have re-cycled his ideas. As a substitute for fixed jobs and standard careers, knowledge workers will develop ever-shifting portfolios of self-employed project work, much of it in fluid teams and co-operative networks or partnerships. Knowledge workers will not have fixed workplaces but will be highly mobile, many of them with home-based operations. While working life will become more risky, it will also become more varied and more creative. The large hierarchical organisation will dissolve into looser confederate relationships.

Against these bold predictions, there have been quieter voices urging that while some things will change, there will also be much continuity with the past. For Drucker, the original prophet of knowledge work, organisations continue to be needed by professionals because they can network the specialists more efficiently than the market-place. Knowledge workers may be footloose between employers, but it will be in organisations' own interest to develop means of retaining them. Outsourced knowledge services will grow, predicts Drucker, but the companies that outsource will have to learn to look after their external experts as carefully as their internal ones. Others have argued that careers and promotion remain the most persuasive inducements for attracting qualified and talented people. Then again, not all knowledge is portable, and specialised in-house knowledge can only be gained by people who stay around.

The issues emerging from these debates around knowledge work and new technology run through much of this book.

- The role of new technology is investigated through a focus on ICT, the technology which is most widely used and most rapidly expanding. At the end of Chapter One, the scene is set by looking at current rates of ICT usage and extension. Most of the subsequent chapters involve an ICT sub-plot.
- Chapter Four examines what organisations are doing about career opportunities. Are they fostering them or winding them down? Are they ripping out career ladders through delayering, are they shrinking the management jobs which many aspire to, or are they developing and extending them to offer opportunities and hold on to expertise? Do workplaces which are advanced users of ICT – hence more dependent on knowledge workers – provide more or fewer career opportunities?
- Are organisations serious about offering employees, including middle management, a long-term future? Chapter Four also assesses this question, looking at policies around pensions and benefits, and personal development, as tests of corporate intent.

- Part of Chapter Five considers changes in work-space and workplace, such as teleworking or working from home, that are facilitated by ICT.
- Part of Chapter Six considers the potentially great increase in detailed control over individuals' work and performance, which becomes available when they are networked into an ICT system.

Management's cultural revolution

The kinds of change so far stressed – intensifying competition and burgeoning technology – seem to come from outside and then press in on the organisation and on its people. But this is one-sided. An external change only becomes a pressure when it is brought inside the organisation. Competition exists in the market-place, but what ultimately counts is how the organisation, the management and the individual change their behaviour in response. New technology emerges, but then has to be adopted and adapted. This can happen slowly or rapidly, reluctantly or eagerly, clumsily or adroitly. The way an organisation, a management or a workforce encompasses change depends on its habits, its style, its *culture*. If change is now accelerating in the workplace, this has to involve a change in culture as well as in context.

A striking difference between current experience and previous eras is that management, at least in the more successful firms, no longer waits around for changes to hit them. Change is *promoted* by the organisation, and it is promoted continuously. This message comes across loud and clear from our own case studies in a varied mix of organisations, small as well as large. Change is now too rapid for management to sit tight until it is pushed into action.[29] The organisation must continually be on the move, adapting to external change but at the same time pressing towards its own change objectives. Continuous change is part of the current management culture. This is not by any means confined to the business world. Government departments and agencies, for instance, are typically swept by reorganisations at intervals of 12 to 18 months and are continually involved in massive changes of methods and procedures resulting from new ICT systems.

The crucial importance of the organisation's people has been underlined at several points in this chapter, and the capacity for continuous change evidently depends on people as ever. A new leading model of how to manage and motivate people came to the forefront in the 1980s. It involved ideas about team-working, communication, involvement, individual development, continuous learning, pay for performance, and personal empowerment and responsibility. These ideas, and the management practices which help make them happen, have been progressively incorporated into mainstream human resource management (HRM), which has come to replace the more limited idea of 'personnel'.

It is important to stress that none of these ideas is, in itself, particularly new. Those with an interest in business history can trace them back to such unlikely sources as World War II research on morale in the armed services, or British coal-mining in the 1950s. As early as the 1960s, large innovative companies were experimenting on green-field sites with new forms of organisation and new motivational approaches. What worked eventually became the stuff of HRM. Another key influence was the rise of Japanese manufacturing, and the challenge of their management ideas, which stressed continuous improvement rather than working to standard. Some ideas, such as 'quality circles' (now often referred to as work improvement groups) were borrowed directly from standard Japanese practice.

What was new, at the outset of the HRM movement, was the belief that only a comprehensive change in the approach to managing people would equip organisations to compete internationally.[30] More recently this has grown into the idea that there is a 'best practice' in developing HRM to produce effective innovation and performance. In the USA, especially, claims have been made that when certain bundles of HRM practices are brought together and animated by a clear strategy, the result is a 'high performance work system' (HPWS) which delivers major rather than minor gains for the organisation, and also benefits employees. Eileen Appelbaum and her colleagues have carried out research, involving detailed case studies and surveys in the steel, clothing and medical instruments industries, and produced impressive evidence in support of this view.[31] As yet, however, the evidence for Britain remains less convincing,[32] perhaps in part because British organisations have gone less far in implementing these ideas.

Whatever their effectiveness, HRM practices and the search for HPWS have themselves become a source of change. Such practices provide a model which many organisations now seek to imitate and pursue. Adopting such practices as open communications, consultative systems, or team-working organisation, obviously in itself involves a large effort by managers and other employees. But this effort is believed worthwhile, indeed essential, to develop a workforce that can cope effectively with continuous change.

This development poses issues which are addressed and answered in the following chapters. Throughout, we investigate what are the factors that are either speeding or delaying adoption of HRM/HPWS practices at the workplace.

- The 'intelligent flexibility' discussed in Chapter Three itself involves a range of the classic practices of HRM/HPWS, notably team-working, multi-skilling, and individual development. We ask how rapidly these practices are spreading and in what circumstance they are being adopted.
- Various aspects of performance management, such as appraisals and pay for performance, are covered in Chapter Four as part of the review of

career development policies. Appraisals are further discussed, from the viewpoint of controls over performance, in Chapter Six.

- Communications and consultation have in the past been regarded as a weak area in British management: how far is this weakness now being addressed? The answers can be found partly in Chapter Four, with further discussion in Chapter Ten (see next section).

Alongside the goals of improved performance and adaptation, HRM has inherited a goal of fair treatment of employees which was central to old-style personnel management. Central to this, at least in many large employers, is equal opportunities policy which endeavours to remove discrimination towards women, minorities, and disadvantaged groups. Increasingly, this branch of corporate policy has moved out of the welfare wing and towards the front office of HRM. Making best use of the skills of those formerly given second-class treatment, or even excluded from jobs, is seen as a way of increasing the pool of talent, and of adapting the organisation's services to a diverse population of customers. Moreover, under the shadow of external regulation (see below), organisations' chances of staying in control in these areas depend on their taking the initiative themselves.

- Chapter Seven focuses initially on the desegregation of jobs on lines of sex. How far are employers recruiting women into jobs formerly done only by men, and *vice versa*? Where is this process taking place most rapidly and where is it lagging?
- Chapter Seven then goes on to look at work-life balance and family-friendly policies. What flexibility over hours do employees get? What help do they receive during the years when they have young children? What priority does management attach to further steps in this direction?
- Chapter Eight investigates the broader issue of diversity in recruitment – older workers, returners, unemployed people, disabled, those with poor English, and ex-offenders. What kinds of organisations recruit from these groups? Is this kind of recruitment linked with exploitation or with progressive HRM practices?

Experts usually stress that the effectiveness of HRM practices depends on them being combined systematically rather than used piecemeal. The workplace has to reach some critical mass of HRM innovation before it gets the real benefits. This idea is followed up in Chapter Nine, which considers how practices are combined into 'strategies'.

- The centre-piece of Chapter Nine is an assessment of how many workplaces are now following a recognisable HRM/HPWS strategy, and what distinguishes such workplaces from others.

- Chapter Nine also looks at some other people-related strategies – both 'lean and mean' and welfare-orientated. The question asked is how far such strategies are compatible with HRM/HPWS or whether they are distinct alternatives.

Regulation's come-back

The pressures of market competition and of new technology on employers' working practices are for the most part indirect, and leave employers ample room to develop their own choices and strategies. Alongside these, however, there are renewed pressures from government regulation of the workplace, which in a direct way constrain what employers must do. Familiar examples are the National Minimum Wage, the Working Time Regulations, or new provisions requiring equality of treatment for part-time and temporary employees. Furthermore, the Employment Relations Act 1999 re-established routes for unions to gain recognition at workplaces where they have sufficient support from employees, even where managements are reluctant. Employees meanwhile have been making extensive use of legal routes to press their grievances or claims against employers. Individual cases mediated by ACAS[33] have been running at about 165,000 per annum in recent years, and 2000/1 saw a sharp peak in cases reaching an Employment Tribunal – up 30 per cent on the previous year.

It is no coincidence that this movement towards a renewed regulation of the workplace, which comes from the European Commission (EC) as well as from the British government, is taking place at this time. It reflects the anxiety of governments about the recently growing global dimension of the competition which we were focusing upon earlier in the chapter. Governments are especially concerned about the massive power of global business alliances which can make use of low-cost labour from countries around the world, thus side-stepping governments' attempts to set minimum wage levels or to raise working conditions. Regulation embodies governments' determination to stay in control of social and employment policies, rather than permit global competition to rule the roost.

However, the ultimate effect of State regulation can be unexpected, especially when employers counter-attack. This can be illustrated by employment contracts, which are more regulated in most European countries than in the UK. In Spain, for instance, temporary employment has soared to constitute one in five jobs, largely because employers have sought an unregulated corner of the job market to escape severe regulation over hiring and firing for permanent posts. In Italy, another country which has long attempted to make jobs secure through the statute-book, one in four jobs now exists beyond the pale of statutory regulation, and the government there has recently felt obliged to legalise and place limits upon some 30 types of non-standard labour contract.[34]

So how will British employers respond to the rising tide of regulation: will they conform, evade, or pre-empt? The biggest test, perhaps, is still to come with the implementation of the Directive on Information and Consultation (ICON), due to start in 2005. Management's response to regulation is considered in detail in Chapter Ten. That chapter consists of four main strands:

- What changes has management made following the Working Time Regulations (WTR)? How often have working practices been changed as a result, and where has this happened?
- How hard is management being hit by employee litigation?
- What is the impact of having a recognised union at the workplace? Do unions appear to hinder or help the various management practices and strategies discussed in the previous sections?
- Is there a growth in consultative committees in advance of ICON? If so, where is this growth taking place – for instance, in unionised or non-union workplaces?

Finally, regulation is a type of change which specially puts pressure on those who manage people. Throughout Chapter Ten, therefore, we ask how each aspect of regulation affects the time-pressures that managers experience.

Finding out about change in the workplace

We have now outlined the ideas and questions behind the research. We have also indicated where to look for the answers to the questions posed, in the coming chapters. In this final section we briefly sketch how the research was carried out, and explain how the findings are presented.

To get answers to our questions about people policies at the workplace, we carried out a national survey of British employers in the second half of 2002. This covered 2000 workplaces, ranging in size from 5 to 7500 employees, in both the private and the public sectors. This is called the Change in Employer Practices Survey 2002 (CEPS-02). More details of the survey are provided in Appendix 1. In this and subsequent chapters, key findings from the survey are shown in the form of simplified charts, and a smaller number (mainly where wording is complex) in table form. Appendix 2 explains more about how the tables and charts have been calculated.

What makes the survey *unique* is its emphasis on change. At each workplace, the manager responsible for HRM or people policies was asked a wide range of questions about changes which took place recently – most of these questions referred to the preceding three years, some to the last 12 months. In addition, she or he was asked about changes which were *likely* to take place over the current year, and especially about *planned* changes. In all, about half the questions in the interview relate to change. So, as well as giving a snapshot of people policies at each workplace in 2002, the survey provides a view of where the organisation is coming from and where it is heading.

In presenting the findings, we also frequently refer to another national survey, this time of employees, which we carried out in 2000/1, with the title Working in Britain in the Year 2000 (WIB-00). This *companion survey* (as we will usually call it) is particularly useful in cross-checking results from CEPS-02 to test their reliability.

There is one point which it is particularly important to understand before dipping into the charts and the other results which we will present. Most workplaces are very small, but a large proportion of total employment is concentrated in a small number of large workplaces such as the major manufacturing plants, local authority offices, universities, and hospitals. If we simply counted workplaces, then the large employers would be swamped by the multitude of very small employers. This would give a very misleading picture of how changes affect employees, as those in larger workplaces would in effect vanish from sight. To prevent this, we weight each establishment by the number of employees there. Suppose for instance a workplace is the average size, it will then be counted just once (weight of 1). If it is twice the average size, it will be counted twice (given a weight of 2), while if it is half the average size, it will be given a weight of one-half.

Our results accordingly are equivalent to counting the employees at workplaces rather than just counting the workplaces themselves. When we say, for example, that '70 per cent of workplaces practice such-and-such policy', we could say more precisely that 'the workplaces practicing this policy cover 70 per cent of employees'. The less precise wording is followed, because it is far less tedious for the reader, but the tables and charts contain a reminder that the results are based on proportions of employment, rather than proportions of workplaces. There is one chapter (Chapter Ten) where the results are differently calculated: the reason for this is explained there.

As a curtain-raiser, the rest of the present chapter offers a simple outline of the main background changes which have recently been taking place in British workplaces. This will provide an initial impression of the relative scale of changes from one group of workplace policies to another. But at this stage there will be no exploration of the reasons for change, or of how one kind of change is (or is not) connected with another. That will follow later. Managers' expectations about changes in the immediate future will also be considered in the following chapters, rather than in this one.

Background 1: Competition and confidence

A good place to start the story is with the growth or contraction of workplaces. We claimed earlier in the chapter that Britain's businesses have been performing well, but is this how managers see things? And how confident are they about the immediate future? Everything else is likely to be coloured by these perceptions.

The managers' replies, covering the period 1999–2002, are in accord with the national trend of growing employment.[35] True, one in four have experienced contraction, but twice as many (one in two) have experienced growth, and for one in four there has at least been stability in numbers.[36] On the whole, then, recent experience has been good.

There are however large industry variations (Chart 1.1), with marked contraction apparent in the engineering industries. In contrast, a more positive experience of employment growth runs right across construction and services. This includes the public services, which suggests a recently improving deal from government despite the general public perception of continued under-resourcing.

Chart 1.2 shows the same question with comparisons by size of workplace – small (5–24 employees), medium (25–99 employees) and large (100 and over). A clear surprise, bucking the trend of many years, is that large workplaces are contracting no more often than small workplaces, and a little more often they are actually growing. Moreover, the large establishments are also – for obvious reasons – more than twice as likely to be relocating part of their business, either elsewhere in Britain or overseas, than in the case of small establishments.[37] When this is taken into account, their growth advantage in these recent years becomes still clearer. Small is beautiful no more – or large is lovelier.

Does recent experience carry over into confidence about the future? The survey interviews were taking place against the background of a sliding stock-market, and anxiety about war in Iraq. Yet confidence

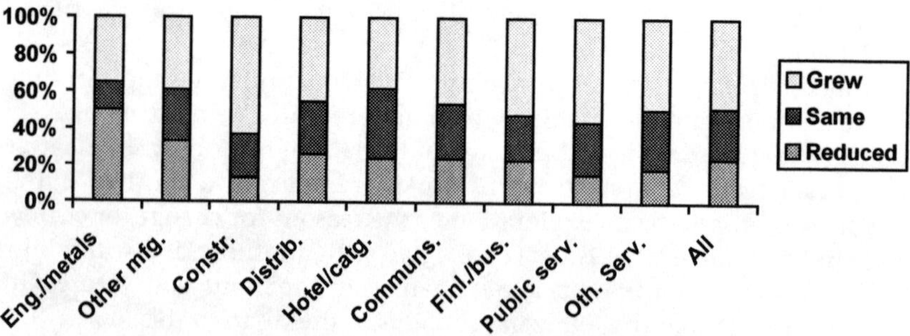

Chart 1.1 Change in employment 2000–2, by industry group
Note: Column percentages, weighted by employment. Full key to industries (left to right): Engineering and metal manufacturing; Other manufacturing; Construction; Distribution and repair; Hotels and catering; Post, communications and transport; Financial and business services; Public services; Other services (leisure/personal service, etc.); All. Agriculture, extraction and utilities not shown because of small numbers, but included in All.

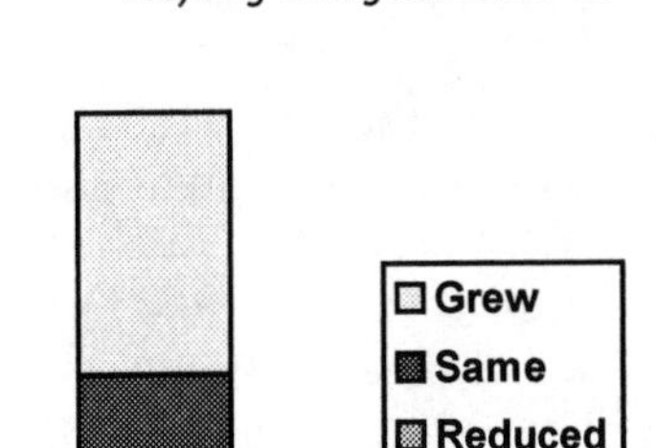
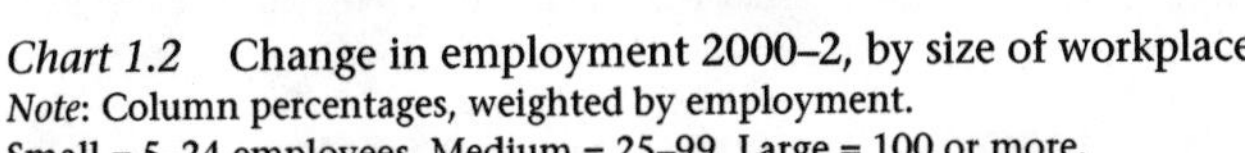

Chart 1.2 Change in employment 2000–2, by size of workplace
Note: Column percentages, weighted by employment.
Small = 5–24 employees, Medium = 25–99, Large = 100 or more.

remains strong. Over one third say they expect their employment to grow over the coming year, while only one in 11 expect it to shrink. These figures probably reflect a general mood, rather than forecasts for particular industries, since industry differences are negligible. This mood of confidence indicates a more robust frame of mind among British managers than was usual in the past, when pessimism tended to set in at the first sign of a downturn. With this confident mind-set, managers are likely to feel positive about pursuing and achieving change at the workplace.

Background 2: Technology's advance

Earlier in the chapter we presented a picture of rapidly advancing technology, especially ICT, but how far is this supported by recent experience? Chart 1.3 shows managers' estimates of how many employees are using 'PCs or other computerised equipment' in their jobs, in small, medium-sized and large workplaces.

A striking point from the chart is that already at one in three workplaces there is a complete penetration of ICT to every job, or something very close to that. Moreover, these fully-wired workplaces are evenly spread across the small, medium and large size-groups. Equally striking, at the other extreme, is how few workplaces are virtually without ICT: only one in 20 overall, and just one per cent in the large workplaces.

The figures provided by the managers can be used to make a rough estimate of what proportion of employees, nationally, are using ICT in their jobs.[38] The estimate which we have derived is, *around two-thirds*. This is very close to the figure obtained from the companion survey of employees (WIB-00), where 65 per cent of employees said that they currently use PCs or computerised equipment in their own jobs. There is no reason to suppose, then, that the managers' estimates are exaggerated. Using ICT is very much the norm in British workplaces.

Has the situation reached a plateau, or is ICT still continuing to advance? To gauge this, managers were asked to judge how much change there had been over the preceding three years. Chart 1.4 shows that ICT use has been increasing during this recent period in one-half of the workplaces, and in one-quarter it has increased a lot. The rate of increase has been particularly high in large workplaces, but less in small workplaces.

More interesting, though, is to see where that growth has been taking place, compared to the current level of ICT usage. This is shown in Chart 1.5. The greatest rate of increase has taken place in workplaces which

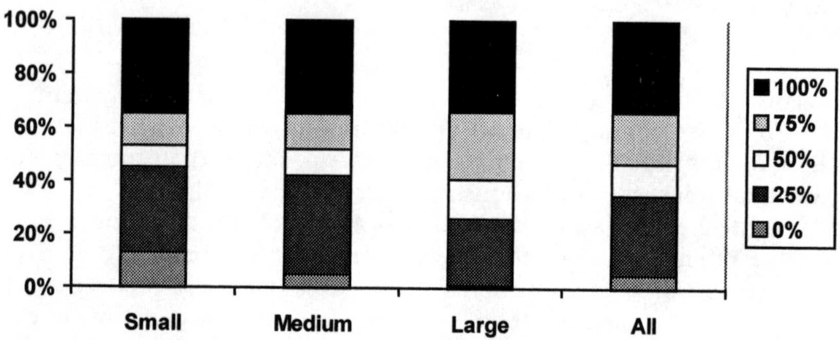

Chart 1.3 ICT usage* by employees at workplaces of different sizes
* The proportion of employees using PCs or other computerised equipment, estimated to the nearest 25 per cent (see legend at right of chart).
Note: Column percentages, weighted by employment.

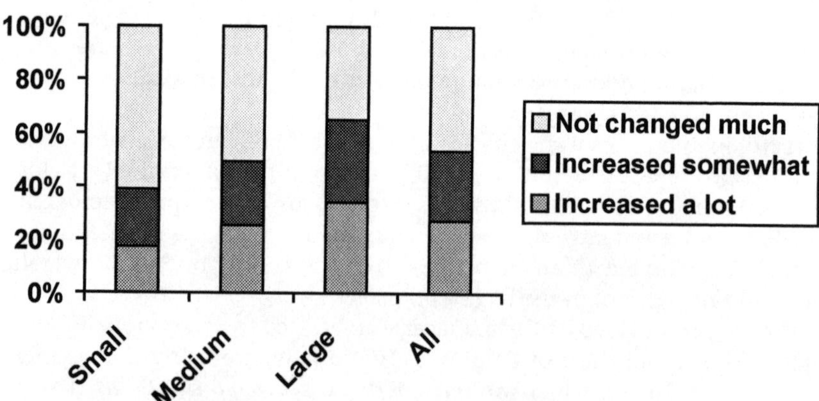

Chart 1.4 Change in ICT usage, by size of workplace
Note: Column percentages, weighted by employment. Response 'Decreased' not shown: it was given by one per cent in all size groups.

Chart 1.5 Change in ICT usage 2000–2, by present level of use
Note: Column percentages, weighted by employment. Those with (nearly) no employees using ICT are omitted from the chart (five per cent of the sample).

have now reached around 50 to 75 per cent utilisation of ICT by their employees. No less than seven in ten of these have been advancing on the ICT front in recent years. There is however a relatively low rate of change in workplaces which have a low utilisation rate, suggesting that these may move only slowly along the ICT learning-curve in the future. About half the workplaces with nearly 100 per cent staff coverage by ICT have also experienced no change in the past three years, indicating that they reached saturation coverage at least three years ago.

It would therefore be going too far to claim that *all* organisations or *all* jobs are going to be ICT-based in the near future. In around one in three workplaces, ICT plays only a minor role and will probably continue to do so. However, in the remaining two thirds, ICT is already pervasive or is rapidly becoming so.

Background 3: Managing people

Against this background of business confidence and rapidly advancing technology, how are managers faring in their responsibilities for people? Strikingly, nearly two in three overall (62%) say that compared with three years previously more time is now being spent by management on personnel, and only two per cent say less time (Chart 1.6). This increasing emphasis on people is, in fact, *the most widespread change across the whole survey*. There is little difference between industries in this respect, and it is only in the smallest workplaces – those with less than 25 employees – that the proportion giving increased time to people falls fractionally below one-half.

As we suggested earlier, a factor in this pressure on management is likely to be the expansion of regulatory change. Another indicator of this is the amount of money spent on legal advice around employment issues, which has been increasing in three in ten workplaces overall, and in nearly four in ten of the larger workplaces (Chart 1.7). This suggests that many employers are struggling with the implications of changing employment law, coupled with the rising tide of employee complaints.

However, as we also stressed earlier in the chapter, the level of personnel and HRM activity is not set solely by external pressures: in many organisations, HRM policies and practices are now developed internally in a process of continual change. To conclude this introduction to the survey findings, we provide a selection of the changes in people policies that are reported by managers. Immediately upon looking at this information (Table 1.1), the time spent on people management across the whole of industry becomes more understandable. Bearing in mind that the table relates to *changes taking place in the past three years*, both the amount and the range of activity are impressive.

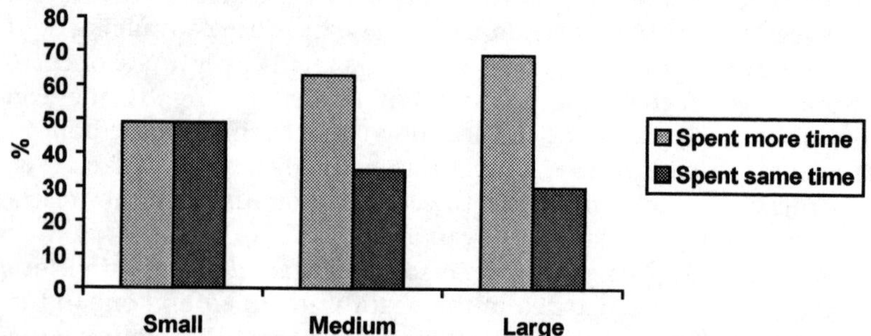

Chart 1.6 Management time on personnel matters, by size of workplace
Note: Column percentages, weighted by employment. Management time refers to change over the past three years. Response 'Spent less time' not shown – it was given by two per cent of small workplaces and by one per cent of medium and large workplaces.

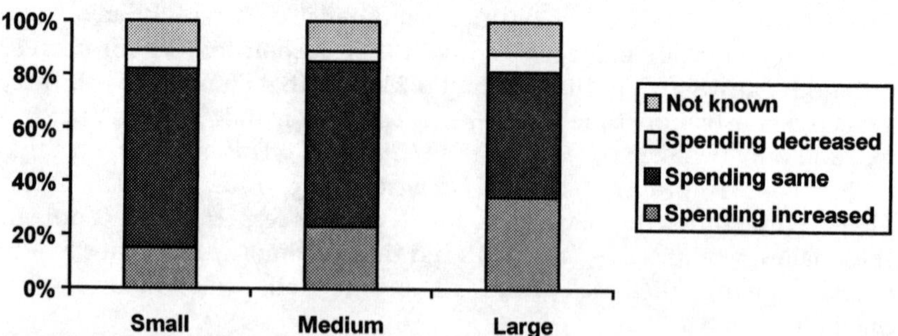

Chart 1.7 Change in spending on legal advice, 2000–2 (by size of workplace)
Note: Column percentages, weighted by employment.

Table 1.1 Selected changes in people practices in the past three years

	Increased	*Decreased*
Training to cover other jobs	50%	2%
Variety of work that staff are expected to do	48%	2%
Amount of job rotation	30%	1%
Team-working	28%	2%
Individual performance assessment	39%	1%
Group-based incentives	21%	3%
Proportion of managerial/professional staff	28%	13%
Number of management grades	24%	10%
Number of employee grades	21%	7%
Outsourcing of activities previously done in-house	24%	n.a.
Introduction of teleworking	11%	n.a.
Encouraging some staff to work at home	11%	n.a.
Harmonisation of conditions of employment	26%	3%
Use of agency staff	32%	25%
Outside contractors in place of own employees	18%	n.a.
Temporary employees	14%	10%
Casual workers	6%	6%
Freelance (self-employed) workers	5%	3%

Note: Row percentages weighted by employment. The response 'no change' is not shown.
n.a. = not applicable/not asked.

The initial impression is of a tumult of change with no obvious pattern or dominant theme. Explanation of these, and many other, changes will follow in the coming chapters. These will, for instance, consider what kinds of workplaces are experiencing each type of change, and how far the various kinds of changes tend to go hand-in-hand.

But we can surely say already that management is not focusing all or even most of its efforts on one group of policies, but seems to be mixing together a wide and varied range. We can guess that the future implications for both management and employees will also be varied, both across jobs and workplaces. Understanding those future implications, with both their down-side and their up-side, is a main task of this book.

2
Flexible Labour at Its Limit?

Employers' organisations often extol the virtues of a flexible labour market. Every British government since the time of Margaret Thatcher has emphasised that Britain has such a labour market, and has claimed this as one of our advantages in international competition.[1] But what does the phrase 'flexible labour market' mean, what is the nature of its advantage, and does that advantage apply to employees as well as to employers?

Broadly speaking, a fully flexible labour market is one where an employer and an individual worker are entitled to agree on any kind of employment contract without constraint. The ultimate in flexibility is if the contract can be for any hours (few or many, fixed or variable), can be terminated on either side without notice and without penalty, and can have any possible arrangement about pay and other benefits and conditions. Real examples of unlimited flexibility tend to look less attractive than the theory. In a past era, for instance, many dock workers were employed on a completely casual basis, a situation which led to violent conflict, while nowadays illegal refugees jump into vans for a day's building work at illegally low wages.

In general, there are limits to flexibility, even in Britain. For instance, redundancy provisions impose some financial costs on employers who terminate jobs for that reason; notice periods for termination of employment contracts are regulated by employment protection law; there is extensive legislation concerned with unfair dismissal; there is a National Minimum Wage, and previously there were Wages Councils which set minimum wages in particular industries. None the less, Britain's labour laws are much less restrictive for employers than in other European countries, except Denmark and perhaps Ireland. Elsewhere in Europe, for example, laws prevent either very short or very long hours being worked, forbid short-term contracts, or make it extremely difficult to dismiss an employee at all. British employers can in principle benefit from the absence of these constraints – but how much of an advantage is it?

The value of flexibility to employers is at its clearest when competitive conditions are volatile or unpredictable. If demand for products or services rises rapidly, but uncertainly, it can be useful to bring in 'pairs of hands' on a temporary or casual basis. If demand then falls suddenly, the employer's cost can be reduced if the workers no longer needed can be sent away at once. Where work can be farmed out to a freelance or homeworker, this can save overheads as well. So, much of the advantage of a flexible labour market for employers stems from the cost reductions of having workers when they are needed but removing them when they are not needed. In short, expendable labour: labour that you use and throw away, as the Italians put it.[2] Of course, this approach cannot easily be applied to jobs where a substantial amount of in-house training and experience are needed before employees become proficient.

Other kinds of flexibility, apart from short-term response to market demand, are also important. When demand varies a lot over the daily or weekly cycle, as in many services, part-time employees can be used to cover the peaks without having to pay them for standing idle in the troughs. This provides the employer with an obvious advantage, even though part-time employees are, currently, no less protected than full-time employees and in practice their jobs have been just as secure.[3] Again, employees on fixed-term contracts of two or three years, who could be trainees or perhaps skilled people like construction engineers taken on for a particular contract, are not necessarily in the expendable category. The employer's advantage here is in limiting a longer-term liability.

Being expendable does not sound much of an attraction to the individual worker. Yet some people at some times in their lives do prefer to work on a casual or temporary basis – students are a case in point. Catherine Hakim, one of Britain's leading authorities on women at work, has even argued that many of the women who fill a majority of the flexible jobs do so out of personal preferences.[4] In principle at least, nobody is obliged to accept short-term work if what they want is a more permanent job. In practice though job-seekers in Britain can lose their benefits if they turn down a temporary job, and if there are many temporary jobs vacancies but few permanent ones, it may be the only way to get a foothold on the jobs ladder.[5] Similarly, it seems that many people have been reluctantly obliged to accept part-time jobs because of a shortage of full-time jobs,[6] even if for others part-time work is an appealing option because it fits in with family or educational schedules.

So if the number of flexible jobs fits the number of people who currently prefer them, everyone stands to gain. But as employers expand their use of flexible employment, more workers can be forced into a situation which has no attraction for them. On the other hand, as the job market becomes tighter through good economic conditions, employers are put under more pressure to offer full-time permanent jobs to those who want them, and to cut back on their use of flexible labour accordingly. According to a review conducted by the TUC, this has indeed recently been happening, with the proportions of unwilling part-time and temporary employees in decline.[7]

One further idea has loomed large in both political and academic debates about flexible labour. It is that this kind of job may be concentrated in a certain type of employer, making the conditions for employees who work thereabouts particularly unfavourable. For instance, flexible labour may be particularly appealing to employers whose costs mainly consist of wages and salaries, and who compete chiefly on cost rather than quality. Obvious examples in the private sector would be catering or cleaning services, but public services which are subject to rigid cost budgets, such as care homes, might also be affected. If such areas develop high levels of flexible labour, such as temporary or casual staff, then this may also drive down the wages and conditions of regular staff there.

Another possibility is that up-market employers with a highly-skilled workforce may be able to increase their profits by buying-in less-skilled services they need from the low-wage sector, rather than employing people internally to do the work. They may even go further, by consciously cutting out sections of their workforce that are not part of their core business, so as to replace them with lower-cost services from outside. Indeed, management journals have been replete with advice on how to define and prioritise an organisation's core competences. So there develops a link between outsourcing and downsizing.

It is the combination of these implications from flexible labour, and their mutual knock-on effects, which has led some to see a gloomy future, or at least a very different one, for the world of work. Extreme predictions include those of Ulrich Beck, who sees a world stripped of secure employment and reduced to grinding poverty for all but the super-powerful, and of Charles Handy who envisages that people will have to put together portfolios of work rather than jobs, while organisations become loose-knit federations rather than tight structures.[8]

But much of the foregoing consists of ideas and assumptions rather than hard evidence. Previous attempts to test the ideas have often found it surprisingly hard to come up with support.[9] Some of the conclusions from this earlier research are that:

- the extent of flexible labour use has been exaggerated
- employees with flexible contracts are less dissatisfied and cynical than often assumed
- employers often do not use the supposed advantages of flexibility in a strategic way or even very effectively.

In addition, the assumption that flexible labour means low-skilled, low-wage jobs is now known to be highly one-sided. For example, professionally qualified employees, such as research scientists and engineers, ICT specialists, teachers, and nurses, form a large proportion of temporary employees and one that has been growing particularly quickly.[10] Yet it would be premature to write off the ideas until more evidence is in. Recent research in Australia, for instance, seems to show clear links between the use of flexible labour and a decline in employment in the same firms.[11]

Our survey of workplaces, carried out in 2002, provides a new opportunity to look at the hard evidence on flexible labour. This chapter checks how British employers are currently using flexible labour, and where this type of practice is headed in the immediate future.

Where is flexible employment located?

The CEPS-02 survey reveals one stark fact: it is impossible to find a 'flexible free' zone. This point needs to be read carefully: it is *not* saying that most jobs (or even many jobs) are now of the flexible variety. An employer may hire labour on flexible contracts, but only for a few jobs or very occasionally. None the less, the sheer range of workplaces which make some use of flexible labour – however limited – carries its own message. Virtually all employers have this kind of flexibility in their kit-bag ready for use. For that reason alone, though, it is surely outdated to imagine that employers who have flexible labour policies are a ghetto area of the jobs market.

- Four in five workplaces[12] have some part-time employees.
- Four in five workplaces use at least one of the following arrangements: temporary staff supplied by agencies; their own temporary employees; people employed on a casual basis; freelance (self-employed) workers; homeworkers or outworkers.
- Four in five of the workplaces with *no* part-time employees use at least one of the other categories of flexible labour.

In addition, there is another type of flexibility which in its own right is almost universal. This is the use of outsourcing – that is, of putting-out on service contracts work which could be done by employees. As recently as 1998, outsourcing was described (in the British context) as an interesting new development common in local authorities, privatised utilities, government agencies and some very large private sector organisations (however, it is possible that in the absence of comprehensive data at that time the extent of outsourcing was not fully understood[13]). The representative data which we have for 2002 show that it has actually been adopted in *every* part of industry.

- More than *nine in ten* (93%) of the surveyed workplaces are outsourcing at least one type of service
- One half of workplaces are outsourcing *four or more* services.

- Nearly one in five say they have *recently* used outsourcing to take on work previously done by their own employees.

The most usual types of outsourcing are cleaning, catering, and security, which used to be done in-house by at least larger employers a generation ago. Added to these now are less familiar kinds of outsourcing, some of which involve much higher, indeed professional, levels of skill:

- training (43%)
- printing and copying (31%)
- ICT (26%)
- recruitment (20%)

Once again, care must be taken over what these figures mean. A workplace will be counted in the figures even if its use of outsourcing is only occasional and small-scale. What is most interesting, all the same, is the penetration of the outsourcing *idea* into new types of activity. The prominent position of training and recruitment as outsourced services suggests that the HRM function as a whole is being seen, in many organisations, as at least in part a non-core activity. Broadly consistent with our figures, the CIPD journal *People Management* has reported that 42 per cent of 'large' firms are outsourcing 'some' HR functions, while British Petroleum (BP) is an example of a leading blue-chip employer that has completely divested itself of internal HRM, contracting the whole function to an external consultancy.[14] More generally, it is clear that outsourcing is moving beyond the familiar realms of building maintenance, catering and cleaning services into services involving high-level administrative and technical competence of various kinds. This type of development is likely to pose new issues for management, both in terms of those who purchase the outsourced services and those who provide them (see Box on page 27).

Apart from part-time working and outsourcing, the other types of flexible labour crop up with greatly varying frequency across workplaces. Agency staff are used on occasion by more than half, temporary employees by just about half, casual workers by one in three, freelancers by one in seven and homeworkers or outworkers by one in 14 (see Chart 2.1).

Industries and flexible labour

What are the circumstances that favour each type of flexibility? Part-time employees are concentrated in the service industries, accounting for more than four in ten of the workforce in distribution, hotels and catering, and for more than three in ten in public services. But industry differences are wholly unimportant for the other kinds of flexibility, such as agency staff, temporary or casual employees, or outsourcing. Temporary employees are found in the public sector as much as the private – as already indicated by

Outsourcing an administrative function

At present, there are few in-depth case studies about outsourcing which examine it from the viewpoint of the service provider. One major case study, however, appearing in 1999, was authored by C. Bruce Kavan and colleagues. They looked at the outsourcing of an invoicing and credit collection service, focusing on a firm which specialised in providing this type of outsourced service and its relations with a number of clients. The findings indicate some crucial issues which can arise when outsourcing extends into the administrative area rather than being confined to simple services such as cleaning or building maintenance. The authors conclude:

- The business systems and methods of the service provider have to fit with those of the client company, but it is often *not* the best solution for the provider simply to 'retro-fit' their service to what was there before.
- Developing the approach to be adopted under outsourcing needs considerable management effort on both sides. When this is achieved, outsourcing becomes 'strategic' and can contribute to enhanced performance for the client.
- It is often assumed that a service provider will itself employ many staff on a temporary or freelance basis, and this was so in this case. However, this created numerous difficulties, since an employee who can work effectively to meet the goals of both the client and the service provider needs to be particularly skilled and motivated. As outsourcing advances and becomes more strategic, the proportion of temporary staff involved are predicted to fall.

Source: C. Bruce Kavan, Carol Stoak Saunders and Reed E. Nelson, Virtual@virtual.org, *Business Horizons*, September–October 1999, 73–82.

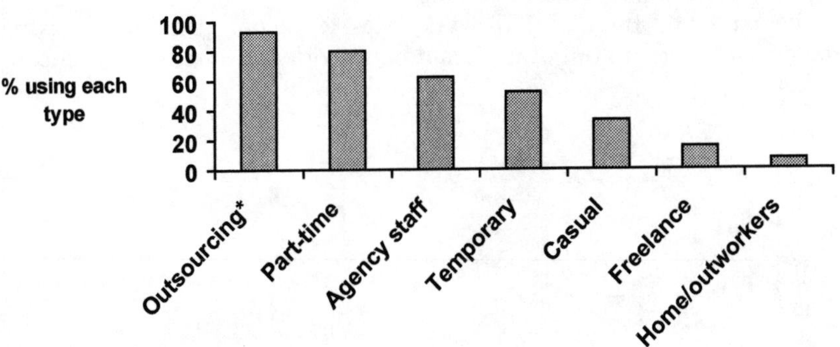

Chart 2.1 Prevalence of different forms of flexible labour
Note: Cell percentages (each bar is a separate percentage of all workplaces), weighted by employment. * One or more types of outsourcing.

reference to teachers and nurses, for instance. This lack of separation between the industries merely underlines the opening message: flexible labour is everywhere.

ICT and flexible labour

One circumstance linked to flexible labour usage is surprising, at least at first sight. It is having a high proportion of staff who use information and communications technology (ICT).[15] High-ICT workplaces are more likely to have people on temporary contracts, to use agency temps, and to use self-employed freelancers. They are also more likely to be replacing full-time with part-time staff, to an increasing extent. These findings are summarised in Chart 2.2. High-ICT workplaces are also above-average users of outsourcing, which will be discussed in the following section.

This increased use of flexible labour by the high-ICT workplaces seems to torpedo the idea, outlined in Chapter One, that they are centres of knowledge competition with an intensified need to develop highly-skilled knowledge workers. But some of the key skills which high-ICT workplaces require are of a specialist type that can be readily transferred between organisations. This applies, for instance, to a range of computer programming and computer support activities. The use of agencies, temporary contracts and self-employed status therefore, at least in part, reflects the special job market for these skilled ICT professionals, who can command very high salaries in periods when the pressure is on firms to develop new systems. Given the high salaries, employers have turned to fixed-term contracting to limit their liability. The use of such contracts could be compatible with a high emphasis on retaining and developing staff in other categories where firm-specific knowledge and skills are paramount. This possibility will be explored further in the next two chapters.

The tendency for high-ICT workplaces to favour part-time working requires a different kind of explanation, unconnected with external con-

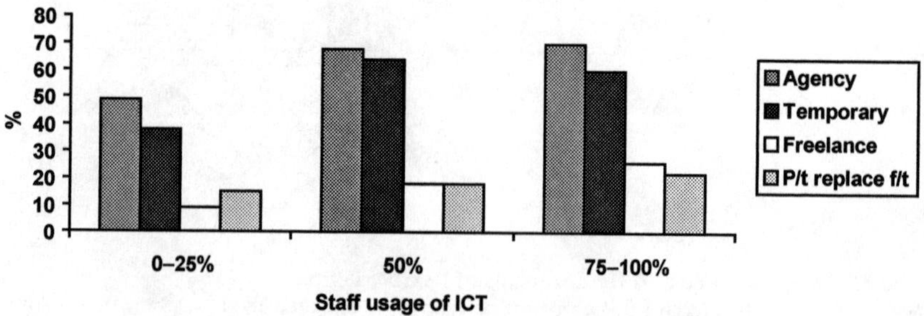

Chart 2.2 Differences in flexible labour use, by level of ICT coverage
Note: Cell percentages (each bar is a separate percentage of the total), weighted by employment. Part-time replacing full-time employees refers to the past three years.

tracting. It could be one facet of a distinctive approach to working hours, among the high-tech employers, and this will be explored further in Chapter Seven.

Substituting for employees?

A question which concerns trade unionists, and probably many employees, is whether flexible labour is used to replace regular jobs. This question can be interpreted in two rather different ways. One is whether the employer has actually cut out some permanent jobs and directly replaced these with temporary contracts, outsourcing or some other flexible arrangement. The other is whether there would be more permanent jobs on offer if the temporary contracts, outsourcing or other flexible arrangement did not exist. The second type of question is very difficult to answer, and it is on the first – direct replacement of former employment – that the survey focused, with three of its questions. The questions can be paraphrased as follows:

- Are there on-site contractors who are doing work which would have been done, three years ago, by employees of the establishment?
- In the last three years, have any activities previously done in-house been outsourced?
- In the last three years, have any former employees changed to self-employed status while continuing to work at the same workplace?

Although the first two questions sound similar, they are different and were interpreted as different by the managers responding to them. Outsourcing is wider than on-site contracting, since many outsourced services can be provided off-site. Indeed, many managers who answered yes to the first question said no to the second: presumably they equated outsourcing with off-site rather than on-site services.

Three in ten workplaces have been replacing some in-house work either by outsourcing or by on-site contractors,[16] while one in 11 has some former employees continuing to work on-site on a self-employed basis (Chart 2.3). Although this is only a minority of workplaces, it is a substantial minority. Outsourcing has already become an important method of substituting external services for internal employment. As most workplaces use outsourcing to some extent, this process could well develop further in the years to come. Of course, this also depends on service businesses being set up to meet the potential demand for outsourcing. Further development will also depend on the nature of competition, as previous research has shown that the use of outside contracting or outsourcing to replace employees most often has cost savings as the main objective.[17]

So outsourcing and contracting-in are not only widespread, they are genuinely shifting employment from the purchasing organisations to the supplier organisations. The survey did not go into the numbers involved, as this would have been hard for managers to estimate reliably. (For some figures about on-site contracting – sometimes referred to as 'insourcing' – see the Box on page 31.) Evidently, though, the potential for a substantial re-structuring of employment seems to be there, in view of the range of activities involved. Indeed, the replacement of activities in many workplaces is already on a large enough scale to impact on total employment there, and Chart 2.4 shows that employee substitution is most common in shrinking workplaces.

Another situation where flexible substitution is also used to an above-average extent is in workplaces with high levels of ICT. One reason for this is probably that the technology makes it easier and less costly to outsource some administrative activities: for example, routine word-processing can be passed to a remote contractor that provides the service on-line. Another reason is perhaps that such organisations are increasingly defining their core competences in terms of ICT and business system skills, and prefer to shift as many as possible of their non-core services outside.

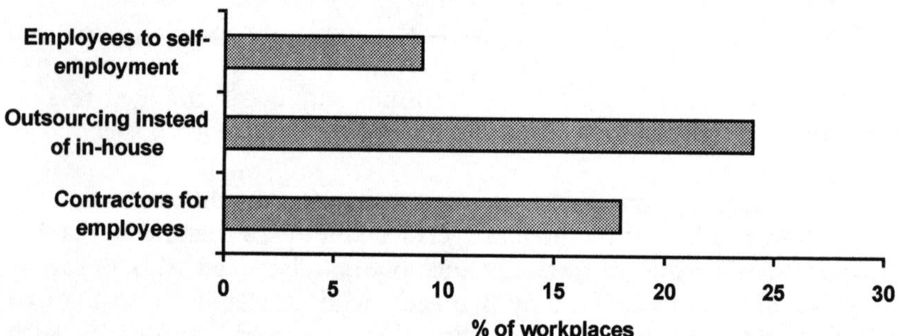

Chart 2.3 Substitution of employees by external contracting, 2000–2
Note: Cell percentages (each bar is a separate percentage of the total), weighted by employment.

Chart 2.4 Employee substitution and change in employment, 2000–2
Note: Cell percentages (each bar is a separate percentage), weighted by employment.

Non-employees on site

The survey assessed one aspect of outsourcing through a question which asked: 'Are there any people who regularly work at your establishment but are not on your payroll, such as subcontractors, agency workers etc.?' This excludes service suppliers who only work off-site, but should include those regularly on-site, including those who work on a self-employed or freelance basis.

- Almost one-half of workplaces (48%) had some non-employees working on site, but at about one in four of these workplaces the manager could not estimate their number.
- Where an estimate was offered, the non-employees on average amounted to about one in eight (12%) of everyone at that workplace.
- Construction has an average of 22 per cent of non-employees but other industries all have similar proportions to one another.
- Across all workplaces the proportion of contracted non-employees to employees is five per cent.
- These figures *exclude* a small number of unusual workplaces where the non-employees greatly outnumber the employees. Nearly all these occur either in construction or in financial and business services.

Where are the changes in flexible employment?

If flexible labour is already so widespread, does that indicate that it is on the way to taking over and becoming the dominant form of employment, as some commentators have suggested? The inference could be the opposite: with flexible labour so widespread, perhaps it is running out of niches and enclaves to take over. The outline information presented in Chapter One (see Table 1.1) already suggests that flexible labour use is not growing so rapidly as in the case of many other people policies. Or, to be more precise, the number of employers with increases in flexible labour is being offset by nearly as many others who are cutting back their usage. This is summarised more fully in Chart 2.5. The suggestion from these figures is that these kinds of flexible employment (which exclude outsourcing) are hitting a ceiling. One factor may be employees' resistance to providing expendable labour in a booming job market where other options are available for them. As noted earlier in the chapter, the numbers taking such jobs unwillingly have been falling sharply, which is indicative of this kind of resistance. Or, as the next two chapters will discuss further, perhaps employers' priorities are shifting and making these types of labour less useful than before.

Yet is this just a temporary lull? Managers were asked whether they expected each of these kinds of flexible labour to grow over the next 12 months. Chart 2.6 shows the proportions expecting increases. To provide a benchmark, the chart also shows the proportion expecting their

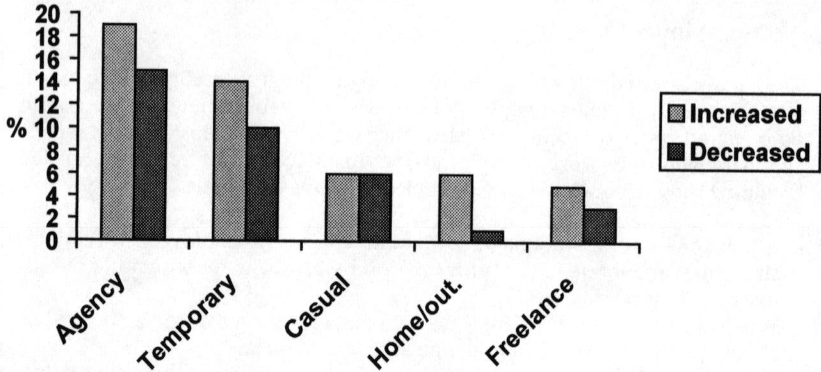

Chart 2.5 Changes in flexible labour use, 2000–2
Note: Column percentages, with the response 'no change' omitted; weighted by employment. Home/out. = homeworkers or outworkers.

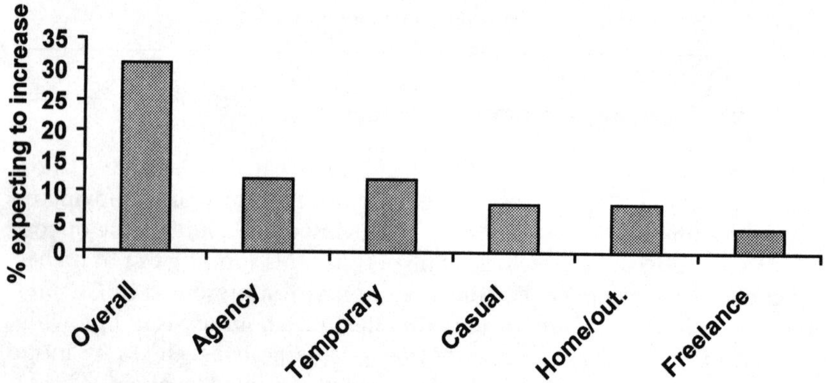

Chart 2.6 Workplaces expecting to increase labour 2002–3
Note: Cell percentages (each bar is a separate percentage of the total), weighted by employment. 'Overall' means total employment at the workplace. Home/out. = homeworkers or outworkers.

total employment to increase over the same period. Increases are expected most often for use of agency staff and for employment on temporary contracts, with about one in eight workplaces looking to each of these. But that is far lower than the proportion expecting their total employment to increase. Other types of flexible work are expected to increase in still smaller proportions of establishments. When the two charts (2.5 and 2.6) are taken together, there is a strong indication that flexible labour, at least of these types and in current conditions, is running out of steam. Indeed, as the majority of growing workplaces do *not* expect to be increasing their use of flexible labour, the indication is that flexible labour will probably decline as a proportion of total labour over the coming year.

A potentially important factor for the future course of flexible labour is the rate at which employers 'convert' from being non-users to users. This can be gauged by cross-analysing the forecasts for the next 12 months with whether the workplace is a user at the time of the survey interview. Those predicting increases in usage over the coming year were made up, broadly speaking, of six existing users for every current non-user, or starter. The starters were therefore few and far between, which in yet another way indicates that flexible labour usage is ceasing to expand.

There is one exception to this, though, and it concerns homeworking. Here, one in three of the managers forecasting an increased usage are in workplaces that do *not* currently use homeworkers. Workplaces with high levels of ICT are also more likely than others to be thinking of increased use of homeworkers. The kind of homeworking these new and high-tech users have in mind doubtless has little to do with sewing sleeves on dresses. They are more probably thinking of the opportunities for remote 'knowledge work' opened up by new communications technology. More on this will appear in the discussion on workplace and workspace policies in Chapter Five.

Flexible labour in combination

Workplaces which use several types of flexible labour in combination – for example, part-time employees, temporary employees, and freelancers – may well be rather different from workplaces which just use one type of flexible contracting. The multiple users may be pursuing flexibility in a more comprehensive and thought-through way, and perhaps place a lower value on their regular workforce as a result. Or of course they may just be more desperate, clutching at flexible labour practices to keep them afloat.

On looking at how each type of flexible labour is combined with other types, one difference rapidly becomes clear. The use of part-time employees is distinct from other kinds of flexibility. Just because so many workplaces have *some* part-time jobs, there is a huge overlap between the simple presence of part-time employees and the presence of other flexible labour. But those workplaces with a higher *proportion* of part-time employees are *less likely* to use agency staff, freelance workers, and homeworkers, as shown in Chart 2.7. In the case of temporary employees and casual employees (not shown in the chart), the level of part-time employment makes no clear difference to usage. Overall, then, relying to a large extent on part-time employees seems an *alternative* to having other forms of flexible labour. This runs counter to a key assumption made by many of the leading authorities on flexible labour and the flexible firm: namely, that all jobs other than full-time, permanent ones form one group that is seen by

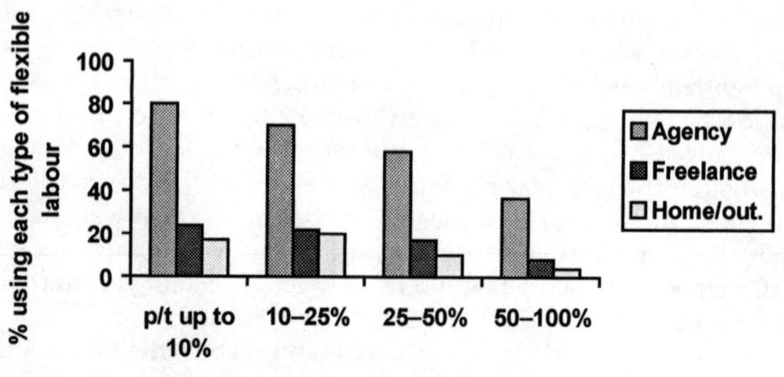

Chart 2.7 Part-time employment versus other kinds of flexible labour
Note: Cell percentages (each bar is a separate percentage of the total), weighted by employment. Workplaces with no part-time employees excluded.

management as distinct.[18] Instead, it seems that part-time employment on balance meets the needs of different types of employers from those that use other types of flexible labour contracts.

The other types of flexible labour, on the other hand, do tend to occur together. This is particularly true of agency staff and temporary staff, but it also applies to any other pair. In short, these types of flexibility are *complementary* with one another. This particularly applies to the less frequently used forms of flexibility: casual employees, freelancers, and homeworkers/outworkers. In the great majority of cases, where these are used there are at least two other kinds of flexible labour being used at the same workplace.

The workplaces which are using three or more of the five types of flexible labour amount to about a quarter (28%) of the total. These seem a particularly interesting group so what more can be said about them? In the first place, there is a definite service industry connection to this kind of multiple flexibility. In financial and business services, and personal and leisure services, nearly 40 per cent of the workplaces are using three or more types of flexibility in combination. This is despite having high proportions of part-time employees in these industries, which elsewhere as already noted is an alternative way of gaining flexibility.

Furthermore, 24-hour opening is linked to multiple types of flexibility (Chart 2.8). Continuous opening cuts across certain kinds of services – hotels, motorway services, hospitals, security, emergency services – and certain types of manufacturing, notably those with continuous process plant. One in four workplaces now keeps open 24 hours a day. Their need for flexible labour has until now received little special attention and analysis but it seems that they may well be an important factor in the future of labour flexibility.

There is also a strong link between multiple types of flexible labour and high levels of ICT (Chart 2.9). This is not only a surprising link but it is much the strongest. If high-ICT users are equated with the most advanced and dynamic section of the economy, in short with 'knowledge work', while low-ICT users are equated with the backward and sluggish sector, then it is hard to square this with the usual picture of flexible labour as a prop for the more primitive, low-cost end of the market. The results indicate that stereotypes are misleading both in the case of ICT and in the case of flexible labour. Much of the work involving ICT use is not necessarily highly skilled, and in some circumstances ICT can be used by management to de-skill jobs rather than increase their skill levels. At the same time, as stressed in the opening section of this chapter, not all flexible labour is low-skilled: temporary jobs exist in large numbers among professional groups, for instance. Furthermore, the same factors which make it relatively attractive to outsource work in high-tech workplaces – discussed earlier in tandem with Chart 2.3 – may also apply to some categories of flexible labour

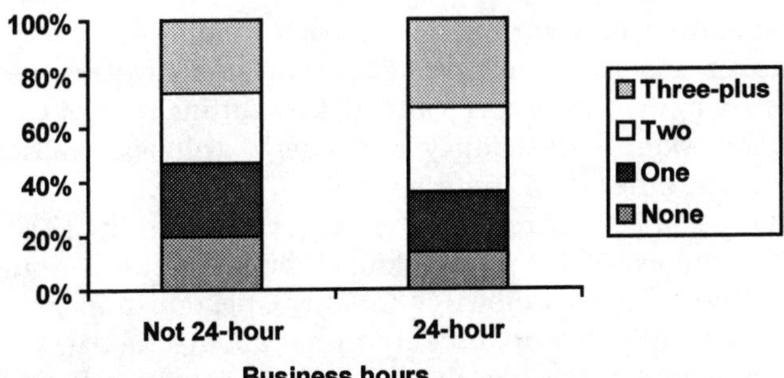

Chart 2.8 Number of flexible labour types in use, by 24-hour operation
Note: Column percentages, weighted by employment.

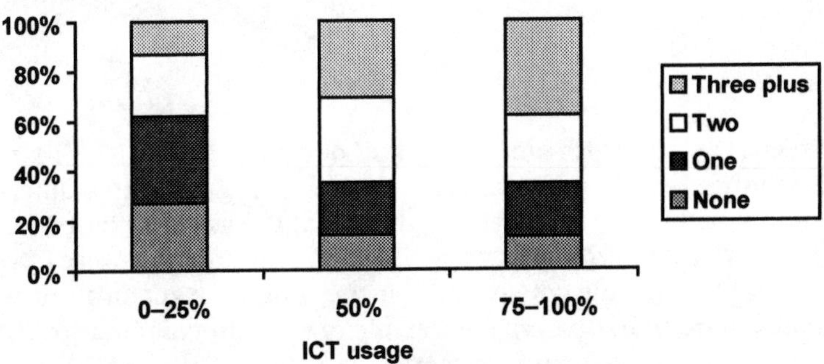

Chart 2.9 Number of flexible labour types in use, by ICT usage
Note: Column percentages, weighted by employment.

contract. For instance, if some ICT-based tasks involve the use of standard software and little or no in-house knowledge, the use of temporary employees becomes a possibility. The results in Chart 2.9 encapsulate how this complex reality balances out across the range of British employers.

How much downsizing?

Another circumstance which is connected to more extensive use of flexible labour is a contraction in total employment at the workplace. Such workplaces use more than the average number of flexible labour practices. They are also, specifically, more likely than others

- to be using employees on temporary contracts
- to be replacing full-time by part-time employees
- to have people working as self-employed for them who were previously employees
- to be outsourcing work to contractors which was recently done in-house.

This combination of a shrinking number of employees and an above-average use of flexible and/or expendable sources of labour suggests a fairly conscious policy of 'downsizing', with a likely cutting-back of commitment to a regular workforce. This policy, or 'strategy', will be examined in more detail alongside other HRM strategies in Chapter Nine.

How many employers are characterised by downsizing? This obviously depends on the exact definition adopted, but something around 15 per cent seems reasonable. As shown in Chapter One, one in four of the workplaces has a shrinking workforce, but only about one-half of these are above-average users of flexible labour. Whatever definition is used, the proportion of 'downsizers' is considerably greater in manufacturing industry, where the main impact of contraction has been felt. Downsizing is not mythical, but neither is it as widespread as sometimes suggested by media pundits.

Conclusions

The evidence about British employers' uses of flexible labour is a mixture of the reassuring, the alarming, and the disconcerting. All three adjectives might be applied to our most basic finding: that the use of flexible labour is virtually universal in British industry. There is no industry, no size of workplace, exempt from this conclusion. Furthermore, the majority of workplaces uses more than one type of flexible practice in combination, and a substantial minority uses three or more.

One reassuring interpretation of this basic finding is that flexible labour practices have become *normal*. They cannot be regarded as solely used by bad employers, indeed their adoption no longer says much about the nature of the employer. In many workplaces, the use of flexible labour is likely to be taking place alongside, and meshing in with, other human resource management practices which may offset their adverse consequences for employees. Later chapters will extensively explore the links with wider HR management.

Another reassuring finding is that flexible labour, contrary to what quite a few commentators have assumed, is not exactly rampaging ahead. Although widespread, recent increases in use by some workplaces has almost been offset by decreases at others, and managers' intentions suggest that further extensions, at least in the short-term, will be at a fairly low level. Flexible labour is reaching a plateau, though it is hard to know whether this will hold in the long-term. Economic growth and a tight labour market may be obliging employers to offer a higher proportion of permanent, full-time jobs – flexible labour may, in other words, be restricted by a lack of takers at present, but could stage a comeback when the economy dips. But there are also longer-term factors. The attractions of flexible labour contracts may be declining, in employers' eyes, as part-time and temporary employees are given greater equality in employment law with regular employees: further changes in this direction were afoot at the time of the survey.[19] Yet another possible explanation is that employers are changing their ideas or priorities about how to achieve flexibility. If they are becoming convinced that the best flexibility is that of well-trained, motivated and adaptable employees, then brought-in flexible labour will not seem so attractive. This possibility will form the main focus of the next two chapters.

Yet there are some reasons for being alarmed about the picture revealed by the survey. If flexible labour use does increase further, it will be doing so from a very wide base. There is no reason to suppose that it is going to be confined to a few sectors of employment while being locked out of many others. The pessimistic idea that flexible and precarious forms of contract will permeate all parts of employment does on this basis have to be taken seriously. However, for this to become a real threat, the widespread use of flexible labour practices would have to be accompanied by an equally widespread withdrawal by employers from developing staff internally for the long-term, which is another issue for the next two chapters.

Another possibly alarming, and certainly striking, point from these findings is the extent of outsourcing (including the sub-contracting of on-site services) which now exists. Of course, much of this has long been in existence, but much is recent. The survey shows that an appreciable part has resulted in the replacement of internal employees by contracted services. The use of outsourcing is partially though not wholly linked with employment contraction; downsizing can usefully be defined as contraction plus outsourcing. In many workplaces, contractors form a substantial proportion of the total head-count. Of course, the development of outsourcing need not be worrying if the employees of the service providers are at no disadvantage, compared with the employees of the firms who formerly did the work in-house. At present, little is known on this score.

Undoubtedly the most disconcerting feature of this chapter's findings is the role played by ICT. Workplaces with high levels of ICT presumably need an equally high level of skills, resourcefulness and capacity for change. There, if anywhere, one might expect to find knowledge workers in learning organisations – circumstances that tilt management away from short-run dependence on flexible labour, one might assume. But one would be mistaken. High levels of ICT unambiguously favour the flexible contracting of labour and the use of outsourcing. Indeed ICT is the factor most strongly pressing in that direction.

One way of explaining this is in terms of core and non-core employees. A high level of ICT, and the accompanying pressures of knowledge competition, may make management focus more closely on core competences while pushing non-core activities outside. The greater the rate of internal change, the more does management wish to concentrate on what is key while relegating the rest to the background. If this is right, then evidently there will be much further development of flexible labour and of outsourcing, in the coming years. On the other hand, the belief that ICT is a gateway to the promised land of high-skilled knowledge work may well be plain wrong. Perhaps much ICT-linked work is of lower skill-level than is so often assumed. Later chapters will help to re-examine this view of what is taking place, by exploring other employment practices of the high-tech organisations. Already, though, we can lay to rest the assumption that new technology offers a high road to better-quality employment. ICT seems set to perpetuate, not render obsolete, the use of flexible labour.

Finally, the lessons of this chapter can be briefly summed up from the viewpoint of the overarching themes that were set up in Chapter One. The extremely widespread use of flexible labour and outsourcing shows that the cost-pressures and uncertainties of a more competitive world have penetrated to virtually every corner of the economy and even affects the kinds of work done by managers and professional staff. Organisations' expertise in using these kinds of flexibility stands ready to be applied whenever economic conditions become more troubled. Moreover, the idea that the growth of new technology would push out this type of labour practice turns out to be completely misleading. And yet there *is* an unmistakable slowing-down in the uses of flexible labour. The following chapters will show how management is switching its attention to other kinds of flexibility and other ways of competing.

3
Intelligent Flexibility

Chapter Two suggested workplaces are reaching a limit in the flexible labour they buy-in. Does that mean that they are running out of options to cope with a changing and uncertain world? What alternative or additional means do they have? This chapter will examine how management is developing its most flexible resource – the individual employee – and will show how that development is moving to the centre of efforts to achieve business flexibility.

Before launching into this part of the story, it will be useful to look back briefly at the type of flexibility reviewed in the previous chapter. Buying-in flexible labour from outside, whether in the form of temporary employees, agency staff, or outsourcing, treats business uncertainty as a numbers problem. The rules for dealing with this numbers problem are straightforward. If there are more orders or more customers, bring in more 'pairs of hands'. If there are fewer orders or customers, scale down the number of workers accordingly. Arrange contracts in such a way that the numbers can be adjusted with the minimum of hassle.

But not all business uncertainty is a numbers problem. The market may shift towards a new kind of product or service, as when CDs put an end to vinyl, or EasyJet and Ryanair challenged traditional airlines with their no-frills service. To meet such a qualitative change in demand requires employees with new skills or capable of learning new approaches. It is unlikely that this kind of change can be met just by buying-in temporary assistance, especially not of the 'pairs of hands' variety. There will have to be targeted recruitment, training and learning, and re-organisation. If the workforce is adaptable and versatile, it will be able to cope with this kind of complex change much better than one where people work in a rigid way. To achieve this kind of flexibility, the organisation must develop its own employees, which takes time. Being able to compete in terms of quality and adaptability was one of the driving forces behind the human resource management (HRM) movement and the search for high-performance work systems.[1]

There are also circumstances when changing demand cannot be met except by the organisation's existing, permanent workforce. An example is where clients expect the attention of a highly-skilled and trusted specialist. Faced with rising demand, the partners in a law practice have little option in the short- to medium-term but to work longer and harder themselves, because additional partners cannot be produced out of a hat. Indeed, anyone managing a business or providing a professional service is going to have to be flexible in the workloads they can carry, as well as in terms of adaptability and versatility. In an era when managers and professionals comprise around four in ten of the whole labour force, this is likely to be a dominant concern for many organisations.

Another case is where staff have to acquire a substantial amount of knowledge that is specific to an organisation, for example service engineers for a particular kind of equipment or telesales staff for an insurance company.[2] Although such work may be of a level well below the professional, it will often still require too long a learning-time for the use of temporary employment or agency staffing to make any sense in terms of costs. Once again, the employer must rely on the permanent staff being able to work more intensively and/or to accept more efficient methods and procedures, when demand increases. And, when demand falls in a particular section of the business, there will often be scope to transfer the staff to other types of work – always provided that they are willing and able to learn quickly and adapt to such a change in their jobs. This kind of internal mobility can help to restrain costs in the face of variable demand.

People are of course inherently adaptable in their everyday lives, so there seems a great deal of sense in trying to use this to provide adaptability for an organisation. In the past, though, the emphasis on task specialisation in the workplace was so strong – as with the worker whose one role was to shape the head of a pin[3] – that individual adaptability was strangled. But many manufacturing companies have been trying to revive it, in the realisation that narrow task specialisation makes little sense when products and processes are changing all the time. One way is for skills to be combined in teams, and for the team members to become, progressively, more versatile and interchangeable. While such team-working is not a new idea, it became a focus of renewed interest during the 1980s when it was sometimes given the title 'flexible specialisation'.[4] In services, too, the importance of having staff who can respond adaptably to customers' needs is obvious. Even in call centres, where staff appear to be drawing on highly scripted answers, detailed case studies have revealed a surprisingly high level of personal ingenuity being needed.[5] The role of trade unions in enforcing the 'one man one job' rule has also been a significant pressure for specialisation in the past, but in recent years they have often played a more positive role in cooperating with change.[6]

So as both task specialisation and union constraints weaken, there is more scope for employers to emphasise the natural route to adaptability: the individual. To develop the individual's adaptability, management can draw upon a wide range of ideas that have each had their turn as flavour of the month: job enrichment, quality circles, multi-skilling, empowerment ... The practical question is, however, whether management can put together a wide-ranging approach which will make a major contribution to the overall flexibility of the organisation. If they can, then flexibility takes on a different character: it comes to depend on the intelligence of the individual employee in learning and coping with change. In short, it becomes intelligent flexibility.

Developing intelligent flexibility

Evidence from the companion survey of *employees*, WIB-00, shows that the day of rigidly defined jobs and tasks is already well past. Two-thirds of employees in that survey said that they sometimes performed a different set of tasks to their usual work, to cope with pressure of work, and more than one in two did so specifically to cover for staff sickness. Two-thirds also received training so as to be able to carry out a range of different tasks according to need.

Despite this apparently well-developed level of flexible working, the further development of individual flexibility is one of the fastest-growing areas of workforce policy.

- About one half of workplaces[7] say that in the last three years their employees have been asked to carry out an increasing variety of tasks.
- The same proportion has given increased training to cover for other jobs.
- In three in ten workplaces there has been increasing use of job rotation systems, whereby an employee takes on different jobs at different times.

All these steps indicate that employers are increasingly using the adaptability of their employees to cope with variation or change in the mix of demand. Moreover, in four in ten workplaces employees are being required to be more flexible over the hours they work, which shows individual flexibility being used to cope with quantitative variations in demand or changing patterns of demand across time.

Not all workplaces are going down this path – one in four are developing none of the four policies just listed. But where an employer is developing one, there is always at least one other under way as well, which suggests a concerted effort in this area. The combination of increased task variety with more training to cover for other jobs is the most common – one in three go for both.

Where are these kinds of development concentrated? Chapter Two showed that with brought-in flexible labour, differences between industries are no longer marked, and the same applies to individual employee flexibility. The search for greater task variety, in particular, is evenly spread across industries. Financial and business services is odd in having a relatively high emphasis on training for job cover, but a relatively low emphasis on formal job rotation. Public services, transport and communications also have below-average interest in formal job rotation schemes.

The complexity of the workplace, as indicated by the number of distinct job levels or grades, is a factor connected with the creation of more flexibility for the individual employee (Chart 3.1). All four kinds of practice to develop internal flexibility are more likely to occur where job structures are towards the complex end. The experience of the many companies which, in the 1980s and 1990s, introduced more flexible organisational structures, including delayered management, shows that middle managers in particular benefited from decentralisation with enriched jobs, more teamworking and more responsibility.[8] Employees in more routine jobs may have also have gained, but to a lesser extent. Here, however, it is tall rather than flat structures which are characterised by a continuing search for internal flexibility. It may be that complex job structures tend to reflect complex services or complex types of production, which create the scope for qualitative changes in the mix of demands going right down the organisation.[9]

In addition, where there is complexity, there tend to be more managers, supervisors and other senior personnel who can manage change and coach less skilled and experienced employees to be versatile. Because they have developed or retained this coaching capacity, such workplaces may have an advantage in creating conditions for additional employee flexibility. Equally, those workplaces which have relatively sparse ranks of managers,

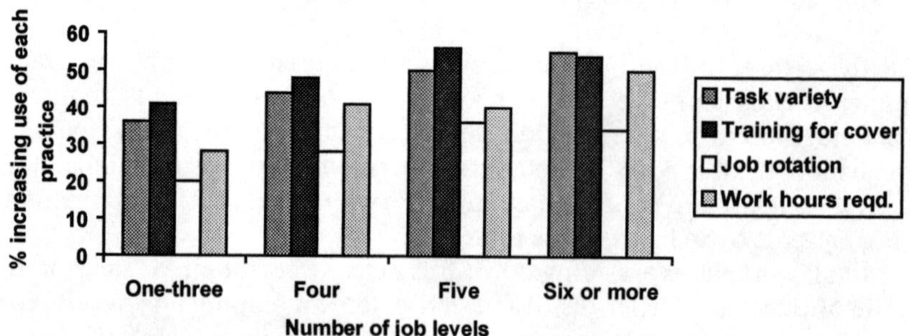

Chart 3.1 Workplace complexity and worker flexibility, 2000–2

Note: Cell percentages (each bar is a separate percentage of the total), weighted by employment. 'Work hours reqd.' means employees are required to be flexible in the hours they work.

perhaps because they had already delayered their structures and moved towards intelligent flexibility during the 90s, do not appear to be as concerned to go further in this direction.

Another important factor fostering internal flexibility is seven-day opening, which is now the practice of more than four in ten workplaces – perhaps indicative of the growing reality of the '24/7 society' that the media talk of. Where a workplace is open every day, the task of managing working time and ensuring that staffing is always available becomes a more demanding one. As would be expected, such workplaces are requiring their employees to provide more flexibility in their own hours of work. Indeed, 46 per cent register an increase in this respect. Less obviously, they are also particularly active in providing training for job cover, with 56 per cent doing this, and in operating job rotation schemes – present at 38 per cent of workplaces with seven-day opening, compared with only 24 per cent elsewhere (Chart 3.2).

So complexity, whether in terms of job structures or seven-day cover, seems a powerful factor in pursuing flexibility through the individual employee. Complex and tall organisations search for the adaptability that delayered organisations sought to achieve in the previous decade.

What kind of flexibility?

Comparing the present results with those in the previous chapter, it is obvious that the policy of intelligent flexibility through the individual employee is forging ahead much more rapidly than the policy of buying-in flexible labour. But with a moment's reflection, it is also apparent that the two approaches must overlap a great deal. After all, when the various kinds of flexible labour, such as temporary or casual jobs, agency staff and

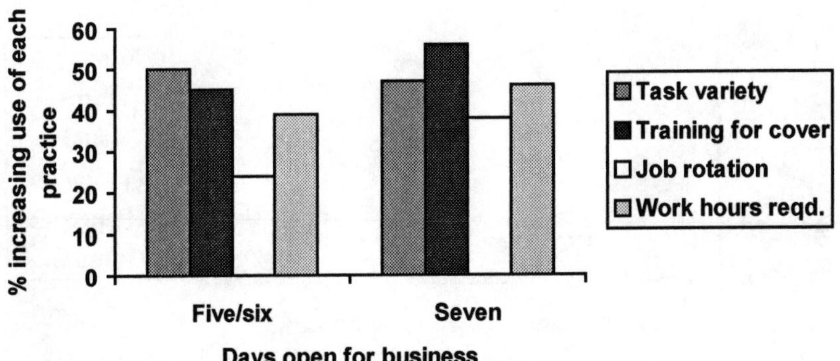

Chart 3.2 Seven-day working and worker flexibility, 2000–2
Note: Cell percentages (each bar is a separate percentage of the total), weighted by employment.

outsourcing, are combined, virtually every workplace is found to be using some brought-in flexibility, even if it is not growing much. At the same time, three in four of workplaces are increasing their emphasis on individual employee flexibility. These two approaches really cannot be regarded as alternatives. They are both so widespread that they have to be regarded as two *complementary* ways of seeking flexibility and adaptation.

The picture can be refined by comparing two flexibility practices at a time, one taken from the flexible labour set and one taken from the adaptable employee set. This produces a much stronger conclusion. Brought-in flexibility and intelligent, employee flexibility do not merely co-exist. They positively encourage one another.

To document this comprehensively would unleash a mind-numbing barrage of statistics. To avoid this, let us focus on just a few examples. Chart 3.3 gives a selection to indicate how the variety of tasks demanded of the employee relates to use of various forms of external labour flexibility at the same workplaces. For instance, of workplaces where task variety has been increasing, 63 per cent use temporary workers, but where task variety has been static, only 42 per cent use temporary workers. Virtually all comparisons of this sort tend in the same direction. Although many are less dramatic, none points in the opposite direction. There is no evidence at all that numerical, external flexibility substitutes for intelligent, internal flexibility, nor *vice versa*. Like some of the findings in the previous chapter, this result overturns a common assumption, that management makes a strategic choice between the external and internal route to flexibility. The reality is that management grabs flexibility from both sides.

A similar picture emerges if the comparison is between the recent changes in intelligent flexibility, and the expected changes in outside or brought-in flexibility over the coming year. To provide an example of this,

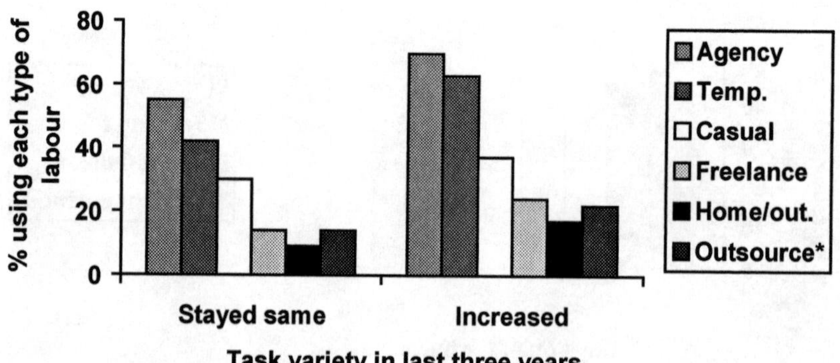

Chart 3.3 How change in task variety relates to external flexible labour
Note: Cell percentages (each bar is a separate percentage of the total), weighted by employment.
* Outsourcing in place of own employees.

Chart 3.4 focuses on training to cover for other jobs. Even where an employer has been emphasising intelligent flexibility, this does not mean that plans or intentions to use external flexibility are in any way weakened. Rather, they generally increase.

Enter the group

Having managers and employees who work flexibly can be specially useful if work is organised in close-knit groups or teams. The idea of a team is, after all, that people support and complement one another rather than operating totally as selfish individuals. This may well mean interchanging roles when needs dictate, and in general pooling resources to absorb and adapt to change. So teams need flexibility, but they also make flexibility easier. By working closely together, each individual can learn about the tasks and skills and ways of working that others have within the team. And by developing cooperation and trust, they can support each other through the pressures and stresses of change. Those are some of the positive ideas about team-working which have led many organisations to adopt it in recent years.[10] (There may be some clouds to spoil this idyllic picture – these will be considered later.)

Both the present employer survey, and the companion survey of employees in 2000, show team- or group-working on the advance in Britain, and perhaps even becoming the norm.

- More than one-half of employees say they work in a group, up by ten percentage points compared with 1992.
- Working in formally designated teams is on the increase in nearly three in ten workplaces, whereas decreases in that kind of work organisation are negligibly few.

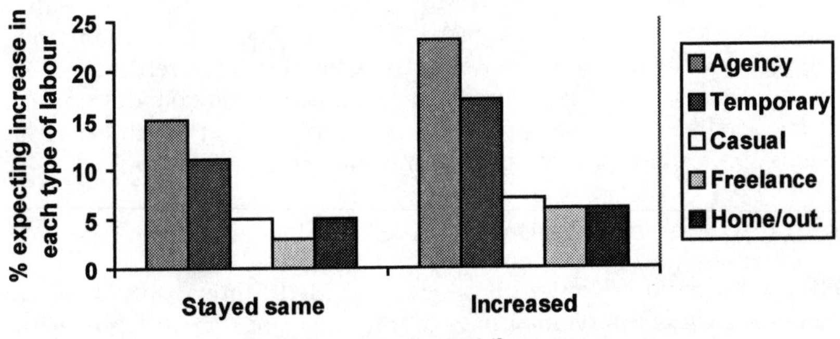

Chart 3.4 How training for cover relates to future use of flexible labour
Note: Cell percentages (each bar is a separate percentage of the total), weighted by employment.

- Nearly four in ten workplaces operate some teams that organise their own work without a supervisor (known as 'self-directed teams').

A rather different form of team is the one which gets together – maybe weekly or monthly – to generate ideas or suggestions for improving the way work is done. These are sometimes called 'quality circles', the name given to them in Japan where they originated and became a driving force for increased productivity. As their role is by no means confined to quality issues, the more general name of 'work improvement groups' seems better.

- According to the survey of employees, three in ten employees now takes part in some kind of work improvement group (which is half as many again as in the early 90s).
- Moreover, one-half of workplaces say that they now make use of work improvement groups to some extent.

These work improvement groups are in themselves a strong expression of intelligent flexibility. Members of such a group must draw on their job experience and use it creatively to identify and solve problems. Work improvement groups can also affect internal flexibility in two further ways. The process of working together breaks down the barriers between teams, sections or departments and makes staff mobility that much easier as a result. And, more directly, many of the ideas that the groups come up with to improve efficiency will be concerned with adapting to change.

The advance of group working and of work improvement groups is strongly linked to the general advance of intelligent flexibility. Among organisations where the variety of tasks that employees perform is increasing, four in ten are pushing forward with formal team-working. Contrastingly, among organisations where the variety of tasks per employee is static, only two in ten are increasing their team-working. This result is typical of others, which are summarised in Chart 3.5. With work improvement groups, the link is not quite so strong because it is a relatively indirect one. Yet it is still clear enough. The flexible individual employee and the cooperative group are complementary developments, both driven by organisations' need for more and still more adaptability.

Pressures, rewards, controls

Perhaps the previous sections have given an idyllic impression of current changes, in which individuals have more varied and therefore interesting work, often combined with team-working that involves greater sociability. But intelligent flexibility is not all jam, nor is life in a team. Recall, first, what is the purpose of these kinds of flexibility. It is to absorb some of the uncertainty and the changeability, which surrounds the organisation and

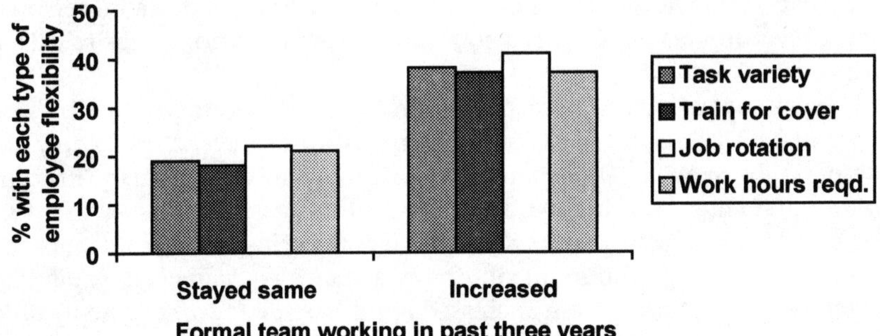

Chart 3.5 Formal team working and individual worker flexibility
Note: Cell percentages (each bar is a separate percentage of the total), weighted by employment.

its product or service. If management decides to delegate the requirement to cope with unpredictability to non-managerial employees, that means that the individual employee, or the team, will have to face and grapple with that uncertainty to a greater extent than before. In doing so they are taking on some of the role formerly played by management. The same applies to middle managers who take on more responsibility delegated from senior management. More adaptability means more anxiety.

This kind of adaptability also, inevitably, means more time pressures. It involves covering for a sick colleague while also keeping up normal tasks, or absorbing extra workload that clients and customers impose. Here, adaptability means doing more work than expected in your normal job. Extra pressures can also emerge in less obvious ways. Enlarging the range of task competences will usually involve some learning time. Perhaps the organisation will make provision for this, but in many cases it will not: being able to learn, while also doing a full-time job, is part of the current idea of an adaptable individual. Jobs that change have a kind of learning overhead, which the organisation is not keen to carry. The adaptable employee will probably never get to the point where the whole job seems effortless, because there will always be new things to absorb. And she will be expected to absorb them, if necessary, in her own time.

As for team-working, the pressures on an individual can be greater than working in a conventional way with a supervisor or more senior manager.[11] Apart from anything else, the team is always there whereas the supervisor or manager is not, and the highly motivated team can be a hard and unforgiving taskmaster. When the team is working long hours to catch up with its tasks or meet its targets, the individual has little option but to go along with the majority. Again, taking part in a work improvement group can involve meeting outside of regular hours and/or volunteering to carry out investigations, or write reports on the issues under review. It takes little imagination to see that these extra tasks are likely to be done in personal time. Accordingly, working in a committed team does not sit easily with a healthy work-life balance.

The employers' survey confirms the time pressures connected with these types of change. As noted earlier, four in ten workplaces say that they are increasingly requiring their staff to work more flexible hours. This will naturally include working extra hours when more senior management so decides. This increase in hours flexibility *demanded by the organisation* is not to be confused with hours flexibility as a *choice for individual employees*, which will be discussed later. Increased requirements to work more flexible hours is twice as common in workplaces where task variety is increasing for employees, as in workplaces where task variety has remained unchanged. Hours flexibility demanded by more senior management is also linked to the increasing use of team-working or work improvement groups (Chart 3.6). An important issue for management in the near future is whether they can continue demanding hours flexibility from employees to support other aspects of internal flexibility. Increasing State regulation of working hours – a topic to be discussed at length in Chapter Ten – may progressively limit the scope to do so. The question is whether this will place still more emphasis upon task flexibility and team flexibility, or will apply a brake to their further development.

Developing rewards

When changes demand more of employees, it is senior management's task to make sure that they respond. Organisations' methods are a mix of more rewards and more controls, but rewards and controls are often hard to tell apart – the rewards are unlikely to be given out without control information that confirms performance. So it is not surprising to find, alongside

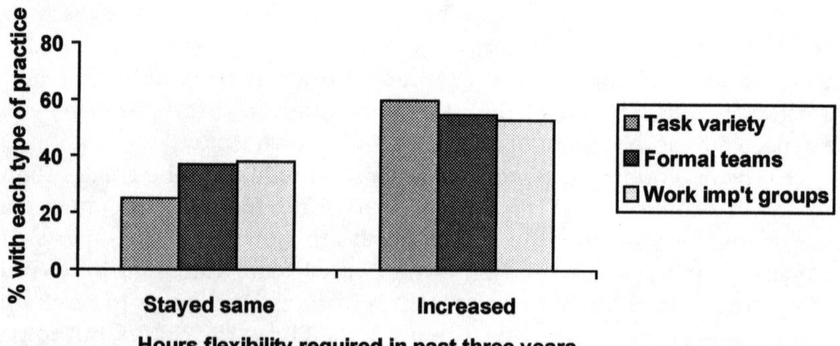

Chart 3.6 How required hours flexibility relates to task variety and team-working
Note: Cell percentages (each bar is a separate percentage of the total), weighted by employment. 'Work imp't groups' means use of work improvement groups.

the changes towards more flexible and responsible employees and teams, a rapid expansion of both rewards and controls. Although the two are different faces of the same coin, controls will be considered separately, and in more detail, in Chapter Six, whereas here the focus is on rewards.

Incentive pay was once the dominant approach to motivation in manufacturing, but with the rise of other ideas it became for a time regarded as old-fashioned. Now the pendulum has swung back and incentive pay is widely seen by management theorists as an essential part of high-performance work-systems.[12] There has equally been a practical development of incentives in Britain, which is viewed as a source of national competitive strength in the recent Porter report.[13]

The expansion in incentive systems is conspicuous in the results of the companion survey of employees. Over the previous decade, a bigger proportion of employees got incentive payments for personal performance, and there was a particularly sharp rise in group incentive payments. The results from the employer survey, in terms of changing workplace policies, are sharper still.

- Individual performance assessment is used as a basis for determining pay in just over one-half of the workplaces.
- One in three of those who do not currently use it are planning to introduce it in the near future.
- Most significantly, four in ten workplaces say they have been increasing their use of individual performance assessment in the past three years.

Not surprisingly, this growth in individual performance assessment particularly accompanies increased demands for employees to take on varied tasks and/or work flexible hours as required (Chart 3.7). To be individually

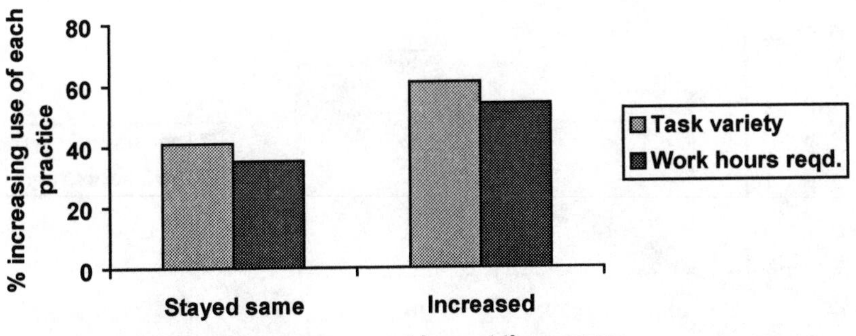

Chart 3.7 Individual performance assessment, task variety, and hours demands
Note: Cell percentages (each bar is a separate percentage of the total), weighted by employment.

rewarded, employees must show they are individually adaptable and committed.

While individualised rewards are flourishing, group or collective incentives are not being neglected even though they are as yet much less common. Two in ten of all organisations say they have been increasing their use of group-based or collective incentives over the preceding three years, and this rises above one in three at workplaces where there has been an increase in formal team-working. As in the case of individual performance assessment, the use of this type of reward is linked to workplaces where more is expected of employees in terms of covering a range of tasks and accepting variable demands on their time (Chart 3.8). This linkage can be read in two ways. Greater change requirements within employees' jobs tend to be backed up by a systematic approach to personal development. And/or, greater change requirements are enforced through tighter management monitoring, via the appraisal process.

Intelligent flexibility, downsizing and growth

How do these kinds of intelligent flexibility relate to competitive conditions? Workplaces that are in more changeable circumstances – *either contracting or growing* – are more involved in the shift to performance rewards than are stable workplaces.

The growing workplaces, understandably, are grasping at every kind of performance enhancement that they can get. So in growing workplaces, the whole range of flexibilities – individual and group – are being pursued to an above-average degree, and the same applies to both individual-level and group-level rewards and controls.

The contracting workplaces tend to operate in a more focused way. They go particularly for appraisal-based pay (45 per cent have this, as against 41 per cent of growing workplaces and 35 per cent of static ones), and they

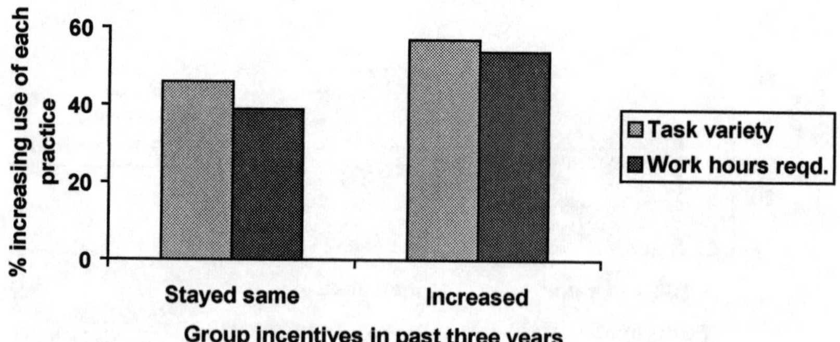

Chart 3.8 Group or collective incentives, task variety, and hours demands
Note: Cell percentages (each bar is a separate percentage of the total), weighted by employment.

also place emphasis on intelligent flexibility to the same extent as in growing organisations. But they have *not* been developing team-working to any great extent. Perhaps with a shrinking workforce they do not have the management resources to take on this kind of development.

This picture tends to confirm the existence of downsizing *strategies*, even though in only a minority of workplaces. Contraction is not a process of fatalistically withering-away, it is a process which, often, involves active policies – it is in these circumstances that 'downsizing' is an apt description. Employees who work in downsizing organisations are likely to be under added pressure, but they also have additional scope to vary and expand their jobs and get recognition for their efforts.

Intelligent flexibility and ICT

The surprise of the preceding chapter was that high levels of information and communications technology (ICT) were connected with the use of external flexibility such as temporary workers and outsourcing, as much as with any other factor. So how does ICT relate to intelligent flexibility? It might seem to be a reasonable guess that high-ICT workplaces would, in many cases, be undergoing rapid change in their processes, services and organisation, and so need adaptable, flexible and creative employees to an extreme. At the same time, because ICT can assist so much with continuous learning, the development of intelligent flexibility should be favoured.

Yet, surprisingly, there are only a few respects in which high-ICT workplaces are developing individual employee flexibility to an above-average extent. On other aspects of internal flexibility, there seems nothing out of the ordinary about them. To understand this, the views of a leading authority on ICT and innovation, Manuel Castells, are helpful. He sees managerial and structural reorganisation moving somewhat independently of technological change. Indeed, Castells notes that the development and diffusion of new and more adaptable organisational models in many cases preceded by a long period the rise of new information technologies. However, ICT subsequently has enhanced the feasibility of implementing organisational change.[14] So it may be that the high-ICT workplaces have *already travelled far* down the road of developing staff adaptability.

None the less, there are some aspects where ICT does prove to be important, and these, flagged in Chart 3.9, all make intuitive sense. Increased task variety for the individual employee is supported in workplaces with a substantial level of ICT, because the software and systems make it easier for the individual to acquire the necessary skills. (An example is the case of journalists who also become photographers with the aid of digital camera technology.) Work improvement groups are common in ICT-orientated workplace because new ICT sits alongside organisational changes,[15] in which innovative ideas from staff are particularly important. Finally,

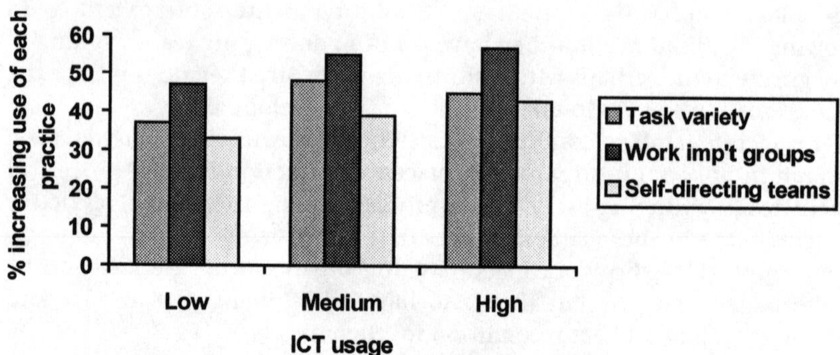

Chart 3.9 ICT coverage, task variety and team organisation
Note: Cell percentages (each bar is a separate percentage of the total), weighted by employment. ICT usage means the proportion of employees using PCs or computerised equipment, to the nearest 25%: Low = 0%–25%, Medium = 50%, High = 75–100%.

advanced forms of team organisation are supported by ICT which facilitates communication and information sharing. In addition, ICT performance monitoring systems, to be discussed in Chapter Six, reduce the risks to the employer of removing direct supervision.

Conclusions

This chapter's picture needs to be put alongside the picture from Chapter Two, for it is only in contrast that its significance can be seen. The previous chapter showed that flexibility that is brought-in from outside is in use virtually everywhere, but is approaching a ceiling or plateau. This chapter focuses on a different kind of flexibility, based on using the adaptability of the individual manager and employee in the regular workforce. Efforts in this direction are developing rapidly and apparently moving to the centre of employers' search for flexibility. This reflects the fact that change is often much more than simple variation in the scale of demand, involving shifts in the type or quality of products and services demanded and the complexity of the organisation needed to deliver them. The intelligent adaptability of the individual employee, encouraged through variable tasks, continuous training, and team organisation, can encompass changes of a kind which mere flexibility in numbers cannot.

But it is false to see the two kinds of flexibility in contest with another, and intelligent flexibility as the eventual winner. On the contrary, the two kinds of flexibility are found more often together than separately, and the conditions which stimulate the one also stimulate the other. It is not a case of 'either ... or' but of 'both ... and'. Employers who have to adapt to an environment of change – and that, currently, is most employers – are seeking for all kinds of flexibility that are available to them.

These conclusions develop those of Chapter Two in showing how organisations are seeking to compete. The sheer extent of employers' search for more flexibility underlines the reality and the urgency of the pressures of an ultra-competitive world. Equally, the particular emphasis on what we have called intelligent flexibility supports the idea of a shift to knowledge work, and of competition on that basis. But even employers pressing on with intelligent flexibility are not forgetting that they can trim costs at the margin by, for instance, using temporary and casual labour.

Another mistake, generally speaking, is to contrast individual flexibility with the development of team-working, another of the main current trends in employers' policies. Team-working adds still more flexibility for the employer, but it requires the individual team member to contribute more as well, so the two tend to accompany one another. There is however one important respect in which individual flexibility and team flexibility differ. Whereas growth organisations seek to combine the two, downsizing organisations focus more on individual flexibility to see them through. Perhaps the downsizing organisations are too busy surviving, or lack the management resources to take on the complex task of team-building. Yet another interpretation is that downsizing corrodes mutual trust and so creates an atmosphere that stifles teamwork.[16]

The implications of intelligent flexibility for employees seem more benign than those of external, brought-in flexibility. The positive implications include more varied – so more interesting – work, more training to support internal flexibility, greater responsibility, and more recognition and reward. But the implications are not, in fact, all in one happy direction. They also include the possibility of more pressure, and more control. For instance, the team can be as much a tyrant as any supervisor. The growth of appraisal systems and group incentive systems reflects employers' efforts to make internal flexibility worthwhile for their employees. But this will not necessarily satisfy employees who want to 'get a life' outside of work, since they tend to face increasingly variable work-demands on their time. Issues of working time and work-life balance are something we will come back to in several of the subsequent chapters.

4
Resuscitating Careers

It was in the early 90s, when Britain entered its second serious recession in a decade, that corporate leaders came out of the closet and admitted secure careers were no longer on offer. A few put forward a substitute policy: 'employability'. This meant that their organisations would at least go on training people, so that when they were axed they could be mobile.[1] In the USA, with its stronger free-market culture, these tendencies emerged sooner and were taken further. 'No long term' became a kind of slogan, coined by Richard Sennett in his 1998 book *The Corrosion of Character*. He argued that the absence of long-term relations at work made employees as well as employers into opportunists and undermined trust and commitment. It was widely noted that staff purges continued widely in the USA even in the booming 90s and in thriving companies.[2] Yet there have also been strong reassertions of the importance of long-term careers, including by US companies familiar in Britain, such as Wal-Mart (owners of Asda) and Citibank. Both are cited in a 1999 article by Sanford Jacoby, in which he concludes that the unexciting reality is 'less long term' rather than 'no long term'.

Debates about career futures are also intense in Britain, as illustrated by a report published by the CIPD in 2002, a few months before the CEPS-02 survey.[3] Here six experts put forward widely diverging views (see Box on page 55), ranging from Richard Donkin of the *Financial Times*, who sees a future where career ladders have disappeared and most professionals market themselves internationally on a freelance basis, to consultant Wendy Hirsh, who sees career development re-emerging as a central activity of the organisation to meet its business needs, and being extended systematically to cover all employees rather than the favoured few.

On both sides of the Atlantic, the move to kill-off the old corporate career promise was associated, in the perceptions of many, with use of external flexible labour and outsourcing. The greater the reliance on these external and variable resources, the less would employers need to concern themselves about their regular employees. In the past two chapters, however, it has been shown that brought-in flexibility seems to be

Expert views from the CIPD careers scenario

As part of the CIPD's review of the future of careers, six experts – four from Britain and two from the USA – gave their opinions. The following is a resumé of the British experts' views based on Daniels and Schramm, 2002a.

Richard Donkin, *Financial Times*, envisaged a future dominated by self-employed, freelance careers, with individuals marketing themselves through professional networks and sometimes having several parallel occupations. Management will be a universal skill rather than a specialism, and career thinking will have disappeared along with career ladders. This situation will provide a better fit to enhanced family priorities.

Wendy Hirsh, researcher and consultant, contrastingly saw career development as a central concern of organisations with individuals being shaped to meet business needs. Elements in career development practice will include feedback on individual progress, advice and guidance, and job assignments which provide learning opportunities. Importantly, career development will be extended to all employees.

John Mockler, head of HR at Tate Britain, was concerned about the talent gap in Britain, especially for public sector employers. This reflected past failures to invest in personal development. As one element to fill this gap, he proposes greater use of the experience of older workers and the development of careers beyond 50.

Helen Wilkinson, consultant, emphasised the growth of knowledge industries and more generally of small business and self-employment. People would move across companies, working on a project basis in a world of outsourcing. This would in part reflect individuals' mistrust of corporate employers who had previously reneged on careers. Organisations would need to think how to rebuild relationships in the absence of internal careers.

approaching a limit while flexibility through greater use of individual adaptability and team-working – what we call intelligent flexibility – is a rapidly rising force. This new emphasis seems out of keeping with the 'no long term' slogan. After all, why train and coach people to be versatile, with all the cost that entails, if you mean to let them go before long? But perhaps the problem is more on the side of the employee, especially if she or he is a professional with highly valued business knowledge. As Peter Cappelli has argued, the job market now penetrates within the organisation and seeks out such people, rendering internal career structures ineffective.[4] Indeed, a theme of the business press at the end of the 90s was the talent war raging between companies.[5]

Yet how better to retain talent than to offer the talented long-term prospects? For that matter, what neater way of obtaining a supply of talent than to develop it from the ranks of existing staff? While boards of directors not infrequently justify their high rewards by the need to recruit the best in the marketplace, recent research shows that in Britain at least, the CEOs of leading companies tend to be higher-paid when promoted internally than when recruited on the open market.[6] This suggests that, even at the highest level, retained talent tends to be a more valuable asset than externally recruited talent.

This chapter focuses on the careers debate, looking at what is currently taking place in British workplaces of all sizes and types. It also seeks to get behind the rhetoric of career policies by examining what employers are doing to encourage and reward employees to remain attached to them in the long term. A crucial aspect of our inquiry is to assess whether job openings are really being created, especially at management level, so as to give employees tangible career prospects, or whether employers are making airy promises with little substance.

Careers reclaimed

Whatever the situation ten years ago, the great majority of British employers now claim to be offering careers and supporting them with internal promotion policies. In all:

- Two in three[7] say that they have career ladders which are open to most employees.
- Seven in ten say that they recruit internally for management or professional posts if possible.
- Six in ten say that they recruit internally for other vacancies if possible.

In the two preceding chapters, little in the way of industry differences was uncovered. But here they loom large. Career ladders are offered less in manufacturing and utilities, which might have been thought of among the blue-chip careers of yesteryear, than in the service industries, some of which have been regarded as the chief repositories of dead-end jobs. Chart 4.1 shows the industry differences: it is not only financial business service or public services that have (or claim) career structures, but equally

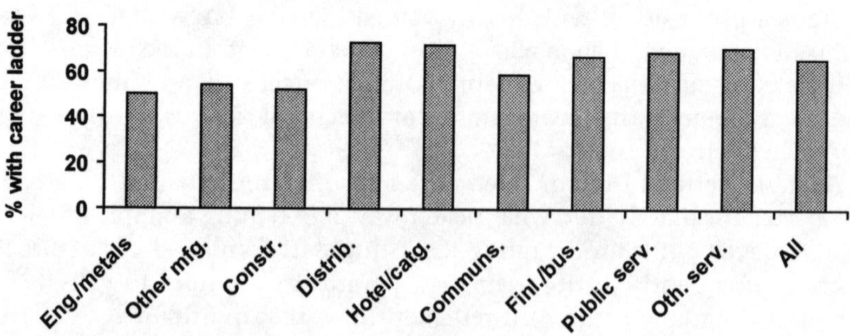

Chart 4.1 Career ladders offered, by industry
Note: Column percentages, weighted by employment.

distribution, hotels and catering, personal and leisure services. This is indeed a remarkable turnaround.

Sceptics might say that these figures are inflated by managers seeing their own organisations through rose-tinted spectacles. The myth of the soldier with the field-marshall's baton in his/her knapsack comes readily to mind. However, so far as the industry results are concerned, there are reasons for believing the turnaround in favour of services to be plausible. Whereas in the past this sector largely consisted of small independent establishments, it is now dominated by large chains which have the resources to develop employee skills. In the USA, for example, the retail sector has played a leading part in re-establishing a commitment to staff development and internal careers,[8] and in Britain also the leading retailers have played an important role in systematic training and in the development of National Vocational Qualifications.[9] British retail chains are widely regarded as among the best-managed and most innovative in the world. And a high rate of innovation generally implies an emphasis on skills and adaptability.

On the other hand, the industry results do not seem to tie in completely with the idea that careers are for highly-skilled knowledge workers. Financial and business services would have many staff who fit this description, but distribution, hotels and catering much less so and it is hard to believe that they are major bidders in the professional jobs market. It seems more likely that, for them, internal career structures are needed to find good managers and supervisors under tight competitive conditions and, more generally, to develop and retain the skills needed to run their expanding businesses. The growing dominance of chains over small independent operators may also imply a need for more middle managers to play the co-ordinating roles in these industries.

There is nonetheless a link between careers and the need for knowledge workers. Notably, employers with high levels of ICT usage across their workforce are on average more likely to be offering careers than those with lower ICT use. Career ladders exist in around seven in ten workplaces which are in the top third of ICT usage, but in only six in ten workplaces with a middling or low ICT usage. High-ICT users also turn out to be attached to some other policies for retaining staff, which are considered shortly.

There is in addition striking support for the overall picture from the companion survey of employees, carried out in 2000, and a similar employee survey of 1992.[10] In both these surveys, employees were asked whether they thought their best chances for the future lay in staying with their present employer or in moving on. In the earlier year, only about one quarter of employees below the management/professional level saw their best chances in staying, and more than twice as many in moving. By 2000, the position was reversed, with the majority of these lower-level employees now seeing their best chances in staying, not moving. At higher levels, where presumably prospects have been better all along, there was little change. So unless there is widespread delusion among employees, there has been a truly remarkable shift in the internal opportunities on offer.

Deferred benefits

Organisations that are serious about careers have usually backed them up, in the past, with financial benefits that particularly reward those who stay long-term. The two most widely used benefits of this deferred type are occupational pensions, and sick pay that is more generous than the State scheme.[11] So one check on how serious employers are about their career claims is to look at these benefits. Occupational pensions, in particular, have become a focus of media and public attention since 2001. As the sliding stock market placed the pension funds under intense pressure and thus exposed companies to risks of insolvency, there were much-publicised cases of schemes being closed to new entrants and/or of the pension entitlements being downgraded. Under these circumstances, maintaining an internal pension scheme becomes a promising test of an employer's commitment to a long-term relationship with employees.

In probing this issue, one should be conscious that pension coverage at the workplace may often be partial. Employees may opt not to join, and more fundamentally the employer may not offer a worthwhile scheme to all categories of employee. It is impossible to judge how effective the provision is in practice without a specialised inquiry. However, the survey at least makes a distinction between benefits that are available to 'most' employees and those that are only available to 'some'. It seems reasonable to assume that where a benefit is available to 'most', then it remains a major commitment by the employer. For instance, an occupational pension scheme which has been closed to new recruits can hardly be described as available to most employees.

In the light of our results, the recent pensions panic seems a little exaggerated. Around two-thirds of employers in the survey provide an occupational pension of some type to *most* of their employees, and this proportion rises to more than four in five in workplaces with at least 100 employees (Chart 4.2). This tallies reasonably well with findings from the companion survey of employees (carried out in 2000/01) where about two-thirds reported having an occupational scheme available to them. So occupational pension provision apparently remains the norm, at least for the time being. The longer-term tendencies are another question.

The survey did not ask whether a pension scheme had been wound up, or whether the employer's provision was changing from a defined benefit (salary basis) to a defined contribution (money-purchase) form. These have been the two adverse developments signalled in the media. However, information on these questions is already available in the reports of OPRA (Occupational Pensions Regulatory Authority). In each year from 1999 on,

Chart 4.2 Occupational pension provision by size of workplace
Note: Column percentages, weighted by employment.

the total number of live schemes fell, but all these falls were concentrated in schemes with less than 100 members, and the number of large schemes (1000 or more members) actually *increased* over the period. Nearly all the schemes offering final-salary or similar defined benefit pensions are large, while employees in smaller schemes are nearly all on a money-purchase basis. While some employers with large schemes are moving to money-purchase schemes, which reduce their exposure to the stock market, by the time of the OPRA annual report of 2002 this was still barely visible in the statistics.[12] This of course is no reason for complacency: others have followed suit subsequently and there is a real risk that many more will do so in the coming years, as has already happened in the USA.[13]

The proportion of workplaces having their own sick pay scheme for *most* employees is very similar to the proportion offering occupational pensions. Nearly three in five workplaces offer both. In addition, deferred benefits are much more likely to be on offer at workplaces which also claim to have career ladders in place (Chart 4.3). So, in the majority of cases at least, the employers' career claims do appear linked with long-term commitments to employees as a whole.

Where career opportunities are real

Although the majority of workplaces have career ladders in place and support them with internal promotion and deferred benefits, this might still be no more than good intentions. The reality of career opportunities depends on jobs being vacant to fill at higher levels, not just on the mechanisms for filling them. Similarly, long-term benefits only pay off for people who stay long-term, and these will be few if there are no prospects. So what are the opportunities in this real sense?

Notice that the answer depends on the existence of higher grades or levels as well as the existence of job vacancies. If almost everyone is at a single pay or grade level, the existence of vacancies will not do much for individual prospects. In delayering, whole grades – usually at supervisory or middle management level – are stripped out, leaving a flatter organisation as well as a leaner one. Inevitably this means fewer potential slots for those below to move into, thus lowered prospects and increased difficulty in retaining skilled and experienced people.

Career ladders, the survey shows, are in fact drastically curtailed at workplaces with very simple structures, up to three job levels (Chart 4.4). But, from four job levels upward, there is not a great deal of difference in the proportions thinking of themselves as offering careers.

Of course the number of job levels in many organisations may not be the result of current management choices, but just a legacy from the past. In around one in three workplaces, however, the survey shows grade structures as an area of active employer policy during the past three years. The

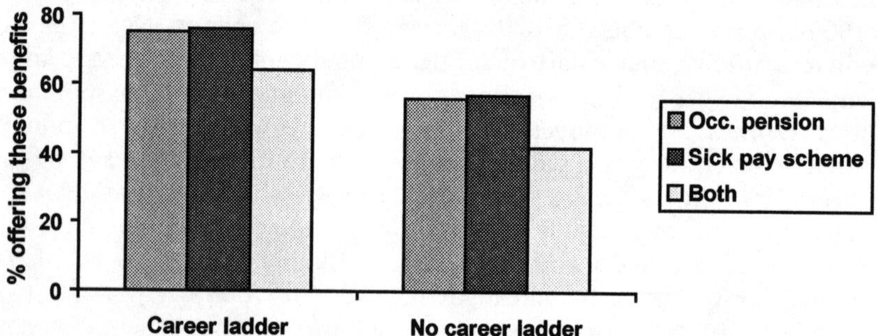

Chart 4.3 Relationship between career ladder and deferred benefits
Note: Cell percentages, weighted by employment. Sick pay scheme means employer provision beyond the statutory level.

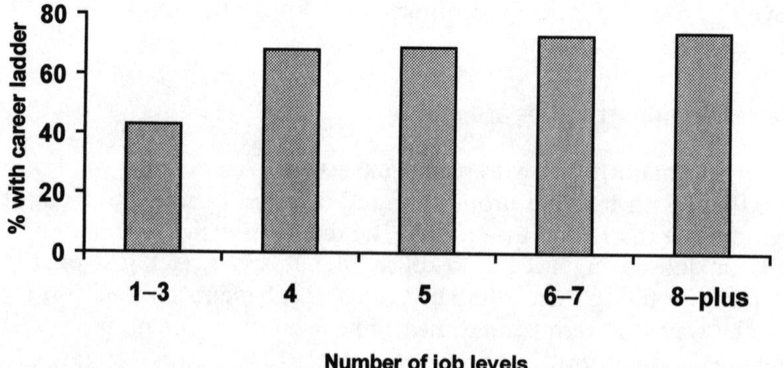

Chart 4.4 Relationship between number of job levels at workplace, and career ladder
Note: Column percentages, weighted by employment.

overall direction of change is clear: grade expansion, rather than delayering, is in the ascendant. Some slimming-down of grades continues to take place – with management grades in one in ten workplaces, and with below-management grades at one in 14 – but increases in the numbers of grades outweigh these cases *by more than two to one* (Chart 4.5). It seems that the move towards flatter organisations and broader grades, which was evident in the late 1980s and early 1990s, has been short-lived.

So one of the conditions needed to improve career opportunities is met. But what of the other: have the actual numbers of jobs available increased? Chapter One provided an initial answer to that, showing that the total number of employees is growing in far more workplaces than it is contracting. Here we can add to that by considering change in the *proportion* of jobs *at management level,* a question crucial for real prospects. In about one in eight workplaces, the proportion of management jobs is being cut. But in twice as many, it is being expanded. The overall picture, then, is a positive one for individual opportunity. On balance there are more management jobs to fill, spread across more management grades. And there are more stepping-stones in the form of sub-management grades, as well. The many employees who see their best chances within the organisation are *not* deluded.

Growth hormone

What factors underlie management expansion and a proliferation of job levels? At a superficial inspection it seems to depend on a strange assortment of industries: construction, financial and business services, public services, personal and leisure services. On closer examination, this hodge-podge has something in common: recent growth. And this single factor explains much of the change in this area – a veritable 'growth hormone' for

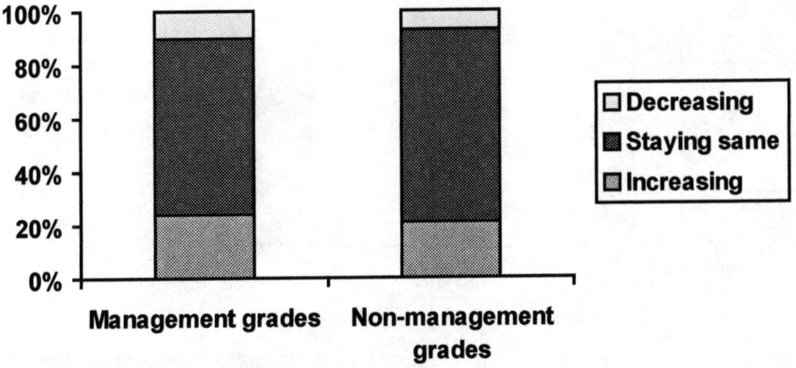

Chart 4.5 Changes in grade structures, 2000–2

Note: Column percentages, weighted by employment.

careers. Expanding management and extra job grades mostly occur where there is growth (Chart 4.6). Where there is contraction, conversely, the opposite tends to happen. There is a warning here not to be carried away by the current improvement in internal job opportunities, which possibly depends too much on economic conditions, and could be sent into reverse by recession.

Size surprise

Growing larger helps employers to beef up their management, and as noted in Chapter One, large workplaces are more likely to have grown recently. So it is natural to suppose that large workplaces have developed their management the most and are offering the best career prospects. But it is

(a) Proportion of management jobs

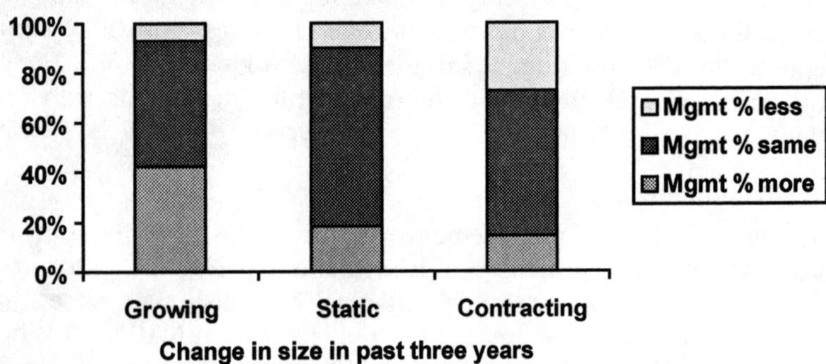

(b) Number of management grades

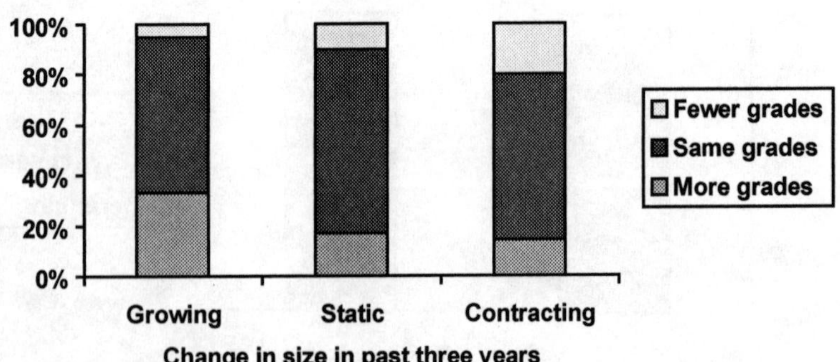

Chart 4.6 Promotion opportunities in growing, static and contracting workplaces, 2000–2

Note: Column percentages, weighted by employment.

not so. On the contrary, the biggest workplaces are *less* likely to be doing so than medium-sized establishments. For example, 35 per cent of workplaces with between 50 and 100 employees have seen an increase in the proportion of managers, but this drops to 29 per cent in workplaces with 500 employees or more.

Perhaps the reason for this result is that delayering is more deeply rooted in the large workplaces. They may be thinking about the next opportunity to rationalise even when growth is pushing them the other way. Certainly, these large workplaces are more likely than others still to be shrinking their management in terms of the relative numbers and the grade structures (Chart 4.7). Among the minority of large firms (500-plus employees) who have contracted overall, one in three have recently been engaged in delayering their management. But the extent of this kind of employer policy should not be exaggerated. Currently, it is very much a minority approach, although it could of course become more prominent in another recession.

ICT boost

If employers want to strengthen their management for long-term reasons – notably the shift to knowledge-based competition – this could provide a further explanation for the higher management proportions and extended management ranks observed in the survey. Especially, the expansion of management could be linked to the advance of ICT, placing greater demands on management and offering greater opportunities for the change-agents of innovation.

The *level* of ICT use in the workplace (that is, the proportion of employees working with the technology) is *not* connected to the expansion of management. But *recent increase* in the level of ICT use does seem to be part

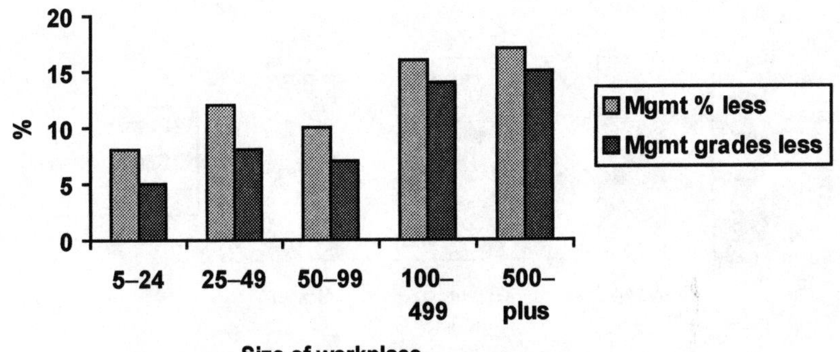

Chart 4.7 Size of workplace and management delayering, 2000–2
Note: Cell percentages (each bar is a separate percentage of the total), weighted by employment.

of the explanation. As shown in Chart 4.8, management growth is particularly enhanced in workplaces where ICT usage is growing *fast*. One in four workplaces have fast-growing ICT, so this makes a substantial difference. But it is still not nearly as large a factor as the overall growth of the workplace.

Supporting careers

Employers claiming to offer careers inside their organisations have now passed several tests of their sincerity. They do on the whole offer deferred benefits, they have put in more rungs on the career ladder, and they have created more room in the upper storeys. One further check needs to be made. Do the employers who offer careers and career structures, also have

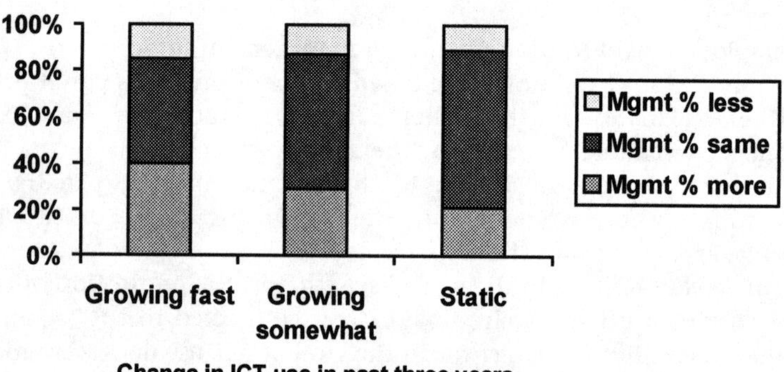

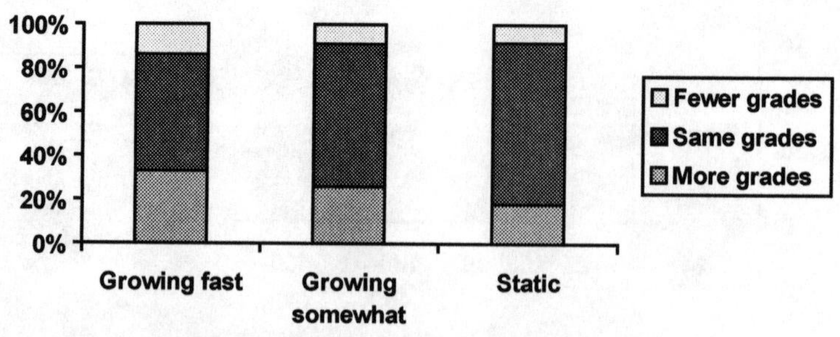

Chart 4.8 Promotion opportunities in relation to changing use of ICT
Note: Column percentages, weighted by employment.

clearly visible methods of developing and motivating employees to progress?

Appraisals

Appraisal, already referred to briefly in Chapter Three, is a long-established practice with origins in pre-War years. The practice has gone on spreading in an unspectacular but steady way. In the past decade or so it has become unquestionably the most widely used method of reviewing individual performance and stimulating employees to develop themselves and shape their own prospects. According to the companion survey of employees, nearly three in five employees – inclusive of managers – take part in an appraisal system of some kind.[14] Appraisal is used in a variety of ways, not just as the front end for incentives and salary reviews, but also as an input to decisions on promotability, and as a means of planning and reviewing training.

The CEPS-02 survey confirms that most workplaces now use appraisals in some form. It is the bedrock of human resource management (HRM) throughout Britain.

- Three in four apply appraisal to most of their employees.
- One in ten applies appraisal to specific groups, probably managers or professionals in the main.
- One-half of those limiting appraisal to specific groups plans to extend its use more generally.
- Four in ten of the minority without any appraisal system are planning to introduce it.

Because appraisal is so nearly universal, it is used by the great majority of the workplaces which do *not* claim to provide career ladders, as well as those which do. Even so there is a clear statistical relationship: workplaces without appraisal systems less often have an expanding management structure. Non-appraising workplaces seem a backwater where not much change is taking place, whereas the more typical workplace is managing a lot of change and is using appraisal as one of its standard tools to do so.

Involvement

Another way in which management tries to develop long-term commitment is by arousing employees' interest in and involvement with the organisation.[15] Of course this approach can be tried even without any career development opportunities, but it perhaps makes more sense where the employer wants employees to stay and get into a career relationship. Much of the involvement that employees experience depends on the skill of managers and supervisors in a one-to-one or one-to-group setting – processes too subtle to be captured in the workplace survey. Instead, the survey asked about the use of briefing meetings and groups, one of the most widely used methods of building involvement, and one which previous research has shown to be effective.[16]

Briefing groups are now used as widely as appraisals, or even a little more widely. Nearly nine in ten of the workplaces (88%) say that briefing meetings are in use, although they do not necessarily cover all types of employee. The companion survey of employees reports seven in ten employees actually taking part in communication meetings of this type, which is reasonably consistent with the employer survey's result. Workplaces that do not brief their employees, like those which do not appraise them, seem to be backwaters with limited career opportunities. Only one in three claims to offer a career ladder and the other indicators are also down.

So organisations which offer careers, and have widened the career opportunities by expanding job structures at management levels, also back this up with relevant human resource policies which constitute the current standard. Where this standard is not met, career opportunities tend to be depressed.

Conclusions

Gloomy predictions about the collapse of job security and the end of careers have abounded in recent years. But this chapter has established that careers are alive and well in the majority of British workplaces. Not only do employers profess to offer them, they are backing up the claim with an expansion of management-level jobs and through enlarged job structures. And these enlarged career opportunities are being supported by systems of staff appraisal and involvement which have become virtually standard. All this chimes well with the development of individual adaptability and team-working organisation which was described in the previous chapter.

Some scepticism might still be in order: if managers want to paint a favourable picture of their organisations, how better than to portray them as a world of opportunity? This argument could be convincing, if there had not been such a large and favourable swing, over the past decade, in *employees'* own views about their prospects – specifically, employees at job levels below management. Putting together the history of the early 90s, the employee perceptions then and now, and current management claims about career policies, one can come up with a simple interpretation. The recessionary early 90s were a time of acute insecurity when many employers reneged on career promises and sought a relationship with employees that was based on no commitments.[17] But after years of steady economic recovery, with tight job markets and rapidly advancing technical change, it makes sense for employers to restore a longer-term relationship which delivers continuity and motivation. A case example of an organisation (a

Changing policy on retention and careers: the case of a law practice

A leading commercial law partnership in London had for some years assumed that it would have a high turnover of its junior staff. Although salaries are high, work pressures are typically severe, since corporate clients expect very high standards both of quality and timeliness in the services. Moreover, there are far more capable staff at junior level than opportunities to become a partner.

By the late 1990s, however, the job market became tight and it was difficult even for a prestigious law practice to attract the type of young staff it required in sufficient numbers to replace the many leavers. There was also anxiety about maintaining succession. After discussion among the senior partners, the HR manager was asked to carry out a review to see how retention could be increased.

The HR manager identified several issues which were exacerbating turnover, including very long working hours and a lack of positive practices to encourage women to adopt a career perspective. Desire for a better balance between work and non-working life was an important factor for younger professionals. It was decided to develop policies that would recognise the need for greater work-life balance. A clear commitment was also made to supporting internal careers, including broadening individuals' experience and creating more intermediate posts below the level of partner.

Source: background case study for Future of Work project.

large law practice) which changed its mind on this score is outlined in the Box above. Quietly, quietly, careers are back.

There is however a noisome fly in this otherwise sweet-smelling ointment. If the demise of careers can be followed by their resuscitation within a decade, cannot another swing of the economic cycle bring things rapidly back to where they were? Cannot employers, in short, call off careers once more? Some of this chapter's findings indicate that this is not mere paranoia. What has driven employers to enlarge managerial ranks and grades is, first and foremost, *growth* – growth which can disappear in months. And even in this economically favourable climate, a significant minority of *large* employers continues to hack away at its managerial structures in the process known as delayering. If this process takes hold again more generally, the career hopes of lower-level employees will once more recede.

What is needed to put career policies on a sounder footing is a business case which is strong enough to survive even a recession. The advent of knowledge-based competition, hence the growing importance of knowledge workers, seems to provide such a long-term business case. With the growth of professionals and managers as a group (already touching 40 per cent of all workers), their distinctive needs and aspirations become a priority. Those needs and aspirations have always been closely allied to careers. Again, as organisations become more thoroughly permeated with ICT and related technology, they have the opportunity to change in far-reaching ways which require the adaptive involvement of all kinds of workers, and a particularly massive managerial effort.[18] Only organisations able to retain their capable and experienced employees are likely to make the most of this kind of opportunity for innovation.[19]

The findings of this chapter suggest that such a change in the business case may be under way, although perhaps still at quite an early stage. Employers with large proportions of professionals have awoken to the reality of the talent war. High-ICT workplaces are also more likely to offer career ladders, a sign which points in the desired direction, although the difference is not great. Most importantly, the expansion of managerial jobs is clearly related to increasing levels of ICT in the workplace, and especially to rapidly increasing ICT. As yet, the impact of ICT is much slighter than that of brute growth. That could change as ICT develops further. But, in the light of the evidence on ICT and flexible labour presented in Chapter Two, one cannot be too sure about this. The long-term skill content of ICT-based work may be lower than has been assumed. In that case, the link between ICT and career structures may continue to be governed by medium-term pressures of change, weakening in the longer run.

The findings of this chapter have, however, revealed a different and more important source of opportunities in Britain. The consumer service industries, for so long regarded as a dead-end in career terms, now put themselves forward as champions of careers. This is not mere posturing. These industries are now in many ways taking the lead in terms of competitiveness, efficiency and innovation. They include numerous world-class firms. They are not usually thought of as 'knowledge businesses' because they do not compete primarily on technology nor do they employ large numbers of the professionally qualified. But perhaps it is the conventional idea of knowledge work and knowledge workers which is at fault. For these firms do need considerable management and specialist skills to run them effectively and to carry through the continuous change in which they are involved. Knowledge and skills of these types, we suspect, have a large in-house component. Accordingly these firms need to retain capable employees and develop the required knowledge and skills themselves. The premier position of the service industries in the career stakes is the strongest reassurance available about future opportunities. It is also one which casts much new light on the diverse nature of knowledge work.

5
Shrinking the Workspace

The previous three chapters have portrayed a new portfolio of policies across many workplaces, with external flexibility balanced by a more intelligent kind of internal flexibility and complemented by a reassertion of careers and development. Despite a number of question-marks which still hover around, the picture is one which many will find broadly encouraging or reassuring, in its promise of reconciling flexibility with continuity at the workplace. We now turn to another aspect of working life where new management approaches seem urgent, and consider the progress of innovation. This too turns out to have some connections with issues of flexibility.

Many employees carry out a miserable morning commute each day, retracing their journey wearily home each night. The social costs in terms of road accidents, fatigue and loss of family time are appalling, while the energy and environmental costs are enormous. With huge numbers of workers engaged in knowledge or information work, and new communications technology making it possible for that kind of work to be done virtually anywhere, why must the old ways continue?

There is another particularly simple fact which may make employers think again about work locations and workspace. That is the rising cost of a square foot of workspace. At the end of the 90s and beginning of the 2000s, city-centre commercial rents rose at double- or triple-inflation rates each year, and now often stand at around £30 per square foot, even excluding the extreme case of London where prime locations can be far more expensive.[1] In our case study research we have seen how this issue has pushed its way to the forefront of employers' consciousness. Partly, perhaps, this is because they are coming to the end of savings in labour costs. For instance, we showed earlier how the use of brought-in flexible labour seems to be reaching a limit. Overhead savings are the new frontier for the cost-cutting organisation – and within overheads, the costs of premises loom large, especially at a time of growth and expansion.

The simplest answer to this simple pressure is to squeeze people into a smaller space while retaining essentially the same work system as now. For the employee, this only holds out the promise of more discomfort: offices in London are already far more cramped than in comparable European capitals.[2] But it is possible that employers will link up the workspace problem with the changing profile of their workforce and their technology. And they may also see a link with the growing employee discontent with (lack of) work-life balance.[3] It is when these links are made that ICT comes into the picture, as the enabling technology for the remote knowledge worker. This combination suggests a solution involving less commuting time and more family time for the employee, and reduced space needs (with linked reductions in service costs) for the employer. Flexibility over workspace then becomes an added dimension of the flexible organisation, and one with particular promise for employees.

Is this reality or fantasy? The Box on the facing page highlights some of the employers who are making it a reality. The rest of the chapter considers the more difficult question of *how widespread* the change could become. It also places the more innovative solutions to the workplace/workspace problem in the context of more humdrum but perhaps equally important business policies concerning layout and location.

Shifting the problem to another place

Businesses will not do something complex if there is a simpler, less costly solution. Faced with persistently rising commercial rents, a natural business response is to reduce workspace requirements in the expensive locations by shifting activities to areas where rents are lower, or by outsourcing the activities and leaving the contractors with the headache. The 2002 survey found a considerable amount of action under both these headings. Of course, it is likely that such shifts are focused on non-core activities while leaving the core business in the prime location.

A little more than one in six of the workplaces relocated some of their activities during the period 2000–2: 13 per cent did so within Britain, and seven per cent relocated some activities overseas. Overall, one in six workplaces carried out such partial relocation, including some with both domestic and overseas forms. Overseas location may of course be seeking new or less costly sources of skill, as well as lower overheads. The proportion with overseas relocation is a little lower than the one-in-ten who are recruiting staff into their workplaces from overseas (discussed in Chapter Eight).

Furthermore, one in eight workplaces currently has plans for relocation in the near future, either home or abroad. About four in ten of those with future plans of this type have already carried out some relocation recently, so it does not seem to be a one-off event but more a continuing process with one piece of relocation being followed by another.

In this process, the leading player is financial and business services, itself the largest industrial sector of the British economy. Here one in five work-

Space, place, profit: employers in search of solutions

The combination of advanced ICT and more flexible staff location can reap large business benefits. A particularly detailed example is given in a case study by Mahmoud Watad and Frank DiSenzo, 2000 who studied a medium-sized firm providing business services to the pharmaceutical industry. A new approach was introduced for the sales force, which involved providing each salesperson with a laptop computer and creating a central computer system for processing orders and providing information and communication services. The sales staff, equipped in this way, ceased to work from a central office and instead worked from home. Although the investment in hardware, software and training was substantial, about 30 per cent was offset by savings in office costs and a further ten per cent in direct staff savings. The main benefit, however, was that sales staff after the changeover spent an additional 15 per cent of their hours with customers, and this was conservatively estimated to translate into an additional ten per cent of sales revenue. Overall, sales rose by 21 per cent. Following this successful innovation, home-based teleworking has been extended to some other staff in the company.

In the UK, perhaps the most publicised office innovation has been British Airways' Waterside HQ, opened in 1998 after many years of development. Described by Hugh Pearman in the *Sunday Times* as 'the world's biggest nursery school', but with mobile phones and laptops in place of scissors and paints,[4] Waterside embodies a new idea of workspace without private offices. Communication points are distributed around the complex, allowing people to plug-in and work anywhere. The emphasis is on informal meeting areas encouraging staff to network, and so stimulating the flow of ideas. (For further details, see Michael Syrett and Jean Lammiman, 2000a and 2000b.)

Carol Glover, 2002 outlines smaller-scale but related office developments at BP Exploration (Aberdeen), Solway Healthcare, and Talkback Productions. BP Exploration is notable in recognising that office restructuring involves work restructuring, and that individuals differ in their preferred ways of working. Accordingly in its development, staff were given choice, within limits set by business needs, of working from home, working in a fixed office, or using variable facilities. Given this choice, about one-third of staff appear to have opted for a substantial change in their ways and places of working.

places has recently been engaged in relocating some activities, and one in seven has plans to do so in the near future. Much publicity has been given to the relocation of call centres in the Indian subcontinent, where there is a large surplus of highly educated workers: these call centres are often twin to a UK call centre to provide 24-hour service cover.[5] Among the factors making this possible are a high level of existing investment in ICT, a technology which melts away the barriers to business dispersion, along with the obvious attractions of much lower pay-rates and premises costs. The industry also has diverse and rapidly changing business opportunities and may use relocation as a means of placing itself where these opportunities emerge, in a growing world market for services.

Outsourcing

As Chapter Two showed, nearly all workplaces are making use of some kind of outsourcing – getting support services from outside rather than maintaining internal staff for this purpose. One in four workplaces replaced some employees by outsourced services within the past three years.

Outsourcing of this type is a large element in the downsizing strategy: nearly one in three workplaces with reduced numbers of employees has carried out some outsourcing, a significantly higher proportion than either growing or static workplaces (see Chart 5.1). But outsourcing is much more than just a part of downsizing. It is frequently practiced in all kinds of workplace, including those where ICT is at a high level or where the use of ICT is increasing strongly (Chart 5.2). This theme, with changes in the location of work being linked to new technology, will recur throughout this chapter.

The disappearing office

Although many employers are keeping down the pressures on space by partial relocation or outsourcing, this in no way takes the space pressures off the remaining staff. In fact, relocation or outsourcing policies usually go hand in hand with other policies to economise on workspace.

The basic method, used by every home in the land when space becomes cramped, is to move the furniture around. In the workplace, though, it is not just furniture but all the equipment and machinery which cause congestion. The point particularly applies to manufacturing, but even in paper-pushing offices the pressure from accumulating hardware has doubtless been aggravated by ICT. Reorganisation of hardware to free up space took place in a little under half the workplaces in our survey (45%) within the past three years.

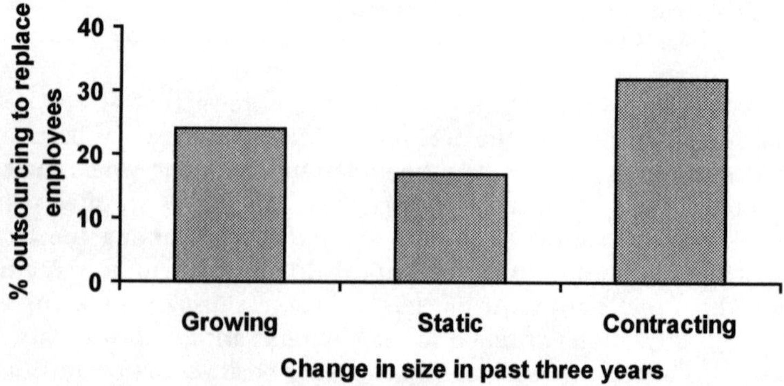

Chart 5.1 Outsourcing to replace employees, and overall change in employment
Note: Column percentages, weighted by employment.

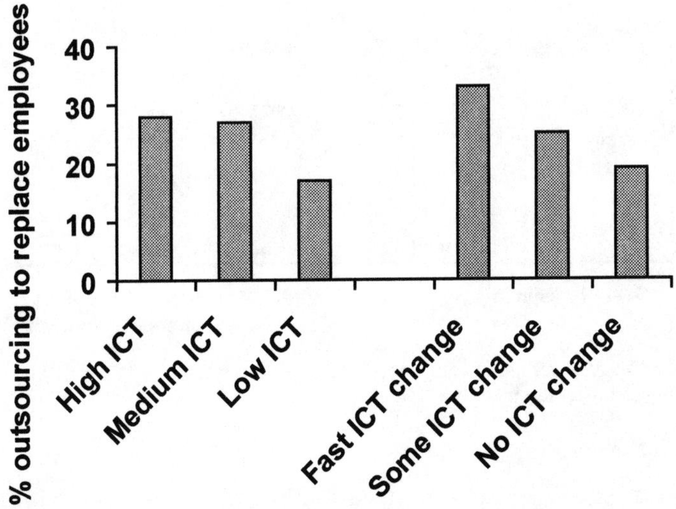

Chart 5.2 Outsourcing to replace employees, ICT use and ICT change
Note: Column percentages (two separate analyses side-by-side), weighted by employment. 'High ICT' = around 75–100% of staff use PCs or computerised equipment, 'medium ICT' = around 50%, 'low ICT' = around 0–25%. 'ICT change' refers to rate of increase in use of ICT over past three years.

This rises to nearer six in ten in manufacturing businesses and financial/business services, industries where hardware is particularly prevalent.

To go beyond this never-ending reorganisation of facilities, management has to consider more radical ways of using space. In our survey, we focused particularly on efforts to economise on office space, where (as the results confirm) a great deal of activity is taking place.[6] The oldest approach to economising on office space – so long-established that it can hardly be regarded as an innovation – is the open-plan office. Although there have been many debates over the years about the efficiency of open-plan layouts, they have continued to be used and to spread throughout most medium-sized and larger workplaces.

One might guess that, by now, they have reached their limit, but one would be wrong. Nearly three in ten workplaces (28%) say that they have been *increasing* their use of open-plan. And one in five plans to make *further* use of open-plan in the coming year. Once more the leaders are financial and business services (over four in ten increasing their use), here accompanied by manufacturing (over one-third).[7] Both growing workplaces and those with high or increasing levels of ICT, are also above-average developers of the open-plan solution (Chart 5.3). With such strong growth on an already-large base, it seems very likely that the old partitioning into small personal offices will soon have disappeared except for the privileged

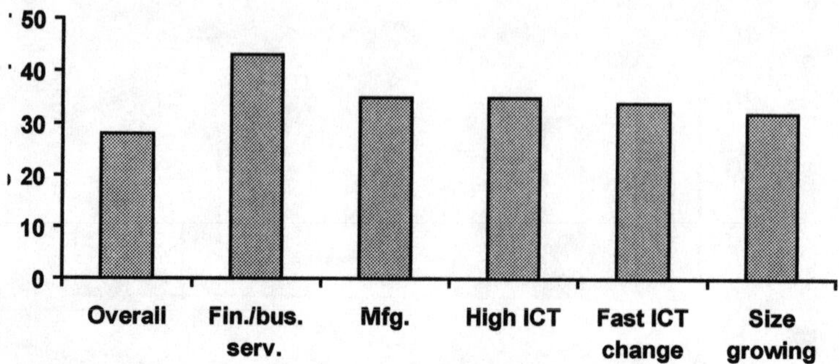

Chart 5.3 Above-average development of open-plan offices
Note: Cell percentages (each bar is a separate percentage of the total), weighted by employment.

few. Not even those staff who have confidential discussions with clients will necessarily be exempted. Many organisations ranging from banks to Jobcentres have shown that it is feasible to conduct potentially sensitive client discussions in an open-plan setting.

The development of open-plan offices has virtually killed off the idea that an office is a private domain for an individual – an idea exemplified by the lingering convention of knocking before entering. The worker in an open-plan office has personal space but it can be walked through by all co-workers, and what she or he is doing is open to view. The office in this respect has become like the factory floor.

The next, and more radical, step is to take away the personal space of the office worker or professional. The leading idea for achieving this is *hot-desking*. In its most sophisticated form, this depends heavily on technology. The office – open-plan, of course – is equipped with work-stations, which may or may not look like conventional desks, but no work-station is allocated to any one person. Usage is either first come, first served, or by pre-booking. The information which the individual needs for her/his work is stored in the networked computer system, and/or in portable devices like laptops, work organisers and mobile phones. In cruder versions, much of this technology may be absent and the individuals have to carry all they need with them.

Hot-desking potentially saves space in two ways. Suppose, for instance, that generally about one in three of the office's occupants are out working elsewhere (for instance, with clients, or at internal meetings). Then the number of work-stations can be considerably less than the number of occupants. Secondly, hot-desking creates incentives for the individual not to delay paperwork, or keep personal copies of files and documents, knowing that these have to be lugged around. The aim is to hold information electronically or in a common filing system. As such, hot-desking can be seen as a step towards the mythical paperless office.

Of course, like many innovations, the idea has been around for many years without being given a fancy label. For example, sales representatives or delivery drivers, out on the road most days, would have a couple of shared tables in a corner where they could come in to tidy up their paperwork. But these are small-scale applications, and the interesting question is how far the general idea can travel. The indications are, a long way, and perhaps rather quickly:

- Hot-desking is now being introduced at one in four workplaces.
- One in eight are planning to introduce it, or extend its use, in the coming year.
- Current users include one in seven workplaces with between five and 24 employees, small enough for the whole operation to be run in this way. Three in ten workplaces with 100 or more employees are applying the idea, but in these cases only a part of the organisation may be affected.

The rate of change in open-plan and hot-desking is all the more remarkable in view of the restrictions placed on tenants, and the dearth of innovative commercial property services, which prevail in Britain – see Box below.

Property market constraints on change

In a 1999 article, Virginia Gibson and Colin Lizieri considered the rapid rate of change in work organisation, especially in large companies, and speculated about the likely implications for space needs. They expected that the observable changes in work organisation would lead to more intensive use of space, and a reduced demand for fixed office space in terms of square-footage, but an increased demand for 'transient space' to meet temporary business requirements, together with a desire for more flexibility in facilities, layout and financial terms (page 204).

However, these authors also note that the British commercial property market is generally unresponsive to these needs because such property is typically part of an investment portfolio for institutional investors. These are chiefly concerned with the security of their investment and do not see themselves as providing a service to the market, and accordingly are extremely conservative. There has therefore been a sluggish response to new commercial space needs. As this inertia is gradually overcome, the rate of change in implementing innovative uses of space is likely to accelerate. Leverage could come from multi-national businesses with their high rate of change and market power, and from the leads given by entrepreneurial activity at the margins of the property market. The development of serviced offices on short leases is cited as a case in point.

Who hot-desks?

One industry with an above-average level of hot-desking is transport and communications. At first sight this is surprising, since this industry is rarely found at the head of workplace innovators. But it has many employees who spend most of their time carrying passengers or making deliveries, who may also need a part-time office base. So it has good reason to develop shared office facilities to meet these employees' needs. The hot-desking label may be new, but the practice, in this industry, is old.

This is much less so in the case of financial and business services, where more than one in three workplaces reports hot-desking. Because the industry is at the forefront of applying ICT, it is well-placed to adopt this approach in an innovative way. As it is actively using other space-saving policies as well, hot-desking can be seen as part of a concerted effort to contain the costs of premises. Moreover, as the industry with the lowest proportion of employees aged over 40 (a mere one in seven), it presumably has less of a problem in overcoming resistance based on traditional ways of doing things.

The other main factor which is pushing hot-desking along is new technology. ICT not merely stimulates a general atmosphere of change, of which hot-desking is a part, but provides the practical means for carrying out the change. More than three in ten of the workplaces with high levels of ICT already in place are developing hot-desking. This also applies to workplaces where the uptake of ICT has recently accelerated (Chart 5.4).

So it is not hard to predict a continuing development for hot-desking. It is already too widely spread to be thought of as a passing fad, and with further development of ICT the technical feasibility and support for the

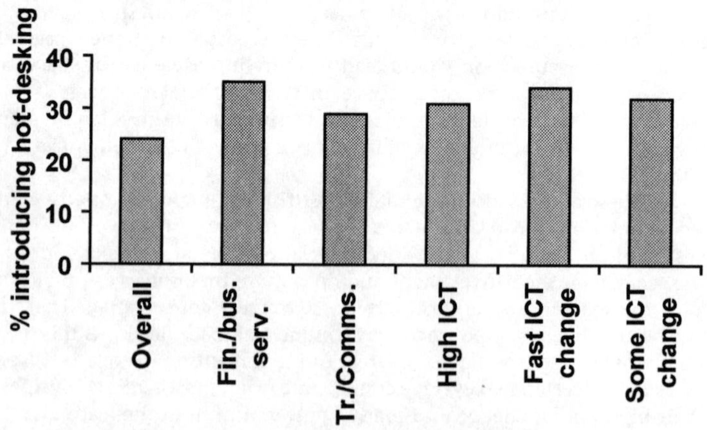

Chart 5.4 Above-average development of hot-desking
Note: Cell percentages (each bar is a separate percentage of the total), weighted by employment.

idea will strengthen. When hot-desking is added to open-plan layout, not much is left of the conventional idea of 'my office' and perhaps not much of the conventional idea of an 'office worker'. From one viewpoint this can be seen as a loss, but from another as an opportunity. The employee, no longer shackled to a particular office cubicle or desk, can perhaps gain more freedom to get the work done according to personal preference and business advantage.

Working at a distance

Perhaps the most radical way of getting rid of rental costs is to locate employees on someone else's premises, including their own homes.[8] Once more there is nothing inherently new about this idea, since even in the modern industrial period a proportion of production work has been put-out to homeworkers, who carry out operations like stitching or packing, which require little equipment and can be separated from other stages of the process. Or, at a managerial or professional level, there is nothing new about taking home paperwork as a solitary, after-hours task. What is new, however, is that administrative and professional employees, who work *collaboratively* in complex organisational systems, may now be able to carry out some or all of their work without being present in an office. This they can do through such means as mobile communications, portable computers, and networked computer systems.

One version, which initially received the most attention, is teleworking. Here the employee is carrying out the work-tasks in one place but the output from those tasks appears at another, distant place. In principle, this is no different from employees sitting at work-stations around a building and sending through information which appears in a central computer. The main difference is simply in the length of the connecting wire. Teleworkers may work from home, or they may go into a local Internet facility to connect to a remote organisational centre, which (as noted earlier) may even be in a different country.

Teleworking is like a regular job, wholly carried out at a place remote from the employer. Another option is for the employee to have a home office as well as a work-base at the organisation's centre, and to operate flexibly between them. This is often referred to simply as 'working from home'. This flexible approach can be particularly useful for employees who also travel about for part of their time to visit clients or attend outside meetings. The new technology makes it possible for the employee to remain continually in contact with base, and able to feed back updates from home or while on the move.

Our survey shows that one in nine workplaces has recently been developing teleworking, and exactly the same proportion has been encouraging the growth of working from home. In the near future, it is the latter which seems likely to pull ahead. While nine per cent of workplaces are planning to introduce or extend teleworking in the coming year, 12 per cent are planning to give further encouragement to working from home.

All workplaces have also provided an estimate of the percentage of employees, in an average week, who spend some of their usual working hours working from home: this includes those who are formally teleworkers as well as those who work from home in a more casual way. Overall the estimated figure is small, at three per cent, but this includes six in ten workplaces which have no employees working from home. In workplaces which permit working from home it rises to ten per cent,[9] and at those which are actively encouraging the practice, to 13 per cent. Moreover, one in eight of all workplaces believes that the proportion who work from home will rise in the coming year. Only one per cent believes that it will fall. These are all indications of a potentially important change, albeit one which so far is taking place only in a minority of workplaces.

Unsurprisingly, the financial and business services industry looms large in both teleworking and in working from home. One in five workplaces in this industry engages in teleworking, a proportion which is only approached by transport and communications (one in seven). In the next year, firms from the industry will pull further ahead since one in six plans further use of teleworking while in no other industry is the proportion as high as one in ten. Financial and business services also have the largest proportion of workplaces that encourage working from home, although public services are not far behind. These are also the two main groupings of industries where the planned extension of working from home is most widespread, covering one in six to one in seven workplaces (Chart 5.5).

The lead taken by financial and business services is natural, given its high level of investment in ICT which facilitates remote working of both types. In public services, teleworking has not been developed, possibly because of the high equipment and line costs which are involved, but working from home fits well with the work-patterns of many staff providing care and welfare services in the community.

Workspace changes and work organisation

Debates about work organisation often deploy issues of coordination and control on one side, with issues of individual effectiveness and autonomy on the other. These issues are also very relevant to policies about workspace and location. For example, the traditional layout with small, separated offices has been criticised for limiting both coordination and control. On the other hand, individuals may well be able to work more productively when the interruptions and distractions of the open-plan office are absent.

These debates take on an added significance in a period when teamworking is becoming the key way to organise work (see Chapter Three). For

(a) Recent change in working at a distance

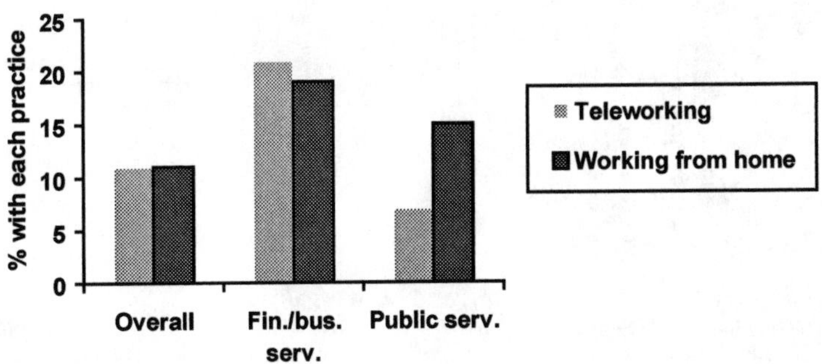

(b) Plans for development 2002–3

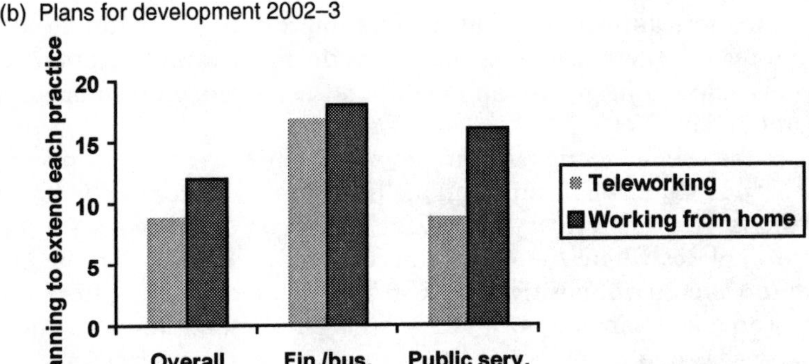

Chart 5.5 Above-average development of working at a distance
Note: Cell percentages (each bar is a separate percentage of the total), weighted by employment. 'Teleworking' means introduction of teleworking; 'Working from home' means encouraging staff to work part of the time at home.

example, both open-plan and hot-desking have been advocated *because* they permit free-flowing contacts between team members and emphasise the group rather than the individual. On the other hand, teleworking and working from home have sometimes been criticised because they interfere with coordination and make people more self-centered.

Organisations recently developing formal team structures are much more likely than others to be extending open-plan workspaces at the same time (Chart 5.6). The same link is evident between open-plan and group or collective incentive reward schemes, or between open-plan and work improvement groups (see also Chapter Three). Hot-desking is similarly

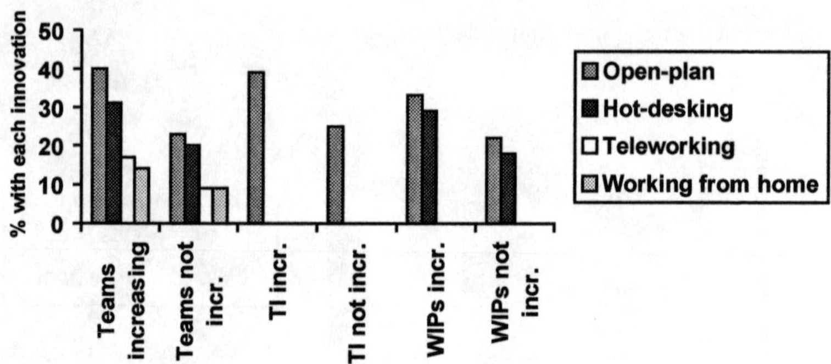

Chart 5.6 Work-space innovations and team organisation
Note: Cell percentages (each bar is a separate percentage of the total), weighted by employment. Bars are only shown where there is a difference between workplaces increasing and not increasing team practices. 'TI' = team incentives; 'WIPs' = work improvement groups; 'incr.' = increasing in past three years.

connected to team-working and to work improvement groups, although less strongly. It therefore seems likely that the move towards team organisation is going to fit in with and maintain the movement into open-plan and hot-desking.

But is the team-working tendency going to inhibit working at a distance? It seems not. Teleworking and working from home are more likely to occur at workplaces where formal team organisation is on the increase.[10] It is true that workplaces where the other aspects of team organisation are being taken forward do not positively foster teleworking or working from home as they do open-plan and hot-desking arrangements. But they are not particularly averse to them, either. It may well be that the developments in communications are removing the barriers to working from home, even where there is a strong emphasis on teams. If employers have reasons for developing teleworking, or working at home, then they do not on the whole see team-working as an obstacle.

The other main tendency in work organisation that was discussed in Chapter Three is towards more flexibility over tasks and time demands. Employers that are pushing ahead with these kinds of internal flexibility are also more likely to be going for all kinds of innovations in workspace (Chart 5.7). However, two other aspects of flexibility – training for cover, and job rotation – are linked only to open-plan office developments, and not to the other types of workspace innovation.

We can therefore interpret the workspace changes through several of the distinctions which have just emerged:

- Open-plan offices are connected with all kinds of change in work organisation and are probably part of a general 'culture of change' which has

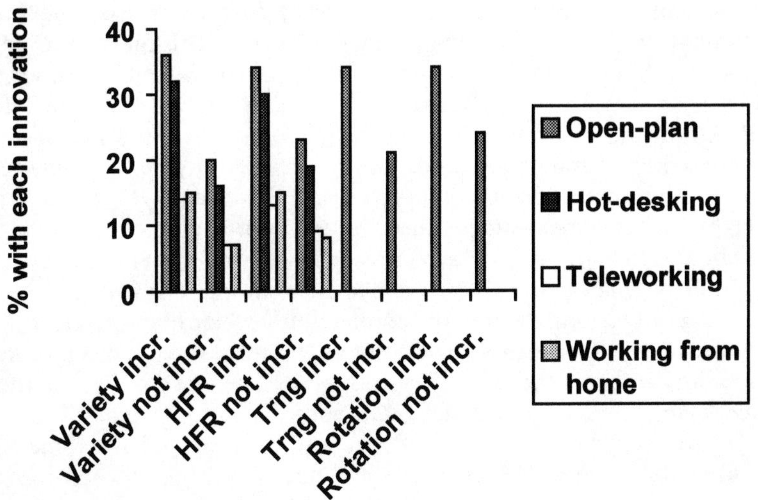

Chart 5.7 Work-space innovations and internal flexibility
Note: Cell percentages (each bar is a separate percentage of the total), weighted by employment. 'HFR' = hours flexibility required; 'Trng' = training to provide cover; 'Rotation' = job rotation scheme.

repercussions in terms of team organisation, individual working, and broader human resource systems such as training.

- Hot-desking is used more specifically to support both the development of team-working organisation and the growth of individual work flexibility, but is unconnected with broader human resource systems.
- Teleworking and working from home are more connected with fostering or supporting individual flexibility than with team-working, although they are not incompatible with the latter.

Is 'flexi-time' helped by 'flexi-space'?

We have just seen that innovations in workspace are all connected to the growing flexible regime inside workplaces, including demands on the employee to work flexible hours. Is it also possible that employees will have increased personal choice over their own hours, resulting from flexibility over work locations? This is most plausible, of course, when the employee works from home. But working at home may not mean freedom from control. Innovations in workspace such as hot-desking or working from home are brought in with the aid of a new technology which gives management, potentially, more ability to monitor the work which is being done at a distance. The individual employee may then have to put up with more control as the price of more choice over where and when to work.

What employees want above all, in terms of personal choice, is flexi-time working (this will be elaborated in Chapter Seven). This means the ability to vary starting and finishing times from day to day, within limits, so as to achieve contracted working hours over a period. This kind of personal flexibility is much more likely to be available for employees below management level in workplaces with two kinds of workspace innovation: hot-desking, and working from home. In workplaces with hot-desking, the overall one-in-eight chance of flexi-time hours being on offer rises to almost a one-in-five chance. In workplaces which encourage working from home, the basic one-in-eight chance of flexi-time rises to a one-in-four chance.

We can only speculate how the connection develops between flexi-time and flexi-space. Evidently, it could move in either direction. Once flexi-time hours are installed, workspace usage may become sparser, leading to space-saving ideas like hot-desking. Or, once the conventional ideas about workspace start to break down, it may also be easier to overcome rigid thinking about work-times. Either way, more choice over when to work appears to go with more freedom, or more improvisation, over where to work.

Conclusions

In designing our survey, we judged that the restructuring of workspace would be a new focus for management innovation. The survey's findings amply confirm this. And it is evidently not just a matter of saving on rental costs by squeezing square-footage. Changes to workspace are part of wider patterns of change and are connected to some of the major developments in work organisation that were discussed in previous chapters. They are implicated in downsizing, team-working, and intelligent flexibility.

Not only have recent changes in workspace been substantial, but it is relatively easy to predict that they will continue. This can be partly based on employers' own plans that they spoke about in the survey. Stronger evidence, though, is that the changes have been taking place in the finance and business services industries, with their long record of persistent growth, and more generally in workplaces which are high users or developers of ICT. It is the technology of communications which stimulates, permits and guarantees the continuing development of new forms of workspace.

The changes in workspace that have been documented in this chapter include both long-established and newer types. Among the older, the relocation and outsourcing of activities are very widespread but show no signs of petering out, while open-plan offices are being extended so rapidly that they will surely become – if they are not already – the standard form of office space. Teleworking, which is not exactly old but not exactly new either, is advancing steadily though unsurprisingly.

The newer and more radical workspace policies are hot-desking, already established as a major force in office design, and working from home, which though on a much smaller scale appears to be gaining ground. These developments can best be seen in a perspective which begins where the traditional office gives way to open-plan. First the privacy of the small office is dissolved, then (with hot-desking) the personal 'ownership' of a space and its contents gives way to a form of collective space, suitable for team organisation and mobile technology. Yet this change makes the individual employee in a way more self-contained, and less dependent on the props and supports of the office, although continuing to work closely with colleagues. Working from home (implicitly, *part of the time*) extends the independence of the individual still further, while using technology to maintain work connections.

In this last stage, especially through working from home, the individual can gain significantly in terms of personal choices over time as well as over place of work. Depending on how the individual uses these choices, there seems a chance of achieving an improved work-life balance through this channel. For that, most people will be prepared to trade-off some office space and status.

The trouble with this, however, is that working from home is never going to be available to all or even the majority of employees, other than in some highly professionalised organisations. It is essentially an option for the employee with a range of flexible, usually highly-skilled, tasks and roles which are not tied to one place for their performance. Many jobs, especially lower-skilled and routine ones, will never meet the criteria for working from home. For them, other pathways to improved work-life balance must be sought, and these will be discussed more extensively in Chapter Seven, Meanwhile, the changing workspace or workplace options for some may become a source of dissension or grievance for others.

As usual, we conclude by suggesting how the findings of this chapter relate to the main themes sketched in Chapter One. The more efficient and innovative use of workspace, which so many organisations are pursuing, is partly motivated by a search for lower costs. This is a further sign of the continuing competitive pressures and financial constraints under which most organisations operate. In addition, though, the workspace developments are closely linked with the advance of ICT – indeed, the links are much closer here than with the developments covered in the three preceding chapters. The changing approach to workspace and workplace reflects not only this technology but also the knowledge work and knowledge workers that the technology serves. As organisations experiment with workspace, they are also seeking to use their knowledge resources more effectively.

6
Extending Management Control

According to the preceding four chapters, many of the trends which have recently been developing in the workplace are benign. Employees tend to have more variety in their work, many more now work in teams which are given increasing responsibility, and career opportunities are being expanded. To cope with competition and uncertainty, organisations are relying less on bringing in short-term, dispensable helpers and more on the versatility and willingness of their permanent workforce. This is supported by development of human resource management practices, including training, job rotation, and communication. In short, employers are showing through their policies and practices that, once more, they value their managers and employees and want to develop them. There is even a prospect of more freedom over where employees work, possibly contributing towards an improved work-life balance.

However, this does not mean that the organisation is relaxing control. When senior management develops and empowers employees, or delegates more responsibility and decision making to them, they very probably expect some positive results from these moves. Even the most participative organisations, such as employee cooperatives, soon learn that control systems, and responsibilities for acting upon them, have to be maintained if the enterprise is to survive. When an individual is given more autonomy in a job, that means that she can make the decisions on her own but it does not mean that nobody should know what those decisions were or what were the outcomes. Autonomy implies responsibility, and responsibility involves scrutiny. As earlier research[1] has abundantly shown, more autonomy can, and does, co-exist with more control.

The interesting question is *how* control is going to be exercised. The general trends in background conditions, discussed in Chapter One, suggest plausible answers to this question. Competitive pressures on the business (or, in the case of the public sector, greater cost and budgetary pressures) are likely to be passed on to the individual manager or employee in the form of an increased emphasis on personal performance, backed by a variety of rewards and sanctions. The first part of this chapter will review the survey findings which relate to this prediction. Since many aspects of motivation can also be seen as forms of control, much of this material is also covered, from the motivational angle, in other chapters and can be dealt with quite briefly here.

What is *new* about control is the opportunity provided by the rapid development of information and communications technology (ICT), another important background pressure discussed in Chapter One. This development in technology makes it possible for the organisation to monitor progress and performance in a far more detailed way, and at much lower cost, than would ever have been possible in the days when control equated to personal supervision. The case of call centre staff has attracted particular attention.[2] The modern electronic switchboard, coupled to computers, permits individuals' work to be measured almost costlessly and with a precision undreamed-of in shop-floor production systems.[3] The call centre manager can spot hour-by-hour or even minute-by-minute anyone who is dallying between calls or is lavishing too much time on a customer. But this is only one very obvious example of what is potentially a much wider development, one which affects managers and their performance targets as much as it affects front-line staff. The survey provides an overview of how ICT-based control is being applied throughout the economy and the workforce.

Control and motivation

Control, as already pointed out in Chapter Three, is the other face of motivation. Employers provide incentives of various kinds to ensure that employees devote their time and focus their efforts on the organisation's interests rather than their own. These incentives can be seen as motivators which produce more effort, or effort of the desired kind. But they can also be seen as controls,[4] because they are almost always linked to some kind of system for checking that the incentives really are generating performance. Whereas Chapter Three stressed the motivational side of incentives, this chapter concentrates on the control side and the changing methods of achieving that control.

White-collar incentives

Historically, and as recently as the 1980s, incentive pay was chiefly of two kinds: commission paid to salespeople, and – much more importantly in terms of the numbers affected – various types of piecework or output bonuses paid to shop-floor production workers. Both these forms of incentive evidently have a large element of control attached to them since payment depends on measuring what is sold or produced (and often comparing this with pre-set targets or standards). Indeed, the extent to which the main tasks of the job could be measured has usually been taken as the key consideration in deciding whether to incentivise pay. For this reason, people working in professional, managerial or white-collar jobs (except those directly involved in sales) in the past were generally excluded from incentive pay. Their jobs were just too complex and too hard-to-measure.

With the shrinkage of jobs in the manufacturing sector and the huge growth of white-collar and professional jobs, incentive pay might have been expected to wither on the vine. But the opposite has happened. As already noted in Chapter Three, after a period of declining popularity with senior management, incentive pay has recovered much ground in recent years – with the approval of many if not all HRM gurus. According to national statistics, the proportion of non-manual employees receiving payment-by-results or other forms of bonus or incentive payments has risen and is not far behind that of manual employees.[5] Furthermore, the proportion of total pay coming from this source is now higher for non-manual than for manual employees, and the actual amounts paid out are much higher for the former since their average earnings are greater. The overall result is that employers are now paying out *four times as much* in performance-related payments to non-manual as they are to manual employees (see Table 6.1). The old assumptions about where incentive pay will be applied have been turned upside down. Even so, these figures certainly *understate* the real change which has taken place, since they exclude performance-based annual salary rises, which apply chiefly to people in white-collar jobs.

The rise and rise of appraisals

How then have organisations squared the requirement for control with this expansion of incentive pay for hard-to-measure white-collar jobs including those at management level? Performance appraisal is one of the main answers. Chapter Three described how this long-established approach has

Table 6.1 Incentive pay for manual and non-manual full-time employees

	Manual	*Non-manual*
Proportion of all full-time employees	30.8%	69.2%
% of each group getting PBR[(a)] or similar pay	18.4%	12.2%
Average weekly payment of PBR, etc. if any received	£59.3	£159.6
Manual/nonmanual PBR, etc. as proportion of total national PBR cost	20%	80%

Note: [(a)] PBR = Payment by Results.
Source: New Earnings Survey 2002 – United Kingdom: Streamlined and Summary Analyses; various tables, own calculations. Excludes part-time and juvenile workers. Weekly amounts include longer period PBR (e.g., monthly or annual bonuses) converted to weekly basis.

slowly but steadily spread to become part of the basic stock-in-trade of HR management. Although originally applied mainly to managers, professionals and other white-collar employees, appraisals are now also part of the work-scene for nearly four in ten manual employees.[6] Appraisals are used in a wide variety of ways, for instance to plan training and development, but it is when they are linked in some way to pay that they become an overt means of control. The CEPS-02 survey shows that appraisals provide at least part of the basis for pay decisions in four workplaces out of every ten, a figure which corresponds quite well to what employees themselves report in our companion employee survey.[7] This figure will incorporate both the use of appraisals for determining shares in an incentive pot (such as monthly, quarterly or annual bonuses), and their role in varying annual pay rises on an individual basis.

On face value this appears to put a large part of incentive pay at the mercy of managers' subjective judgements. However this may be to ignore the links with other changes in the background. These include, for instance, extensive use of targets and objectives (often quantified) for individuals,[8] and behind these the growing availability of performance data from computer systems, to be discussed later in the chapter. Moreover, many employers, especially larger ones, have devoted great efforts over many years to training managers in appraisal techniques and to ensuring that the reviews are carried out systematically. Previous research has suggested that appraisal systems are capable of increasing the pressure to perform which employees experience.[9]

Even when not linked to incentive pay or to salary reviews, the appraisal systems – now used in 17 workplaces out of 20 – give management at least an idea of which employees are performing below the average and which are performing above the average. This information is potentially important in reinforcing motivation and control in a variety of indirect ways, as well as directly through incentives or pay increases. Some of these indirect paths to motivation/control will now be considered.

Promotion and appraisal

The increased opportunities for promotion that were described in Chapter Four provide employers with a means of motivating higher performance. Promotion usually provides much greater rewards for the successful than they can get through incentive pay or salary increases. An appraisal system can convert the motivation for promotion into a control system, if it makes it clear to the individual what type of performance will influence future promotion decisions.

The CEPS-02 survey did not ask any direct questions about the links between appraisal and promotion, but the previous chapter indicates that the use of appraisal is at a particularly high level where genuine promotion opportunities are available. The companion survey of employees also shows that people tend to be aware of this link. Of those who get appraised, well over half (56%) think it affects their promotion chances, and this proportion rises to nearly two in three (65%) among employees who believe their promotion chances are 50/50 or better.

Long-term rewards and appraisal

Similar reasoning applies to other kinds of reward which lie in the future for the manager or other employee who stays with the organisation. These include, most obviously, an occupational pension, the protection provided by an employer's sick-pay scheme, and the cumulative impact of salary increases or increments over the years. The labour economist Ed Lazear has argued that these common features of organisational reward systems are not mere paternalism but provide powerful motivation, if combined with the policy of dismissing employees who 'shirk' in their jobs.[10] Employees are fearful of missing out on these long-term benefits and so make sure that they work to an acceptable level of performance. Of course, the fear of losing long-term rewards will particularly apply to people who are past the mid-career point, plus those who are anxious to have a protected career-track from the outset.[11]

Once again, appraisal provides a method of turning this source of motivation into a method of control. This is particularly so when combined with awareness that, some time in the future, managers and staff could be affected by redundancies through business contraction or merger. If the organisation always has, through appraisal, an up-to-date rating of employees as better/worse performers, then it has a ready means of deciding who will stay and who will go at such a time. However, where performance aims are not clearly communicated, or are not consistently acted on in appraisals, anxiety about future job retention (or about promotion chances) can lead to counter-productive and neurotic behaviour such as 'presenteeism' (the desire to be seen as the last person to leave the office).

Interestingly, workplaces where the numbers employed have recently been shrinking are just as likely to be using appraisal as workplaces where employment has been growing (Chart 6.1). This fits the idea that appraisal can continue to be an effective form of control even where job security is uncertain. It also adds to the evidence that downsizing workplaces are not lacking in HRM practices. It is in the workplaces where employment is static that appraisals are less often in use.

Group control and appraisal

Another way in which management has sought control in managerial, professional and white-collar groups is through the development of teamworking. It is true that the work of a poorly motivated or ineffective person can be 'hidden' within a work-group, especially if the group is protective towards its members, and this suggests more rather than less control.

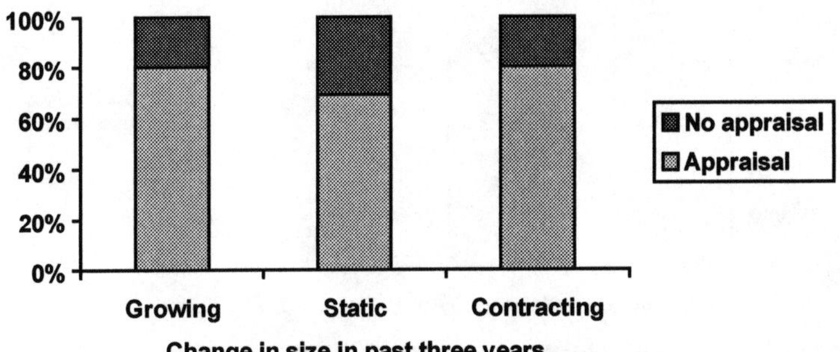

Chart 6.1 Appraisal in growing, static and contracting workplaces
Note: Column percentages, weighted by employment.

However, the performance of an individual is usually more visible to members of a close-knit team than to a superior. In practice, it seems that team-working groups often exert additional pressure to perform on their members. Indeed, one of the dangers of team-working is that these pressures can become excessive, interfering with an organisation's attempts to develop work-life balance policies.[12]

As Chapter Three indicated, team-working – even though by no means a new approach – has been on the increase in a large proportion of workplaces in recent years. The control aspect of team-working has simultaneously been reinforced by the growth of group-level pay for performance, which gives the team an added incentive *not* to shelter an under-performing individual. The companion survey of employees shows that over the 1990s, the national proportion taking part in group-based incentives grew from a mere five per cent (one in 20) to 17 per cent (about one in six). The CEPS-02 survey shows furthermore that one in five workplaces has been *increasing* its use of group incentives in 2000–2.

Increased use of formal teams is much more likely where appraisal is also in use (Chart 6.2), or *vice versa*, suggesting that senior management feels more assured in using teams where the appraisal system provides a measure of control. A substantial part of appraisal now has a group dimension. One in eight workplaces say that when appraisals are used to determine pay rewards, group performance is involved as well as individual performance. This equates to nearly one-third of the workplaces where appraisal is being explicitly linked to pay.

Control through technology

While appraisal is the established orthodoxy for control of employee performance, ICT-based monitoring is the prospective revolution. To recap briefly on what was presented in Chapter One, ICT is already extremely

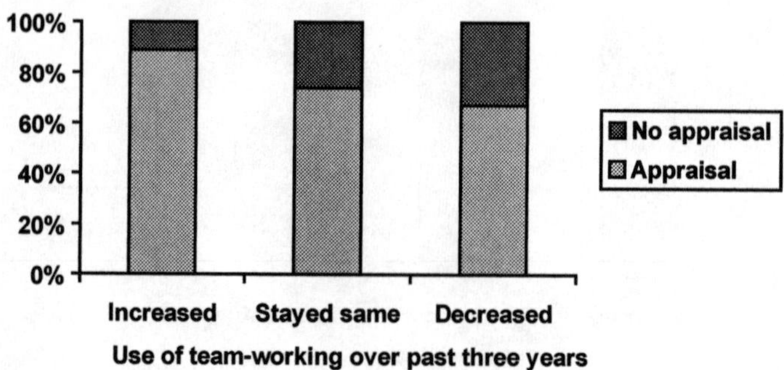

Chart 6.2 Formal team-working and appraisals
Note: Column percentages, weighted by employment.

widespread in British workplaces, and is continuing to be steadily extended, both in terms of employees covered and in terms of applications. At least two-thirds of all employees, at all job levels, and including the smallest workplaces, are using ICT in their jobs.[13]

Coupled to this is the spread of digital electronic recording equipment, as used for example at checkouts or cash-tills, in continuous chemical processes and on assembly lines, in the cabs of commercial vehicles, in telephone systems, and throughout computer messaging networks. It is the linking of digitised records with computer systems that provides the almost unlimited potential of ICT for monitoring work. While such monitoring was formerly hard-wired into some production lines, for instance to provide continuous records of output or defects, the new technology covers a much wider range of employees and is inherently more adaptable and encompassing because it is software-based. Where – much more commonly – control systems were formerly based on paper forms that were laboriously analysed into progress reports or management accounts, the impact of ICT is still more fundamental, creating scope for continuous or short-cycle rather than weekly or monthly checking.[14]

It is impossible to devise a single question which covers all aspects of ICT-based monitoring and control. Our nearest approach to this is a question which asks managers whether 'a computer system or automatic data recording system keeps a continuous record of the work being done by any employees'. The wording stresses monitoring rather than periodic accounting, and task performance rather than, for example, attendance or competence.

Two other questions deal with additional specific aspects of monitoring, which may not be completely covered by the more general question. The first asks whether the workplace makes use of EPOS (electronic point-of-sale) equipment, such as are particularly familiar at the supermarket checkout, and are quite widely used by many other types of service business.

Although the primary purpose of EPOS is usually to log sales and update stock records, the technology can also be used to monitor and analyse the performance of sales and checkout staff. The second question concerns the use of electronic time recording (ETR) or time management systems, which are used to monitor attendance and hours worked.

The basic results for all three questions are summarised in Chart 6.3, which also shows differences by size of workplace. EPOS and ETR are each used by about three in ten workplaces, but whereas EPOS is used equally across workplaces of all sizes, ETR has made most of its impact on the employees of the larger workplaces. Continuous work monitoring through ICT is taking place in nearly half the workplaces – a full half in the larger ones, and over one in three of the smallest group.

Coupled with the general question about continuous monitoring through ICT, the survey also asked for an estimate of how many employees are affected. As shown in Chart 6.4, in about one-half of the workplaces with

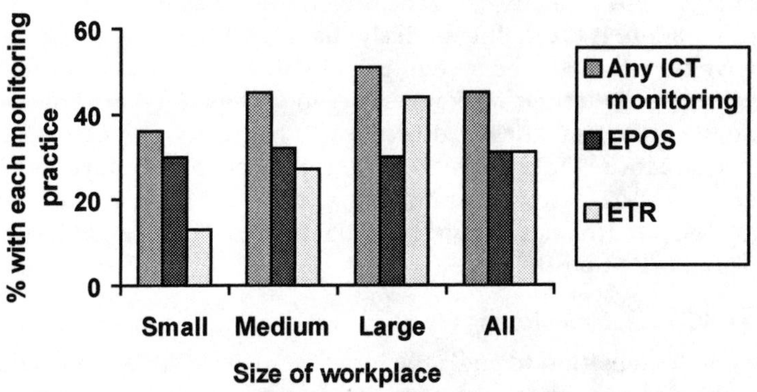

Chart 6.3 ICT monitoring, EPOS and ETR by size of workplace
Note: Cell percentages (each bar is a separate percentage), weighted by employment. EPOS = electronic point-of-sale; ETR = electronic time recording.

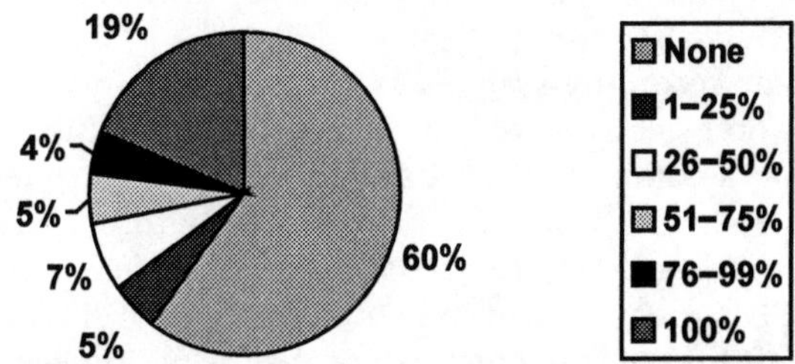

Chart 6.4 Proportion of employees covered by ICT monitoring
Note: Total percentages, weighted by employment. The legend reads clockwise, beginning with None (60%).

this kind of monitoring (one in five of all workplaces), *all the employees are covered*. The remaining workplaces with ICT-based monitoring have widely varying proportions of coverage. Overall, about three in ten employees is currently covered by this type of monitoring, according to management estimates.

Of course, being covered by the monitoring technology does not necessarily mean that an employee is actually being checked with it, or is conscious of its heavy breathing. It is therefore interesting to consider what employees themselves say on the subject. The companion survey (WIB-00) asked employees whether a computerised system kept a log or record of work they did. Just over one half of employees said that this was happening, a considerably higher proportion than suggested by management in the workplace survey. The discrepancy probably arises because managers, in reporting their current practices, disregard systems that are not actively being used. For instance, all employees – including the CEO – using computers connected to a computer network[15] can have all their computer usage logged, but in many cases the organisation has no practical use for this information. It is certainly unlikely that the CEO will be checked on in this way, even though the system permits it. In fact, less than half the employees who said their work was being logged by ICT – or about one in four of all employees – believed that it was being actively used to check their performance.[16] Taken together, the employer and employee evidence indicates that ICT-based monitoring is already a significant presence in management control, but also suggests that it is not being used to anything like the full extent possible.

Where is ICT-based monitoring used?

It takes no imagination to guess the industries where EPOS is entrenched. These are distribution (where nearly three in four establishments are users), hotels and catering (where the proportion is two-thirds), and leisure and personal services (somewhat over two-fifths). In addition, EPOS is more often used where the proportion of part-time staff is high (a distinction which separates retailing from wholesaling in the distribution sector). EPOS is little used in public services.

Electronic time recording systems as we have already seen are mainly used in larger workplaces, and they are also used where there are many job levels indicating a complex type of structure that usually requires more control. Unionised establishments are more likely to use ETR than non-unionised, even after allowing for size and industry differences. In terms of industries, ETR is more prevalent in manufacturing (with around one-half of workplaces in this sector), which is not surprising in view of the tradition of 'clocking-on' which has long existed among shop-floor employees. Among the service industries, though, there are many workplaces using ETR in both distribution and financial and business services (two-fifths of workplaces). The proportions using ETR are very much lower in all other services.

Whereas EPOS and ETR have distinctive patterns of usage across industry, the more general type of continuous work monitoring via ICT is much more evenly spread. Public services have the lowest level of ICT-based monitoring (about one in three workplaces), with most other industries falling in the bracket of around 40–50 per cent of workplaces as users. Financial and business services have the highest rate, with 55 per cent of workplaces; this is the industry where call centres, telephone transactions, Web-based services, and Internet use are further advanced than elsewhere.

Overall the picture is one of a widespread development of ICT-linked monitoring, with public services as the chief exception (Chart 6.5).

The control of work-time

To explore how ICT is applied to control, the simplest place to start is with ETR systems. ETR in its simplest form is no more than a traditional clocking-on device with an electronic mechanism. More sophisticated versions take advantage of digital technology to provide data input to a computer, or have an integral computer programme. This offers more extensive recording options and greater ease and flexibility of analysis.

Over the 1990s, there was an increase in the proportion of employees whose attendance hours were checked by a time-clock or by ETR.[17] This seems strange in view of the considerable shift of employment, over the same decade, towards professional and managerial jobs where 'clocking' has never prevailed. It also seems out of tune with the movement towards more empowered, participative employees. Shouldn't they at least be trusted to work their contracted hours? The point is perhaps that contracted hours are no longer the simple thing they once were, and with a growing complexity of working hours, senior management feels the need

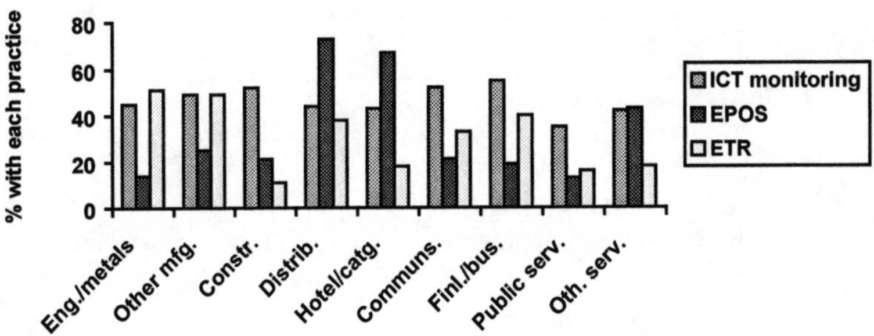

Chart 6.5 ICT monitoring, EPOS and ETR by industry
Note: Cell percentages (each bar is a separate percentage of the total), weighted by employment. EPOS = electronic point-of-sale; ETR = electronic time recording.

for more measurement and monitoring. ETR with its flexibility of analysis as well as recording is then deployed to meet this need.

Certainly the use of ETR is linked to the two main ways in which working hours are becoming more flexible: the organisation's demands on managers and other employees to work variable hours as required, and employees' gain of personal control over their own attendance times through flexi-time working. As shown in Table 6.2, increased use of ETR takes place in both circumstances, and especially with flexi-time working. People probably accept ETR as the inevitable price of more choice over when they work.

ETR also provides time control relating to variable and extended hours, and the associated premium payments or time-off in lieu. Even if pay is not involved, the employer can point to the demands of the Working Time Regulations, which are discussed further in Chapter Ten. Those workplaces with ETR are much more likely to be monitoring working time to conform with the Regulations, than those workplaces that have no ETR (Table 6.2 again). Despite these reasonable justifications for ETR, the technology can arouse strong employee resentment and opposition in some circumstances. This was vividly illustrated in July 2003, when the imposition of an ETR system by British Airways management led to a disastrous wildcat strike of check-in staff at Heathrow Airport.

How is ICT-based monitoring information applied?

As exemplified by the Heathrow strike, it is where monitoring, aided by technology, becomes persistent and obtrusive that criticism is often voiced (see Box on following page). The media reaction to the continuous monitoring of employees' work, notably in the case of call centres, has been generally hostile. Many academic commentators have also seen the development as sinister, drawing parallels with nineteenth-century prisons

Table 6.2 ETR: links to working time practices

	% with ETR
(a) Increased requirement on employees to work flexible hours	36%
– No change in requirement	27%
(b) Flexi-time working for non-management employees	42%
– No flexi-time	29%
(c) Monitor actual hours for Working Time Regulations	34%
– No monitoring for this reason	21%

Note: Cell percentages, weighted by employment.

Dangers of over-control

People Management, the journal of the Chartered Institute of Personnel and Development (CIPD), has published several features in recent years warning managers of the dangers of going too far with monitoring and control.

In the issue of 23 November 2000, consultant Michael Rose criticised the emphasis on controlling people through a multitude of quantified targets. The continuously shifting nature of business requirements, he maintained, makes targets misleading and/or results in an unceasing flood of target revisions. He therefore characterised targets as 'DUMB – defective, unrealistic, misdirected and bureaucratic', and argued instead for a more developmental approach in which individuals are encouraged to seek continuous improvements in their performance.

In the issue of 6 February 2003, Kirstie Ball reviewed several academic contributions to the debate over surveillance. For example, Gary Marx, 1999, was cited as arguing that surveillance was extending in many companies beyond performance to a probing of the fitness of the inner person, through personality testing and compulsory health checks. He maintained that such developments risked making many good employees into 'deviants' while corroding the employer's own ideals concerning relationships with staff. He pleaded for a return to high-quality personal supervision as the basis of control.

where the inmates, kept under constant surveillance by the guards, not infrequently went insane.[18] One of the founders of information science, Norbert Wiener, a half-century ago foresaw the future possibility of extended monitoring and control and looked on it with dismay.[19]

However, case studies of electronic monitoring systems have so far indicated that except in extreme cases managers and employees themselves are essentially pragmatic towards them. If the information generated helps them to do their job better (and perhaps to earn more as a result), they can view the development in a positive light. People can also use feedback information to gain more control over their own work environment or to bargain with management.[20] For example, telephone staff for the Automobile Association (AA) appear to have accepted closer on-line monitoring in their 'virtual call centre' because the resulting increase in performance was necessary to offset the cost of the equipment that made home-based working a going proposition.[21] Again, one of the potential benefits for employees from performance monitoring in call centres appears to be prospects for rapid promotion,[22] which may be connected to better data about who performs well.

The underlying issue is therefore the way the information from ICT-based monitoring is actually used, and who gets it. If the information is confined to management, and is used to assess employees and make decisions about rewards and sanctions, then employees can be expected to be suspicious and fearful. If on the other hand employees get a share of the information, and can use it to their own advantage, then ICT-based monitoring is likely to be much less contentious. Similar issues have arisen over appraisal systems: best practice guides now routinely stress the need to give employees the fullest possible access to the information on which they are being appraised, and the chance to comment on and criticise that information. How far is such a principle also being extended to ICT-based monitoring, which, relative to appraisal, is still in its infancy?

Progress control and individual performance

According to the managers replying to our survey, the main use of ICT-based continuous monitoring is to check the progress of work. This is regarded as a very important or quite important use of the systems in nearly nine in ten of the workplaces where continuous ICT monitoring is present. Moreover, the 'very important' rating outweighs the 'quite important' rating more than two-to-one. Clearly, such a use in itself is uncontentious, since the technology is only being used to do better what has always been done, without any negative implications for employees.

Fewer workplaces use ICT-based monitoring to evaluate the performance of employees, but even so this is a far from negligible proportion. One-half of the workplaces with ICT monitoring are using it to evaluate individuals, and this amounts to one in five of all workplaces. Similarly, three in five of the workplaces with EPOS are using the technology to evaluate individual performance, a higher proportion than in non-EPOS workplaces (Chart 6.6).

A situation in which monitoring might be particularly important, from the management viewpoint, is when employees are working away from

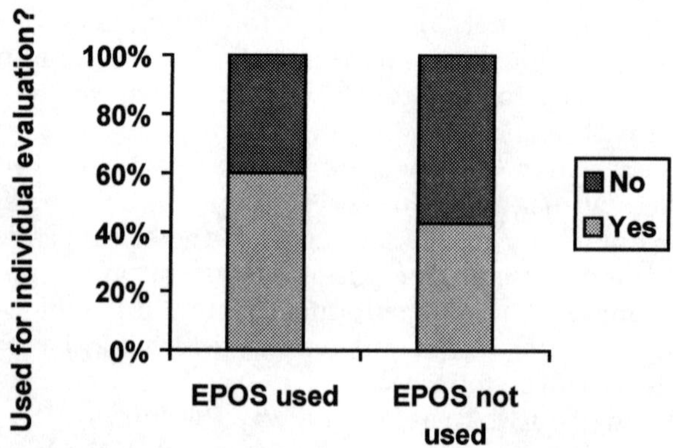

Chart 6.6 Whether ICT used for individual evaluation, in EPOS and non-EPOS workplaces

Note: Column percentages, weighted by employment. Chart excludes workplaces not using ICT to monitor work continuously.

base in a teleworking or working-from-home mode (Chapter Five indicated the growth of this type of arrangement). But is the management in workplaces with this kind of set-up actually more inclined to monitor employees? It seems not, or at least not to any great extent. For example, in workplaces where there is no teleworking, 46 per cent have monitoring by ICT, and this rises slightly to 52 per cent in workplaces where teleworking is being developed. The difference is still smaller for working from home. It may be that these forms of working are often too small-scale for management to be bothered about monitoring. Or the groups concerned may sometimes be so small as to be overlooked in replies about the general policy of the organisation. Extension of monitoring could come when the change towards distance working becomes more widespread. However, recent case study research by Alan Felstead and colleagues[23] suggests that management often remains unclear or confused about their approach to managing home-based employees, and these fundamentals need to be addressed before a clearer policy can be established.

Managers and other employees as users of ICT monitoring information

The biggest question for the future of ICT-based monitoring is the extent to which the employees whose work is being monitored for reasons of performance assessment will themselves share in the information. Without such participation, employees are likely to experience the development as a threatening form of external pressure, rather than as helpful feedback to improve performance. The current picture given by the survey is far from reassuring on this count. In essence, it shows a rather centralised use of ICT-based monitoring information, with senior management in pole position as users, line management in second place, and other employees a long way behind. Despite the lessons gleaned over many years from the use of appraisal systems,[24] the opportunity to use this newly developing field of business performance data in a participative way is not being widely grasped by management.

Chart 6.7 shows the main results, with a breakdown by size of workplace. Overall, three in four workplaces which use ICT-based continuous monitoring are passing the information to senior management, while approaching three in five pass it to line management. But at only one in three workplaces do employees get a share of the information. Larger workplaces are more likely to use the information at line management level, but no more likely than others to involve employees as users. Medium-sized workplaces (25–99 employees) tend to have a particularly centralised approach, with senior management more than three times as likely to get the monitoring information as are their employees.

The desirability of allowing employees access to the monitoring data seems particularly clear if the data are being used to evaluate them. But workplace practice is unresponsive to this point. Among the workplaces

Chart 6.7 Who gets ICT-based monitoring information
Note: Cell percentages (each bar is a separate percentage of the total), weighted by employment. Chart excludes workplaces not using ICT to monitor work continuously.

that use monitoring information for employee evaluation, and among those that do not, the proportion giving employees access is just about the same. It is only where management regards progress information as very important that the proportion involving employees with the information goes up – and then only a little, to 37 per cent.

Monitoring and training

Another constructive use of monitoring information, from the employee viewpoint, is to support on-job training. For example, performance information can be fed back to show progress towards full competence in a job or in a task. The continuity of monitoring made possible by ICT systems, and the immediate feedback which they potentially provide, therefore have great implications for work-based training.

The majority of the workplaces that use ICT-based monitoring are aware of this potential at least to some extent. Four in ten of them say they regard training as a very important application for this type of system, while a further three in ten regard training applications as quite important. There is no difference between smaller and larger workplaces in this respect.

The feedback provided by EPOS systems has been used in training in some industries, notably retailing, for many years. Not surprisingly, then, a higher proportion of workplaces with EPOS – just over one half – says training is a very important application for ICT-based monitoring. In distribution, the proportion approaches three in five, and other industries making considerable use of EPOS systems, notably hotels and catering, and leisure/personal/other services, are not far behind.

These results suggest that as ICT-based monitoring is applied more intensively, training applications will also follow. But although effective training is clearly in the employee's interest, there is little indication of a link from training applications to more employee involvement as a direct use of feedback information. Even among workplaces rating training applications 'very important', the proportion giving employees the monitoring information rises only marginally to 35 per cent.

Conclusions

Control is a crucial requirement of all business and public service organisations. Given the pressure of competition, and the complexity of other changes, it is unsurprising if management responds by seeking more control.

On the ground, therefore, it is no surprise to see a widening array of control methods being deployed. These include performance appraisal systems, teams with their own internal monitoring, and various forms of incentives and long-term rewards. All of the foregoing are methods of control which have long been in existence, but now they are being deployed more widely – indeed, in the case of appraisal, becoming almost universal. As motivational methods increase, they can also be linked to controls via appraisal.

Alongside such established methods there is a new one: the use of ICT to provide continuous monitoring of work. Already familiar at retail checkouts or at the finance industry's countless call centres, this technology is in reality far more widely distributed and may well emerge, over the next few years, as management's central approach to control. What is new is the ability to monitor work at every instant and, furthermore, to analyse the information so collected as frequently and in as much detail as management desires. In principle, all staff who work on-line to a networked computer system can be monitored along these lines, but only a small fraction of this potential for monitoring has yet been taken up.

There are perhaps two main dangers inherent in this new-found technical power. One is a danger shared by all control systems, namely that of concentrating on what is measurable rather than on what is important. The plethora of quantified information that can be generated by ICT-based monitoring systems may blind management to what is missing from the record, such as, for example, the quality of staff's interchanges with customers. Indeed, case studies reveal that only one half of ICT-monitored staff believe these systems cover all important aspects of their work.[25]

The second danger with the technology lies in going too far with it – to a level of surveillance that leaves employees with no freedom in their job. In the long run this mistake is unlikely to persist, because employees who feel excessively pressured will organise in opposition, or will vote with their feet, until a more balanced approach is restored. But while this is being worked out, there can be much grief on both sides, grief that is avoidable if senior management is sensitive to the needs of employees as well as to their own need for control.

An effective way of avoiding conflict with employees, over ICT-based monitoring, would be to make them partners in the use of the information, so that they can use it to develop their own competences and enhance their performance. This is a lesson which should have been learned from the accumulated experience of appraisal systems, if from no other source. As yet, this lesson is being applied only to a limited extent and in the majority of workplaces, management has either not understood or not responded to this opportunity. Addressing this weakness could do much to increase the effectiveness of ICT-based monitoring systems and would help to allay anxieties about the development of this control technology.

The findings of this chapter relate to all four overarching themes of change which were outlined in Chapter One. This is not surprising, because control is a central function of management and has connections with all aspects of organisational change. The sheer extent of control, covering both the traditional methods of appraisal and the newer ones from ICT, in the first place suggests the continuing pressures of cost competition. Moreover, while control based on appraisals is sufficiently flexible and qualitative to accommodate the tasks of knowledge workers, including managers and professionals, this is less likely to be true in the case of ICT-based monitoring. Yet such ICT-based monitoring systems are already covering around half the workforce and appear to be spreading rapidly. This sends a signal that cost and financial control still get a higher priority with senior management than the development of the knowledge-based workforce. More generally, heavy reliance on mechanistic controls, like those offered by ICT-based monitoring, seems at variance with the HRM-driven agenda for developing high performance through commitment and trust. There is a real conflict taking shape here between low-road and high-road approaches to competition and innovation. While control is always necessary, organisations need to think hard and deep about the types of control which will fit their broader strategy for change. Finally, in an atmosphere of mounting public concern about intrusive surveillance, the insensitive development of ICT-based monitoring could rapidly lead to industrial conflict[26] or even to calls for government regulation in this area.

7
Lowering the Sexual Barriers

This chapter looks at the current employment of women in British workplaces and in doing so connects with several of the themes outlined in Chapter One – especially the response to changing competitive conditions and the construction of progressive policies for the workforce.

The great majority of British employers have been experiencing either growth or at least stability in recent years. In these favourable though still competitive circumstances, it is hardly surprising to find that *recruitment and retention* have moved up management's priority list as the job market has progressively tightened. By mid-2002, according to a CIPD survey, 51 per cent of HR managers put recruitment and retention in the top three business priorities, while 28 per cent put it at number one.[1]

In such a climate, employers should be removing all barriers which prevent employees from entering the available jobs or from reaching their potential at work. Among these barriers, none is more obvious, and none has been discussed so much, as the barriers which segregate jobs and opportunities between men and women, generally to the disadvantage of women. The most familiar business case for equal opportunities runs as follows: remove the barriers of sex and you will increase the pool of talent on which future success or survival will depend. This case gains weight when, as now, girls outperform boys in school exams, and women graduates are outnumbering men. At the same time, employers' seriousness in developing people policies that equally meet the needs of women and men is a key test of their ability to act in a socially responsible way and thus pre-empt regulation.

An obvious place to start is with sexual barriers affecting recruitment into jobs. Although there are fierce debates about the reasons for the segregation of jobs by sex,[2] there is wide agreement that opening male jobs to women's entry, and *vice versa*, constitutes a main pathway to remedying the situation. Once that women have equal access to working alongside men in the same kinds of jobs, they have the full force of anti-discrimination legislation in their support, as recently stressed by the CBI.[3] So long as women's jobs are segregated from men's, their ability to take advantage of anti-discrimination legislation is greatly weakened. Moreover, by working in men's jobs women can demonstrate their capabilities and help to break down adverse stereotypes of their worth. For instance, there is now widespread recognition of the achievements of women as managers and business leaders. So the recruitment of women into 'men's jobs', and *vice versa,* is likely to play a crucial part in equalising opportunity.

Alongside this, opportunities for women at work cannot be separated from the way work interacts with family life. The State has intervened to provide women with maternity rights that, at least partially, reconcile having babies with staying in jobs.[4] Over the past 20 years, this together with changes in society's attitudes has had a dramatic impact on women's return to work after childbirth, as already noted in Chapter One (see note 11 there). The result is that more of a typical employer's work-force is made up of women with a young child, or men with a young child and a working wife or partner. As yet, though, there is no comprehensive, national childcare system, unlike in France, Denmark, Sweden and some other countries. Working parents with young children have to cobble together their own childcare strategies from grannies, nannies, nurseries and their own time. Meanwhile British men work on average the longest hours in Western Europe,[5] hindering them from playing more of a role at home, and placing more pressure on their partners.

Accordingly, an assessment of sexual barriers at work also has to consider issues of working time and of family-friendly policies or work-life balance policies. The importance of this issue has been recognised by government, through its Work Life Balance 2000 Campaign,[6] which sought to persuade employers of the business case for work-life balance policies. The Employers for Work-Life Balance forum, run by The Work Foundation, has similar aims and reflects corporate concerns around this issue. The TUC has also given prominence to the topic.[7]

Underlining this point, results from our companion survey of employees, WIB-00, have shown plummeting levels of satisfaction with working hours and workloads, among both men and women, and growing feelings of strain between work demands and family demands. These feelings come from a period when men's average hours have remained persistently high, while those of women with children have risen steeply – with obvious consequences for the total workload of the family unit. This chapter will examine employers' responses to this situation.

How jobs are segregated

Not so long ago, *most* jobs were done either entirely by women or entirely by men. Indeed, many workplaces were either all-female or all-male. Total job segregation of this type is less prevalent but it still exists: in some electrical engineering factories, for instance, you can still walk from an assembly department where all the workers are female to a machining department where all the workers are male. To take a newer example, when you phone a call centre it is usually a female voice that replies, unless you are calling 'technical service' in which case it is usually a male voice. This situation has huge implications, creating road-blocks to promotion, and increasing the inequality of pay between men and women. Indeed, research has shown that much of the earnings disadvantage of women can be accounted for by the concentration of women in particular groups of jobs at workplace level.[8]

There are many familiar examples of jobs or occupations that are mainly held by women, and have poor pay and prospects. These include care assistants, sales checkout staff, or 'dinner ladies' in schools. Traditionally female-dominated professions, notably nursing and teaching, are not known for their generous salaries.

However, women have made progress in entering professions formerly dominated by men. For example, in 1964 women constituted about one in five of qualified practicing pharmacists, but by 2001 they constituted one-half.[9] This reflects the general rise in qualification levels among women, who now obtain more than one-half of all the first degrees awarded. Indeed, the way in which girls out-perform boys in school examinations has become so commonplace as hardly to call forth a comment in the media. Women have also increased their share of employment in the financial and business service industries, which have been and continue to be the power-house for the British economy.[10] Although there are many routine jobs in this industry, it also contains large numbers of 'knowledge worker' jobs such as accountants and financial advisers, lawyers, computer specialists, and business consultants.

Another factor in unequal opportunities is the concentration of women in part-time jobs, and the concentration of part-time jobs in some industries and some workplaces. Research has shown that the depressed hourly earnings of part-time employees, relative to full-time employees at the same job level, is mainly accounted for by workplaces with high proportions of part-time employees, rather than by part-time status in itself. In other words, a part-time employee is likely to get the standard hourly rate for the job in a workplace mainly consisting of full-time employees, but is likely to receive a depressed rate in a workplace where she/he is surrounded by many other people who are also working part-time.[11] In addition, management often uses part-time status as a filter to rule out large blocks of employees from promotion and up-grading opportunities. Nursing is an occupation where this type of segregation has been particularly documented (see Box on page 104), despite lip-service to equal opportunities.

There remain large differences in the proportions of women employees and of part-time employees between industries. These industry proportions are

The career blocks for part-time nursing staff

Nursing has long been regarded as offering good career opportunities for women, on a strong base of professional education and training. Moreover most nursing is carried out within the National Health Service, which like other public sector organisations is formally committed to equal opportunities. Despite this, the minority of men in nursing have much higher probabilities of promotion to the higher grades in the profession. This has been partly explained in an article by Nikala Lane as the result of the systematic exclusion from promotion of nurses working part-time, who constitute about one in three of total nursing staff. Previous studies have shown that most part-time staff are concentrated in the lowest nursing grades, and that promotion is achieved mostly by women who have worked continuously (without career breaks) and on a full-time basis.

Lane's study used a combination of questionnaires and group discussions with nurses, and interviews with nursing managers. She found that nurses working part-time hours had similar qualifications and training to those working full-time yet were almost entirely confined to the lower grades. Among the reasons identified in the study:

- Higher-level posts were advertised as full-time so excluding those only able to work part-time hours.
- Childcare support was lacking and management was unwilling to offer flexibility over shift patterns and rotas.
- After taking career breaks nurses were often compelled to take posts at lower grades than they formerly held.
- Nursing managers – female as well as male – interpreted part-time hours as a lack of professional commitment and assumed that in working these hours, the nurses showed a preference for less responsible work.
- Nursing managers showed no awareness of the frustrated ambitions of part-time staff nor of the constraints imposed by lack of family-friendly practices.

Source: Nikala Lane, 2000, 'The Low Status of Female Part-Time NHS Nurses: A Bed-Pan Ceiling', *Gender, Work and Organisations*, volume 7 number 4, 269–281.

shown in Chart 7.1.[12] At one extreme, public services employ women in nearly three jobs out of every four, while at the other extreme, the engineering and construction industries employ about one in five. The service industries are generally toward the higher end, but financial and business services have close to a 50/50 mix and transport and communication services are mainly male, like manufacturing. The industries with low proportions of women employees also tend to have low proportions of part-time jobs, but the correspondence is only a rough one. The highest proportions of part-time jobs are in hotels, catering and retailing. Public services and financial and business services have lower proportions of part-time jobs than might be expected from the numbers of women that they employ.

What is of more particular interest is workplaces with extreme proportions of women or part-time employees. These are the situations with the greatest implications for equal opportunities, where desegregation would have the biggest impact. Chart 7.2 shows the workplaces with either very high proportions of women – more than three in four employees – and also those with very high proportions of men. Public services emerges as the main location of predominantly female workplaces, though there are also many in distribution and, to a lesser extent, in the other service industries. Construction, engineering and transport/communications are the main locations of predominantly male workplaces.

Similarly, Chart 7.3 gives the industry break-down of workplaces where the majority of employees are on part-time contracts. The picture here is particularly clear: most of the predominantly part-time workplaces are in distribution, hotels, catering and public services. The personal and leisure

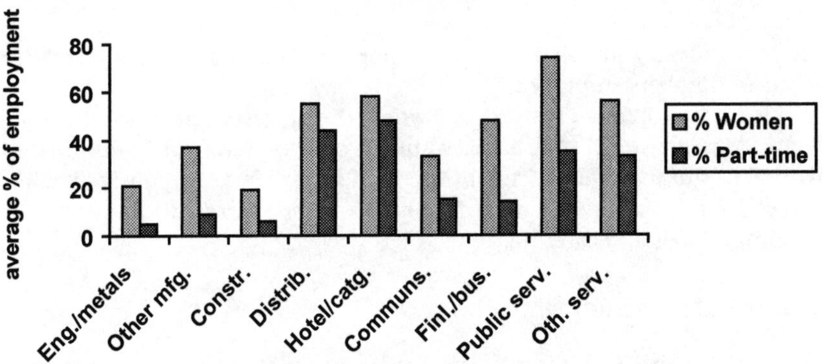

Chart 7.1 Employment of women and part-time employees: industry averages
Note: Cell percentages (each bar is a separate percentage of the total), weighted by employment.

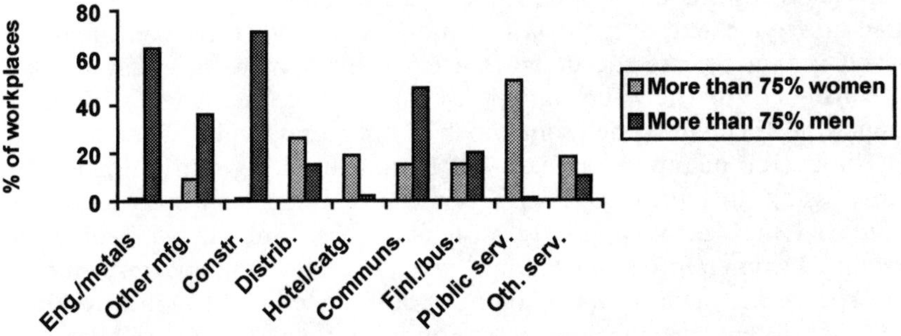

Chart 7.2 Workplaces with high proportions of women or of men, by industry
Note: Cell percentages (each bar is a separate percentage of the total), weighted by employment.

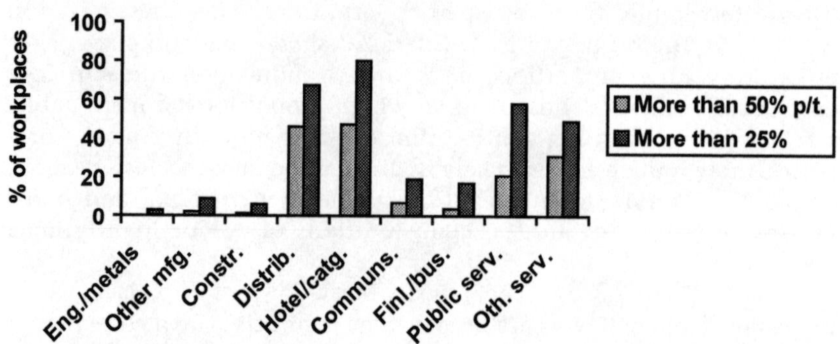

Chart 7.3 Workplaces with high proportions of part-time employees, by industry
Note: Cell percentages (each bar is a separate percentage of the total), weighted by employment.

services industry also has a high proportion, but is a small industry in terms of numbers employed.

This first group of charts suggests where the biggest impacts would come from a desegregation of jobs. Examples would be fewer male-dominated workplaces in manufacturing or transport, fewer female-dominated workplaces in public services and distribution, and more full-time jobs in retailing, hotels and catering.

Desegregated recruitment

Because of the special importance of segregation at job level, our national survey of employers focuses on questions about current or recent recruitment to see if there is movement towards desegregation. The questions ask if women are being recruited into jobs previously done exclusively by men, and *vice versa*. One disadvantage of these questions is that we get no information from about one in ten of the employers, because they have had no recruitment over the last 12 months. The advantage on the other hand is that we use the down-to-earth activity of recruitment to give an insight into the issue, rather than relying on statements of equal opportunities policy which sometimes do not correspond with practice.

The overall picture (see Chart 7.4) is that the desegregation of jobs is progressing, in both directions. Overall 15 per cent of workplaces have recruited men into previously all-female jobs, and 18 per cent have recruited women into all-male jobs,[13] over a 12-month period. One in four workplaces has made a change in one or both directions. And just over one in four say that the questions do not apply to them, because they *already* have *no* jobs that are all-male or all-female. Further research will be required to flesh out the findings, since they do not tell us how many jobs are being filled in this desegregating manner.

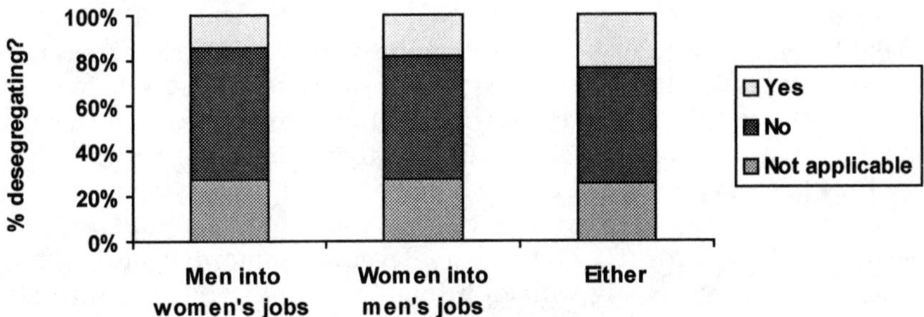

Chart 7.4 Desegregation through recruitment in the last 12 months
Note: Column percentages, weighted by employment. 'Not applicable' means that there are no exclusively male or exclusively female jobs at the workplace.

What the findings amount to is that about one-half of the workplaces have recently done or are doing *something* towards desegregated employment between men and women. But many of these doubtless still have a long way to go before reaching full desegregation. On the other side of the equation, one-half of the workplaces do not claim to be fully desegregated, yet have done *nothing* to change this situation in the past year. A part of that, however, could be because no vacancies have come up in the segregated types of jobs, over that period. Whether the current rate of change is to be considered satisfactory, is of course a matter of opinion. But at least there is change.

Where is desegregation taking place?

In general, the industry differences relating to desegregated recruitment are small. In public services, which has the highest proportion of women employees, recruitment of men into formerly all-female jobs is appreciably above the average, being reported at 23 per cent of workplaces. Manufacturing industry, with its low proportion of women employees, is also just slightly above-average in putting women into all-male jobs: this is reported at 20 per cent of engineering/metals workplaces and at 22 per cent of other manufacturing plants. Overall, the rather weak industry effects are disappointing for those who would like to see positive action by employers to break down the barriers. Where the barriers are highest, on an industry basis, there seems little indication of a major effort as yet.

There is a little more encouragement from looking at desegregation across workplaces with different proportions of the sexes. Broadly speaking, workplaces with very high proportions of women are more likely to bring men into all-female jobs, as shown in Chart 7.5, while at workplaces with low proportions of women, more women are brought into all-male jobs. However, this factor makes more of a difference for men than for women: could this be because the more feminised organisations are more attuned to equal opportunities?

Organisations that are deeply involved in ICT have a particular need to make the most of their people in coping with change, and therefore should have a greater-than-average interest in removing job barriers between the sexes. This is indeed reflected in the results here. In the first place, one in three of the workplaces with the highest usage level of ICT say they have *no* jobs that are done only by women or only by men. This is appreciably higher than the one in four that is found overall. Secondly, those with ICT at a *medium* level are somewhat more likely than others to be placing women into all-male jobs and men into all-female jobs. And thirdly, there is a link between the rate of change towards ICT and the rate of job desegregation. This last is shown in Chart 7.6. It seems, then, that the general movement of industry towards ICT is tending to push down the job barriers for women. But this is not to a dramatic extent, and has yet to make much impression on the huge

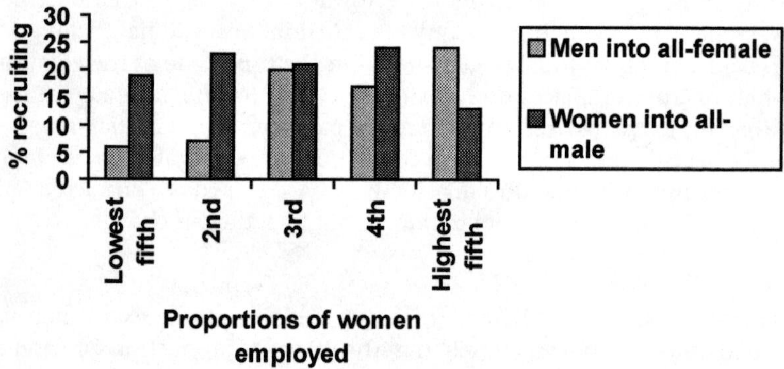

Chart 7.5 Desegregation by proportion of women employed
Note: Cell percentages (each bar is a separate percentage), weighted by employment.

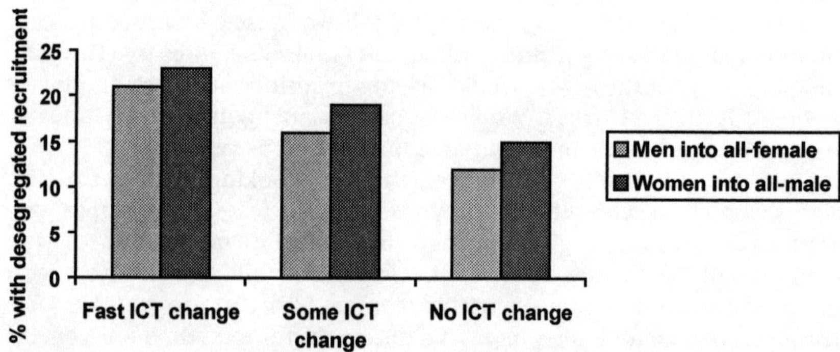

Chart 7.6 Desegregated recruitment in past 12 months, and rate of ICT change
Note: Cell percentages (each bar is a separate percentage), weighted by employment.

differences in the employment of men and women between industries and between workplaces.

Fitting hours to people

Working hours constitute perhaps the biggest barrier to women's careers in Britain. They also create a substantial difficulty for men who would like to give more time to family life. Chapter Ten will look at recent attempts to regulate hours at work, and how these are impinging on management. The present chapter has a different angle on hours, concentrating on the extent to which working hours can be adapted to people's circumstances or preferences. This is flexibility from the employee's viewpoint rather than the employer's, but it can also result in employees becoming more attached to the organisation and more capable of developing a long-term career. This is part of the business case for flexible hours, which both government and employers' organisations have been promoting.[14]

A remarkably large proportion of workplaces claims to offer flexible working hours to employees: nearly four in ten to *all* employees, three in ten to *some* employees. This seems too good to be true, and probably is.

The explanation is almost certainly that the managers answering our survey have included a wide and somewhat miscellaneous range of practices under their idea of flexible working hours. For instance, workplaces with large numbers of part-time employees tend to say they offer flexible working hours. So do those with seven-day or 24-hour opening, which tend to offer some scope for choosing or transferring to any one from a range of shift patterns. Of course that does give the individual more choice than in a workplace which has one rigid set of hours, but it is not what an employee thinks of as a flexible hours system – namely, a system that allows *them* to vary their hours according to their needs. Management respondents to the survey may also have in mind various other policies, like permitting movement between full-time and part-time contracts, favourable maternity or paternity leave, or various kinds of family-friendly provisions which will be discussed later in the chapter. The figure of seven out of ten employers that offer *some kind of flexibility* over hours is very much an upper limit.

The *characteristic* or typical working hours arrangements show a much lower degree of flexibility. The details are shown in Table 7.1. Fixed working hours remain the dominant arrangement. They are used for employees below the management or professional level, at two-thirds of workplaces, and for managers/professionals at four in ten workplaces. Flexi-time hours are the basic arrangement at only one in seven workplaces, whether for managers and professionals or those in other grades. Being able to choose starting and finishing times applies to managers or professionals in the same proportion of workplaces, one in seven, but to non-managers hardly

Table 7.1 Characteristic working time arrangements

	Managers	*Non-managers*
Decide their own start and finish times	14%	3%
Work flexi-time hours	15%	14%
Work fixed hours	40%	64%
No characteristic arrangement – it varies	31%	20%

Note: Column percentages, weighted by employment.

anywhere. These figures tie up well with the companion survey of employees, where two in ten said they worked a flexible hours system, and a further one in ten (mostly managers and professionals) said they decided their own starting and finishing times.

Switching hours

Scope for employees to vary their hours to some extent on a daily or weekly basis is therefore a long way from becoming the standard approach. But though fixed hours dominate, there may be some scope for employees to select a set of fixed hours that suits their circumstances, or to change from one set of fixed hours to another. This, if available, provides some flexibility that can help to match working time to family or individual needs as these change at different stages of life.

One widely available flexibility of this kind concerns switches between part-time and full-time status. In view of the disadvantages of many part-time jobs in terms of pay and prospects, there is a particular benefit in being able to move back into full-time work as soon as it fits personal circumstances. Of workplaces with part-time workers, three in five permit transfer in both directions, and a few more permit transfer from full-time to part-time but not the other way. Something which was regarded as an unusual privilege a few years ago (so that people who wanted to switch hours often had to change employers) is now becoming the norm. The rise of the large retailer, with an insatiable demand for part-time staff, has doubtless been a major influence here.

Fitting in with school

Just under three in five workplaces claim to offer working hours that are convenient for women with school age children. In many cases this claim may not mean much more than that part-time hours are on offer, or in other cases it may refer to the flexi-time arrangements which have just been discussed. But one further positive practice is term-time working. About one in three workplaces now offers this to employees.

The trouble with policies like the offer of term-time working is that women often do not want them because of the large loss of earnings that is involved.

While we record one in three workplaces having this as a policy on offer, another survey of employers, carried out in 2000 (see Terence Hogarth and colleagues 2001: Figure 4.3), reports that only 15 per cent of employers actually had any employees *using* such a provision. Since our sample of employers appears comparable with theirs, it seems that the offer of term-time working is not taken up *at all* in about half the employers offering it.

Overall, progress towards genuine choice and flexibility over hours in Britain seems slow. Although many employers believe that they do offer flexible or convenient hours, the availability of flexi-time systems is very limited, while the ability to choose start and finish times is virtually confined to managers and professionals (and only a small minority of those). Term-time working is again available in only a minority of workplaces, and does not appear to be popular in any case.

All in all, the main type of flexibility offered to women in Britain remains part-time employment. A new surge of part-time employment has been taking place recently. Nearly four in ten of the workplaces have been increasing the proportion of part-time staff, and nearly two in ten have been replacing full-time workers with part-time workers to some extent. This is more to do with the organisation's flexibility than with the employee's flexibility, and has been discussed from that viewpoint in Chapter Two. But for employees too, it continues to be the main if not the only show in town. Unfortunately, as stressed earlier in this chapter, it is a kind of flexibility that often comes at a considerable cost to the individual.

Family-friendly policies – now and tomorrow

Family-friendly policies have been one of the most discussed media topics of the past few years, often seen – rightly or wrongly – as important props for women's careers. In view of this topical interest, and the rising dissatisfaction with work-life balance manifested in the companion employee survey, we expected family-friendly policies to be the focus of a great deal of current management attention. So the survey lavished numerous questions on this topic.

The most widely offered family friendly practices are to help employees with babies and subsequent parental duties, as indicated in Table 7.2. Specifically,

- Three in five provide maternity leave beyond the State minimum
- Four in five allow unpaid parental leave
- Four in ten offer some paid parental leave.

Then there are two policies, term-time working and career breaks, which help mothers (and potentially fathers) to reconcile child-rearing with work over a longer time-frame. Term-time working has already been discussed as

Table 7.2 Availability of family-friendly provision

	% of workplaces
Maternity pay above the minimum	59%
Unpaid parental leave	83%
Paid parental leave beyond minimum	36%
Career break	40%
Term-time working	37%
Information about day care	23%
Financial help with day care costs	11%
Day care provision on site	8%

Note: Cell percentages, weighted by employment.

a form of flexible working time. Career breaks involve longer periods away from work, up to several years, and then a controlled re-entry. Each is available in about four in ten workplaces – a substantial proportion, but unlike employers' maternity provisions, still a minority.[15] Career breaks, however, are likely to be even less popular with staff than term-time working.[16] As well as the loss of earnings involved, women with some justification fear that such breaks will damage their long-term career prospects, whatever their employers may say.[17]

Finally, there are various kinds of employer help with childcare: information, financial assistance, day care provision (créches). These are much less available, covering around one in ten to two in ten workplaces depending on the type of help. Most employers do not see help for an employee's childcare as their concern, even though many do see it as their concern to make it easier for the employee to carry out childcare duties.

Where is family-friendliness found?

Family-friendly policies are not scattered at random around workplaces, but tend to cluster together – employers are more or less family-minded, and if they have one of these policies they are likely to have others as well. So it makes sense to add up the employer's provision across all these policies to create a Family Friendliness Index (FFI). With the aid of the FFI, it becomes easier to see the wood and not the trees, rather than the reverse. The differences which emerge are partly to be expected and partly surprising.

- The public sector comes out top on the FFI.
- Close behind come distribution and hotels and catering, with manufacturing industry lowest.
- The FFI is higher in workplaces with a large proportion of female employees and/or a large proportion of part-time employees.
- Where unions are recognised, the FFI tends to be high.

- Growing workplaces *and* shrinking/downsizing workplaces both have higher FFI than stable/static workplaces.
- FFI tends to be lower where there is 24-hour opening.
- Workplaces with high usage of ICT tend to have high FFI.

One point this conveys is that employers put in family-friendly policies when they come under pressure from within to do so. A reasonable guess as to why male-dominated industries or workplaces do not often have these policies is that the male majority does not shout for them. Unions however help to redress the balance.

Another, rather different message is that family-friendly policies are being taken seriously by employers who are actively responding to change. It is particularly notable that even downsizing workplaces have, on average, quite a positive stance on family-friendliness. Moreover, it is known from previous research that employers with a substantial range of HRM practices also tend to be more active on work-life balance issues and to have family-friendly practices.[18] This is also found in the present survey, but as it is an established finding, we need not go over these results. The broad conclusion is that family-friendly practices are reasonably well established among proactive or strategic employers, as they are sometimes called, but relatively thin on the ground with the remainder.

Future family-friendly policies

As well as asking about current family-friendly policies, the CEPS-02 survey asked employers about any plans or intentions they might have over the following year (that is, the year of 2003). Future plans were checked for eight types of policy, corresponding to those listed in Table 7.2. Each of the questions was confined to newly introducing the policy, rather than extending or developing an existing policy, and so was not asked if the workplace already had the policy in being.

The results, shown in Table 7.3, showed a remarkably low level of interest in introducing new family-friendly policies among the workplaces which did not already have them. As a proportion of such workplaces, 16 per cent were thinking of permitting employees to take unpaid parental leave, the most popular new option. Of the other seven policies, only one was of interest to ten per cent of workplaces (information about local day-care services). These two policies presumably entail low costs for the employer. The other policies, all of which potentially involve significant costs, were of interest to only between six and eight per cent of the workplaces not already having them in place. All these figures, naturally, are still smaller when considered relative to the whole survey.

To get a perspective on how low these figures are, consider results from questions posed in a similar way about the future introduction of various human resource management practices, most of which would involve

Table 7.3 Future plans concerning introduction of family-friendly policies

	Base: those not having policy now	*Base: whole survey*
Maternity pay beyond basic	6%	2%
Assistance with childcare costs	7%	6%
Career breaks	8%	5%
Term-time working	6%	3%
Parental leave beyond basic	8%	4%
Day-care programme for children	6%	5%
Information about local day-care	10%	7%
Permitting unpaid parental leave	16%	3%

Note: Cell percentages, weighted by employment.

much more management effort than the family-friendly practices. The following are the proportions of workplaces intending to develop these HRM practices over the next year, out of those not using them at present:

> appraisals, 41 per cent; suggestion scheme, 19 per cent; briefing groups, 17 per cent; work improvement groups ('quality circles'), 17 per cent; staff committee or works council, ten per cent.

Clearly, the introduction of new family-friendly practices are being given a low priority relative to these other changes, and the predictions for future growth in employee coverage by family-friendly practices must be correspondingly low. In view of the strong evidence from other sources that the conflicts between work and family are of great concern to employees – men as well as women – this seems strange, to say the least.

Conclusions

Change towards equal opportunities, and towards full use of women's potential as employees, is perhaps always slower than one might expect. The pre-existing structures and systems are of massive bulk. Change initially nibbles at the margins and can only gradually eat its way to the centre. New recruitment provides one of the margins of potential change, and it is on this that the first part of the chapter focused. One in four workplaces has recruited women into previously all-male jobs, or *vice versa*, which could be taken as a reasonably positive result – bearing in mind that the period under review is a short one.[19] Another positive indication is that the break-down of sexual barriers to jobs is greater where ICT use is increasing. This suggests that change and innovation help to dissolve the sexual barriers. On the other hand, these positive developments look small when set alongside the great disparities between industries.

If moreover many employers are seeking to widen the employment opportunities of women, why are they not doing more to adopt and develop flexi-time working patterns and family-friendly benefits and practices? Admittedly, maternity and parental leave have been extended beyond the basic statutory level at the majority of workplaces. But this family support, confined to around the time of childbirth, is very much the exception. Flexi-time working, the facility which is most effective for women in combating conflicts between work and family,[20] is available for less than one in seven employees and this proportion seems to be rising slowly if at all. Other family-friendly practices are available at less than half the workplaces, and in the case of childcare assistance, at very few indeed. Most surprisingly of all, planned development for the coming year is at a much lower level than for other, more demanding changes in HRM policy, and this suggests that family-friendliness is toward the bottom of most managements' priority list.

One defence for this neglect could be, perhaps, that the usual range of family-friendly practices and flexibilities are actually rather ineffective. In other words, management is being realistic and honest in rejecting tokenism. The low take-up of policies like term-time working supports this interpretation. Also, countries that have achieved a much higher level of equality in the workplace for women, notably Denmark and France, have not based it on family-friendly policies in the firm, but on public investment in subsidised childcare services. Employers can reasonably point out that if the State is unwilling to make such provision, it is not for them to fill the breach. Given poor public childcare facilities, employers can surely only scratch the surface of the problem – or so it can be argued.

This explanation, however, does not entirely fit with the findings about where family-friendly practices are concentrated. By and large it is the workplaces that are actively pursuing or adapting to change, and those which have well-developed HRM practices, that provide family-friendly practices and are continuing to extend them. This suggests that the absence of such practices indicates less active and less perceptive management, rather than a reasoned assessment of what the practices can achieve. Additionally, evidence from other sources suggests that the private-sector managements who have adopted family-friendly practices are reaping some advantages for the business. A recent study, using information from the Workplace Employee Relations Survey of 1998, identified a variety of family-friendly practices that were associated with improved performance on several outcome measures.[21] For example, where a workplace nursery was provided, staff turnover and absenteeism were lower, while assistance with the costs of childcare was linked not only to lower staff turnover but also to above-average labour productivity and quality achievements, as judged by managers. Flexible working hours provisions were also associated with below-average staff turnover and absence, and above-average management assessments of quality and worker effort.

It seems more likely, then, that the slow advance of hours flexibility for employees, and of family-friendly practices, indicates a blind spot for a large section of British management. The potential advantages in terms of staff recruitment, retention and motivation are either not understood in these employers, or the prevailing management culture in such organisations is hostile to making such changes. The case of NHS nurses, discussed earlier in this chapter, suggests that resistant management cultures can be found even in large public-sector organisations where many of the managers are themselves women. Where management does not perceive the advantages of family-friendly practices and work-life balance, then the costs of making changes will constitute an obvious obstacle, but one which can be overcome through exposure to the evidence of successful practice. It is harder to see the path ahead when management cultures are fundamentally hostile to this type of change.

Finally, the findings of this chapter can be reviewed in terms of the various sources of change which were outlined in Chapter One. It seems that external pressures on organisations, including growth opportunities, a tight job market, and the rapid spread of ICT systems, have been quite effective in lowering the barriers for women's entry to previously male-dominated jobs. On the other hand, there are few signs of improvement in women's longer-term opportunities through increased work-life balance. That suggests that the cultural revolution in management, referred to in Chapter One, remains incomplete and does not yet include, except in a minority of organisations, a full incorporation of equal opportunities. In this area, British organisations seem pushed more by short-term pressures and costs, and less by any strategic aims about the development of their workforce. As a result, they also expose themselves to further government intervention and regulation.

8
Developing Diversity

This chapter continues themes from the previous one, looking at pressures on recruitment and whether these can be met in ways that contribute to socially useful goals. As Chapter Seven pointed out, the economic conditions of recent years have generated a highly competitive environment around the search for staff. A partial recruitment solution which has been widely discussed in recent years is the acceptance of 'diversity' in the workforce, that is, the incorporation of groups that deviate from the one-time benchmark of 'fit white male' employees.[1] Diversity has become an explicit goal for many British employers, driven in part by labour shortages and demographic change, but also by regulatory developments. In addition, it is argued that organisations with a diverse employee base are better positioned to respond to new markets and evolving social trends. At the same time, diverse recruitment helps to satisfy an enlarged equal opportunities agenda which contributes to social and political aspirations.

A wide variety of social groups, apart from women (whose recruitment was discussed in the preceding chapter), face discrimination in the search for work. Individuals may be perceived as 'too old' or 'too young', or to have been out of work 'too long'. Or they may simply be different – disabled or foreign, for instance. Those who have been in prison, or are on probation, face special kinds of exclusion (see Box on page 118). In rejecting the suitability of these diverse job seekers organisations limit the pool from which to select candidates for vacancies, and potentially set the scene for further legal and political regulation of employment.

But under tight labour market conditions, groups traditionally at the bottom of the jobs queue[2] move up as employers cast their recruitment net wider. Under pressure, employers re-assess the criteria which they apply to candidates and find that many of the barriers they erected were unrelated to the real requirements of particular jobs. The job market then begins to provide a solution to what was previously seen as a social issue.

There is also a business competition case for organisations to sustain a diverse workforce.[3] In a continuously changing market it becomes more

Employing ex-offenders

The employment of ex-offenders poses special difficulties for employers, including in some cases legal prohibition. However it is widely acknowledged that the attitudes of management, employees and customers constitute the greatest barrier. Because of this, ex-offenders often conceal their criminal record so that organisations employ them in a state of ignorance – a situation which increases risk. Following the Police Act 1997, and the establishment of the Criminal Records Bureau, employers will now have enhanced opportunities to check criminal records. This is likely to result in greater barriers to employment for ex-offenders unless at the same time employers develop systems for assessing risk in a rational way and employing ex-offenders where it is reasonable to do so.

The Inner London Offender/Employer Intermediary Project is one of a number of initiatives in this area described in a recent CIPD report. Supported by the Probation Service, the project works with employers to identify their recruitment and training needs and to develop programmes for young offenders which match these needs. Employers who take part are committed to recruiting from this source. Training is provided both before recruitment, to make the young people job-ready, and in the job so as to strengthen retention and motivation. Assessment for NVQs is incorporated. There has been particular success in the retail sector, where the London Retail Centre has been involved in training provision. Participating employers include many of the best-known retail organisations, such as Boots, Clarks, HMV, House of Fraser, Marks & Spencer, Sainsbury, Tesco, Tie Rack and Virgin. Outside retailing, participating organisations include Heathrow Express, London Eye, London Underground, and Tate Modern.

Source: Chartered Institute of Personnel and Development (2002c) *Casing it out: Why it can make sense to employ ex-offenders*, London: CIPD.

important to be sensitive to the evolving needs and market potential of a diverse consumer base. For example, an American insurance company (Allstate Insurance) was able to expand its customer base by employing staff from diverse ethnic groups: customers from ethnic minorities felt better served by such an organisation.[4] The expanding over-50 population represents another example of a social group attracting business interest that is keen to access the grey pound: home improvement retailers B & Q have acquired a reputation as leading recruiters from this age-group. The argument for a diverse staff base applies with at least as much force to public services, which by definition must serve all sections of communities which, in Britain, have become highly diverse. There has even been a major project to embed diversity policy into the Cabinet Office, the nerve-centre of British government.[5]

At the same time, diversity policy has had its critics.[6] For example, it is argued that employers widen their recruitment base primarily to push down wage rates and/or fill marginal hard-to-fill slots, and then claim to have lofty moral aims by reference to diversity. In addition, having an explicit *policy* for diversity, it has been said, can actually underline awareness of differences and this can lead to more rather than less discrimination in the treatment of staff. Certainly, the fact that an organisation carries out some recruitment from minority or disadvantaged groups does not in itself show that it is free of discrimination. Neither our survey of employers, nor this chapter, addresses discrimination as such.

Whatever one's views about the ethical case, there is no doubt that diversity policy has become an important element in employers' recruitment. The CIPD's 2002 report on recruitment and retention[7] stated that one in four employers has an explicit policy of this kind, supported by a range of active practices. The most common of these practices are (a) paying attention to a greater range of personal qualities in recruitment and selection – for instance by accepting evidence of skills in place of formal qualifications, (b) appointing people with potential who do not initially meet all the selection criteria, and (c) monitoring gender, ethnicity and other characteristics as part of the recruitment process.

This chapter focuses on recruitment from diverse groups, and investigates where it is taking place (for instance, whether concentrated in particular industrial enclaves). It also examines its links with other aspects of human resource policies. If diverse recruitment is connected with the bringing-in of flexible labour, it may be geared to cutting labour costs. If it is linked to practices that emphasise staff development and adaptability, diverse recruitment can perhaps be seen as part of a constructive human resource agenda. In short, we seek to interpret not only *where* diverse recruitment is taking place, but *why* it is taking place, and how this relates to the processes of change at the workplace which were outlined in Chapter One. Is management engaging in diverse recruitment purely as a reaction to competitive pressures, and perhaps as no more than a short-term expedient? Or is diverse recruitment often part of a wider and longer-term effort to develop human resources and to pre-empt external regulation?

The extent of recruitment diversity

The groups labelled as 'diverse' within this chapter include both younger and older age groups and the recently non-employed. Individuals with a broken employment record may have been involuntarily unemployed for many months or voluntarily out of the labour market to raise a family – a group referred to as 'returners'. People with disabilities, people with a poor command of English, and ex-prisoners or individuals on probation are also included within the concept of diversity used here. The survey did not address recruitment of ethnic minorities as such, since this poses quite complex issues of definition and would require a specialist survey in its own right.[8] But the varied groups covered in the survey should give a fair indication of organisations' stance on diversity.

In the survey of employers, managers were asked, for each one of these groups, whether *any* recruitment from them had taken place during the previous 12 months. This approach establishes *how widespread* is diverse recruitment, but not how large-scale it is since the numbers recruited were not collected.

The survey reveals that diversity in recent recruitment is very widespread. Nearly four-fifths of employers have recently been taking on staff from *at least one* of the groups which often face discrimination in the labour market (Chart 8.1). But there are large differences between the groups, with some much more widely represented than others in recent recruitment (Chart 8.2). Among organisations taking on new recruits in the previous year:

- Two-thirds recruited someone over 50
- Somewhat more than one-half (56%) recruited at least one 'returner'
- About one-half recruited someone under the age of 18

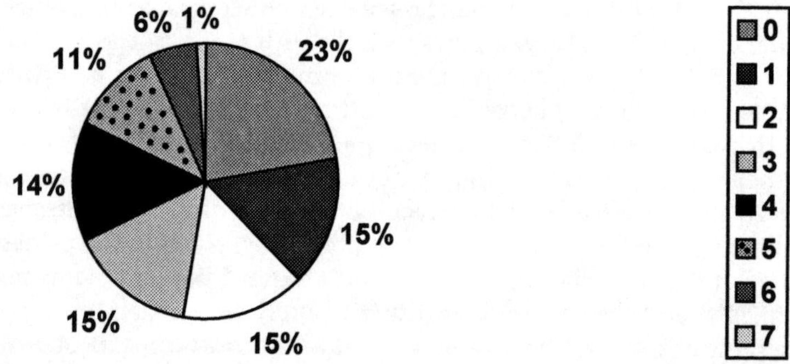

Chart 8.1 Number of 'diverse' groups recruited at workplace (last 12 months)
Note: Total percentages, weighted by employment. The legend reads clockwise starting with 0 (23%). Those with no diverse recruitment include those with no recruitment whatever in the past 12 months.

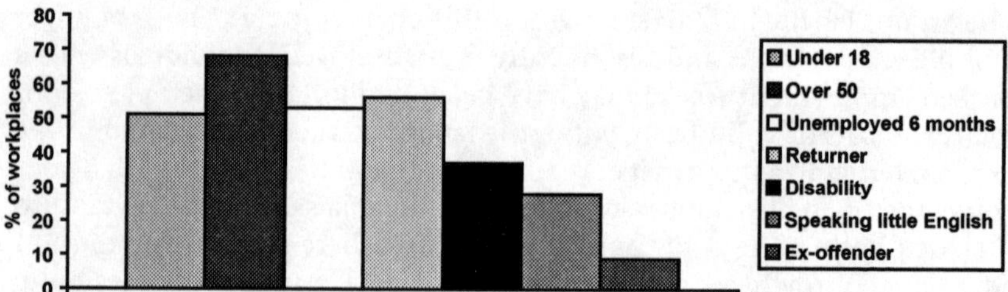

Chart 8.2 Workplaces recruiting from each diverse group (last 12 months)
Note: Cell percentages (each bar is a separate percentage of the total), weighted by employment.

- The same proportion (one-half) recruited someone unemployed for at least six months
- A little over one third (37%) recruited someone with a disability
- A little under three in ten (28%) recruited someone with little English language skill
- Less than one in ten workplaces (nine per cent) recruited an ex-prisoner or person on probation.

Recruiting from just one of these groups might be a casual expedient or an accidental result for that employer, whereas recruiting from several groups over the same period suggests a serious recruitment policy. As shown in Chart 8.1, 15 per cent of workplaces have recruited in just one category, but almost two-thirds have recruited from two or more of the diverse groups under consideration, and just under one-half have recruited from three or more. The general picture, then, is of recruiting across a range of groups by the majority of employers and this supports the view that diversity in recruitment has become, or is fast becoming, part of orthodox personnel practice.

Who are the diverse workforce employers?

Despite the general responsiveness to diversity in recruitment, there remain differences between industries and these reinforce perceptions of the public sector as the leader in this field. Public service employers are most likely to recruit the over 50s, long-term unemployed, returners, and disabled people. Wide recruitment of diverse groups is also found in distribution, and hotels and catering. Businesses which are open six or seven days a week are also associated with higher diverse recruitment levels relative to those which are open for only five days. The construction industry, which has been growing particularly rapidly in recent years, leads in the recruitment of people under 18, and ex-offenders.

This profile of industries with diverse recruitment raises a number of questions. Many jobs in the hotels, catering and retail trades, which tend to demand '24/7' service provision and are thereby particularly hungry for staff, are of the low-wage variety. If such businesses compete primarily on costs, the apparent acceptance of diversity may come at a price for these social groups, the price of lower job quality. However, we should not jump to conclusions, since industries like retailing are now emerging as having well-developed HRM practices including career structures (see Chapters Three and Four). This issue is considered further in sections below.

Another obvious interpretation of diverse recruitment is as a response to widespread recruitment difficulties.[9] Apart from manufacturing, economic conditions have been buoyant as reflected in the fact that nearly half the workplaces have been growing over the past three years, with the remaining half divided fairly evenly between stability and contraction (see Chapter One). The great majority of all workplaces, regardless of growth status, are recent recruiters, but growing workplaces are still more likely to practise multiple diverse recruitment, suggesting some impact of tight job markets. Similarly, workplaces experiencing increased staff turnover during the previous three years are somewhat more inclined to absorb staff from a diverse background (Chart 8.3). But these differences are not large.

The demand for greater equality in recruitment practices comes from a number of sources, including trade unions. The presence of unions did not however enhance the probability of workplaces employing diverse staff.[10] Instead, staff shortages, high staff turnover and needs associated with particular industrial sectors were the primary drivers of diversity in recruitment. This suggests that diversity in recruitment is more a response to economic and job market conditions than part of an imposed equality agenda.

Diversity and flexible labour

Chapter Two showed that flexible labour practices have permeated all sectors of British industry, from the low-skill to the high-tech employer. Users of flexibility are however somewhat more concentrated in service industries especially where 24-hour opening is provided. How does diversity of recruitment fit into this picture? Is there a relationship between the use of flexible labour and diversity? Recruits from these diverse groups could either be placed in temporary or casual jobs, or a multiple recruitment strategy of labour flexibility *and diversity* may be combined to achieve a cost-effective labour supply. In the latter instance diversity may be deployed within the core workforce of secure permanent staff as well as among those with flexible contracts.

The survey does point to a link between the use of flexible labour and the acceptance of diversity, but it is a rather limited one. It is clearly

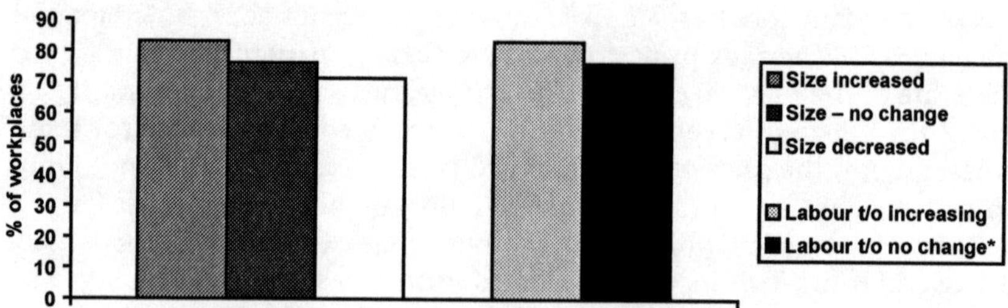

Chart 8.3 Change in size, labour turnover, and diverse recruitment
Note: Cell percentages (each bar is a separate percentage of the total), weighted by employment. Workplaces with no recruitment excluded. 't/o' = turnover. * Labour t/o no change includes decreases in labour turnover.

visible in small workplaces (less than 25 employees), is weaker in large workplaces (100-plus employees), and non-existent in between. In the small and to a lesser extent the largest workplaces, the higher the number of flexible worker groups employed (temporary, casual, etc.), the more likely the recent recruitment of a worker from one of the diverse groups. This suggests that the flexible labour feeds off diverse recruitment and that to obtain employment, people from the diverse groups often have to accept non-permanent jobs. Add small workplaces to this specification, and it begins to look like 'McJobs'. However, for some groups these jobs are not necessarily disadvantageous. Short-term contracts are sometimes preferred by young people, for instance if they are continuing their education or saving to travel the world. Some older people also favour flexible contracts as a means of continuing employment while gaining access to pension rights from a previous employer which could be denied under standard employment contracts.[11] In any case, for large and (especially) medium-sized employers, diverse recruitment turns out to be an issue which is largely independent of using flexible labour.

Diversity and HRM policies

Under current stereotypes, management reliance on flexible labour contracts is regarded as a low-road workforce strategy involving low wages and low skills. However, the results of earlier chapters have suggested that this is over-simple or outdated, since flexible labour contracts are extensively used in conjunction with high-road HRM strategies as well as for many kinds of professional employees. Accordingly, even if there is a partial relationship between diversity and flexible labour contracts it does not of itself show that diverse recruitment builds a lower-skilled, expendable workforce. We must also look more directly at whether diverse recruitment is or is not found alongside the more long-term or developmental HRM practices. If such practices are present where members of the diverse groups are recruited, then these recruits have some chance of developing and making progress.

In terms of the skill-base encouraged by employers, the results are clear-cut. Diversity-seeking employers are significantly *more* likely to be moving towards a professional workforce combined with an increased expectation of staff to acquire multiple job skills, and individual adaptability. Increased levels of training have accompanied these developments in workforce task assignments. While such moves may be associated with higher pressure or work demands, they are also indicators of upskilling. These signs suggest that diversity-seeking employers are committed to their staff, valuing them as a long-term rather than expendable resource. To spell this out further, diversely-recruiting employers are more likely to have

- increased the proportion of managerial and professional staff
- increased the amount of job rotation
- increased the amount of training of employees to cover jobs other than their own.

However, it is possible that employers recruiting from diverse groups still keep them separate from core employees in terms of their treatment and conditions. Indeed, the creation of a multi-tier workforce is one of the fears which has been expressed about diversity policy. This fear will be somewhat allayed if diversely recruiting employers offer good benefits to staff, and if in addition they are moving towards giving such benefits to *all* employees. Such a policy indicates a long-term and inclusive outlook towards staff retention and development.

Inevitably larger workplaces recruit more staff and thereby are more likely to accept or encourage diversity. These larger workplaces are also more likely to provide a raft of benefits. The following analysis therefore takes workplace size into account and within each size category the extent of recruitment diversity is considered.

On this basis, greater diversity of recruitment is associated on the positive side with a greater likelihood of:

- Financial assistance or loans for house purchase

But on the negative side, diverse recruiters are *less likely* to provide:

- An occupational pension scheme
- Sick pay beyond the basic government scheme
- Subsidised or free meals
- Private health insurance

Overall, then, terms and conditions among diverse recruiters do *not* stand out as being good. On the other hand, the workplaces with more diversity in recruitment *more often* claim that their employee benefits are being progressively harmonised across all groups of employees. This suggests that the workplaces more involved in diverse recruitment, although not particularly generous providers of benefits, are seeking to integrate the various employee groups in their terms and conditions. In some cases they may be pursuing what is sometimes called 'downward harmonisation', meaning that some benefits are being stripped away from upper tiers of the hierarchy at the same time as the remaining benefits are more equally shared.

There is also evidence from the survey that workplaces which embrace diversity deploy a range of HRM practices that are widely regarded as touchstones of positive employee relations. To an above-average extent, they are communicating actively to employees, operating employee suggestion schemes, and making use of staff committees or Works Councils for consultation.

Broadly speaking, therefore, it would appear that diversely recruiting employers tend to adopt high commitment HR practices, leading to employability, and encouraging involvement and equality of treatment. We cannot be sure that recruits from the diverse groups share in these conditions, but at least the conditions are favourable to their eventual integration.

Employers can also provide favourable employment conditions by means of another aspect of flexibility not yet discussed – flexibility of working hours. This aspect is examined in the next section.

Family-friendly policies and hours flexibility

Flexibility of hours and family-friendly policies are two approaches which employers can use to provide a supportive environment so as to attract and retain employee groups with particular needs. They have already been discussed in the preceding chapter from the viewpoint of women employees but they can also be important for other groups. For example, part-time and/or flexible hours present opportunities for gradual re-entry to, or phased exit from, the labour market suitable for returners with children and older workers respectively. The demand for part-time work among younger sections of the workforce has also risen, as the number of students has grown alongside educational costs being increasingly passed on to students and their families.

Our survey indicates that recruitment among the diverse groups is enhanced in workplaces with higher proportions of part-time workers. But are these hours being imposed on newcomers, or is management being responsive to the hours that people seek? There is some indirect evidence to suggest responsiveness. Workplaces which recruit from a diverse labour supply are more likely to allow employees to *change* from full-time to part-time hours, suggesting a degree of *choice* over hours worked.

Flexi-time hours are also somewhat more available for all staff in such workplaces, again indicating some choice over time at work (Chart 8.4). However, this apparent flexibility in hours worked should not be exaggerated, for as Chapter Six revealed, only one in seven workplaces permits staff to work flexi-time hours. The prevailing norm for non-managerial staff continues to be fixed hours arrangements.

Comparison of diversely and non-diversely recruiting workplaces also reveals that the former are more likely to have recently increased the replacement of full-time employees with part-time, and to have recruited men for jobs that were previously performed by women (and *vice versa*). These shifts suggest that in the diversely recruiting workplaces, new groups

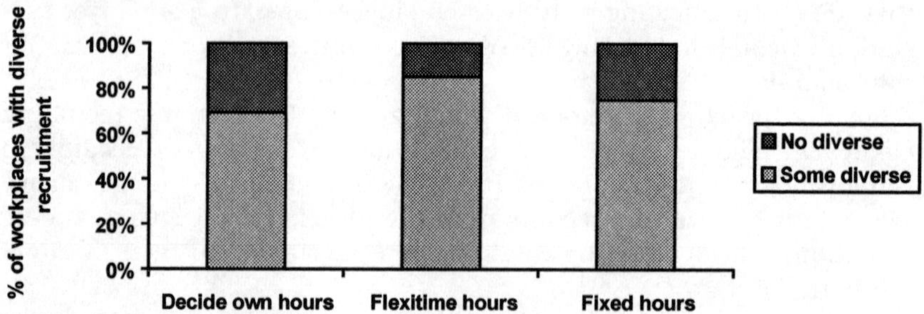

Chart 8.4 Diverse recruitment and working hours of non-managerial staff
Note: Column percentages, weighted by employment.

of employees are increasingly being considered for jobs previously performed by a more limited range of people.

Moving on to other benefits and conditions that may be termed 'family-friendly', we confront a somewhat mixed picture. Once company size and industry have been taken into account, diversely recruiting employers are no more likely to offer assistance with the cost of childcare, parental leave, or maternity pay beyond the basic government scheme. Nor are they more likely to offer career breaks. Therefore, despite being prepared to recruit individuals who have had a career gap, this does not extend to holding open current jobs for those who wish to take a prolonged absence. This negative finding is consistent with the lack of generosity over employee benefits which was noted in the previous section of this chapter.

But while terms offered to new parents are not generous, in some other respects diversely recruiting employers may be interpreted as family-friendly. Term time working is more prevalent among such workplaces, as well as flexi-time hours being more widely available and more likely to be increasing. In addition, these employers are more likely than the average to provide employees with information about local childcare services, and to allow unpaid parental leave. While these are low-cost provisions, they indicate some sensitivity to family issues and some desire to help.

Diversity and ICT use

In Chapter Two a surprising link emerged between flexible labour and high levels of ICT use, dispelling the popular view that flexible labour is confined to low-tech, low-skill sectors of the economy. Is there also a connection between ICT use and diversity – or perhaps between ICT and *lack* of diverse recruitment? This question connects to educational and social debates about how ICT is likely to affect disadvantaged groups at all stages of life. Does ICT offer such groups a fresh chance, or does it set up a new kind of barrier against them?

A positive link could arise because high-tech workplaces tend to be growing and rapidly changing, so they might be expected to be particularly open to recruitment from diverse sources. On the other hand, they may require specific types of skill, and especially familiarity with ICT, and this may pose difficulties to people who have been out of the employment mainstream. The balance between these factors is crucial for the prospects of people from the diverse groups within workplaces that are ICT leaders.

In practice, workplaces which *already have* a high concentration of staff using PCs or other computerised equipment are *less likely* to employ people from the diverse groups than those at a medium level of ICT use. Required skill levels in such workplaces appear to present an over-riding obstacle to diversity. Overall, workplaces with a high staff coverage of ICT recruit from fewer of the diverse groups.[12] There are particularly clear differences for under-18s, people with six months or more of unemployment, and those whose English speaking is poor. The full results are shown in Chart 8.5.

On the other hand, workplaces *rapidly increasing* their use of ICT are *more likely* to recruit from the diverse groups. Here, the need for additional staff appears to override any skill barrier, or it may be that such workplaces are currently laying on additional training to support the extension of ICT and accompanying changes, which makes it easier for them to absorb diverse newcomers. Overall, workplaces with rapidly increasing ICT recruit from more of the diverse groups, by comparison with those which are not changing. Those workplaces where ICT use is increasing at a moderate pace are intermediate in their involvement in diversity. There are particularly clear differences for under-18s, returners, and people with disabilities, as shown in Chart 8.6.

To sum up, it seems that while workplaces are rapidly extending their use of ICT, there is an enhanced opportunity for people from a wide range of groups to gain employment. However, once workplaces have built up to a high level of ICT skills , greater entry barriers confront the newcomer. It could also be that the workplaces which early developed a high level of ICT

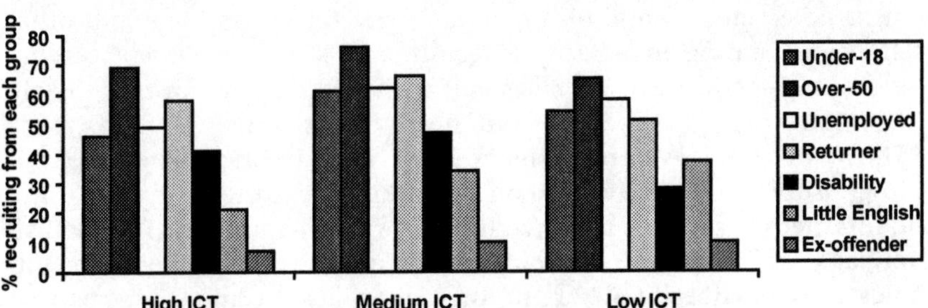

Chart 8.5 Recruitment from diverse groups, by level of ICT coverage
Note: Cell percentages (each bar is a separate percentage of the total), weighted by employment. Those with no recruitment excluded from chart.

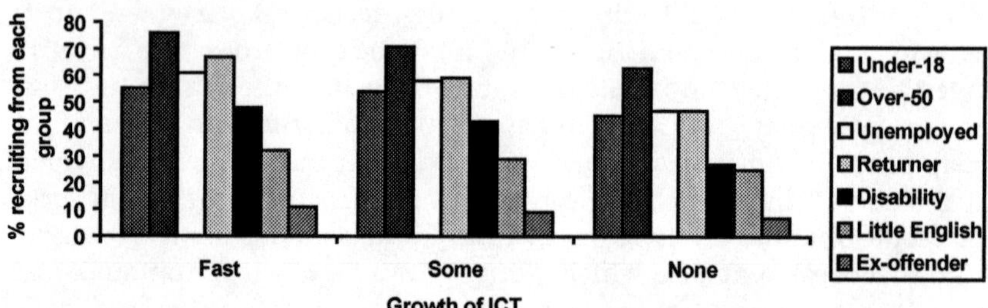

Chart 8.6 Recruitment of diverse groups, by increase in ICT use
Note: Cell percentages (each bar is a separate percentage of the total), weighted by employment. Those with no recruitment excluded from chart.

tend to have a largely professional workforce, and this would present a barrier to some of the diverse groups even without the factor of ICT skills.

Diversity and recruitment methods

It is not immediately obvious what effect various recruitment methods or techniques will have on diversity, or *vice versa*. Recruitment agencies may act as gatekeepers barring the way to potential recruits, especially if they ration opportunities among job-seeking clients according to their position on a scale of presumed employability. Alternatively, it is claimed that such agencies can function as a bridge for some segments of the labour market, counteracting 'resistance to disadvantaged groups'.[13] Yet another recent development in recruitment techniques is use of the Internet. Does Internet recruitment by-pass recruitment obstacles and offer a more direct line between job seekers and jobs, or is it just another barrier to people deprived of access to ICT?

The survey of employers indicates that the traditional variations in recruitment policy no longer make any difference to diversity of recruitment – even if they formerly did so. The presence of internal career ladders, for example, and internal filling of vacancies for professional and other staff, has no bearing on diversity of recruitment. Moreover, workplaces that use external recruitment agencies are neither less likely nor more likely than other employers to recruit from the diverse groups.

The new technology of recruitment, however, is making a difference, and it is a positive one. Nearly one-half of workplaces in the survey are using the Internet for some of their recruitment (see Chapter One for details). Comparison of businesses which do and do not use the Internet to recruit, indicates that virtually all of the diverse groups are more likely to be recruited by workplaces using the Internet (see Chart 8.7). The advantage is highest for people with disabilities. Workplaces which are recruiting via the Internet are twice as likely to recruit from this group, within a 12-month,

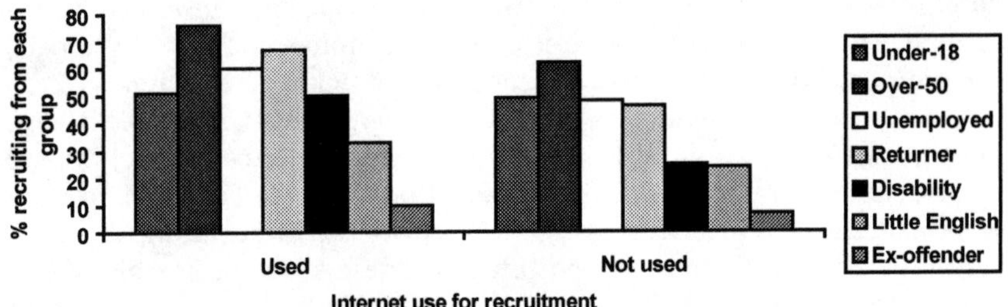

Chart 8.7 Internet recruitment and diversity of recruitment
Note: Cell percentages (each bar is a separate percentage), weighted by employment. Those with no recruitment excluded from chart.

as are workplaces relying on traditional methods of recruitment. But all the diverse groups, with the exception of under-18s, fare better with Internet recruitment. The lack of benefits for under-18s is perhaps because there are conventional routes through which juvenile employees are recruited, and the Internet has not yet made inroads in this area.

Recruiting overseas

In keeping with the emergent picture of employers being pushed toward more imaginative recruitment solutions, they may turn increasingly to overseas recruitment, a step which the British government has recently encouraged to meet skill shortages. Diversely recruiting employers are in fact *four times as likely* as others to be actively trying to recruit from outside the UK. But the scale of this development should not be exaggerated – it remains a minority practice with just ten per cent of recruiters looking abroad for staff. Professional and technical staff are targeted abroad to the greatest extent (by 63 per cent of overseas recruiters), while 30 per cent of overseas recruiters are seeking managerial staff, 13 per cent secretarial staff, and 42 per cent other categories. Just two industries have more than the average ten per cent of workplaces with some overseas recruitment – hotels and catering with 21 per cent looking abroad, and the public service sector with 17 per cent.[14] These are also the industries with the greatest diversity in recent recruitment.

Conclusions

A key finding of this chapter is that change is the friend of diversity. Where workplaces are growing, staff turnover increasing, ICT use accelerating, or work practices changing, diversity of recruitment is more likely to be present. Whether pushed by staff shortages or intensified competition for custom, under these circumstances employers are more open to diversity in the composition of their workforce. In the buoyant climate of 2002, most employers were ready to recruit from the diverse groups considered in this chapter. The other side of this coin is that if economic conditions stagnate, the prospects for people in these groups could quickly deteriorate.

A diverse workforce is also associated with higher levels of flexible labour, but this link chiefly applies to small workplaces – perhaps the McJobs end of diverse recruitment. Temporary, casual or freelance contracts in such workplaces may represent a bridge whereby some disadvantaged groups gain access to employment opportunities. These kinds of flexible labour tend to be associated with low-wage, low-skill opportunities, so recruitment diversity seems partly concentrated in workplaces offering poorer terms and conditions of employment. Further investigation of this point, however, produces mixed messages. On the one hand, diversity of recruitment is more often found in workplaces with heightened levels of job training and other HRM practices that are suggestive of a developmental approach towards employees rather than an emphasis on cutting labour costs to the bone. On the other hand, there are various indications, apart from the use of flexible labour contracts, that employers using diverse recruitment tend to be cost-sensitive and close-fisted. They are on average less likely to offer benefits such as occupational pensions and enhanced sick pay entitlements to their employees, or to offer those family-friendly practices which entail significant costs.

The survey does not tell us whether people recruited from the diverse groups actually get access to the beneficial HRM practices in their workplaces, or whether they tend to remain outside them. Two results provide at least some indirect encouragement on this score. Workplaces with diversity of recruitment are above the average in offering transfer from part-time to full-term hours, and in seeking to harmonise benefits across all employees.

The influence of ICT is again important, but in a less straightforward way than in previous chapters. Workplaces that have already achieved a high level of staff coverage by ICT are relatively uninterested in diversity of recruitment: this could be because of a skill barrier. But rapidly increasing ICT, like other kinds of change, is favourable to diversity. Moreover, the burgeoning field of Internet recruitment enhances diversity, perhaps because it promotes equality of access. This seems potentially a most important development, both from the viewpoint of those trying to climb over recruitment barriers, and from the viewpoint of employers seeking to widen and diversify their workforce.

We can now sum up how diversity of recruitment fits into the patterns and processes of change at the workplace. Much of it, like the desegregation of recruitment described in Chapter Seven, is a response to the pressures of competition in tight job markets. We do not however know how far it is backed up by other policies to ensure that recruits from the diverse groups are given long-term chances: it would need a more specialised study to investigate this issue. All we can say is that workplaces with diverse recruitment are not short-termist in their outlook. To be sure, they tend to be cost-sensitive, but their managements also tend to be active in employee development and in effective communications. So it seems that diversity of recruitment is to some extent being accompanied by a proactive HRM approach. The key point for the future is to establish how much the diverse groups, once recruited, themselves take part in and benefit from this approach. On this depends the value of diversity policy for the corporate contribution to wider social goals.

9
Which Strategies?

Across the last seven chapters, we have described the main areas of changing practice in the management of people at British workplaces. There is little doubt now that change on a massive scale is taking place. But what does this change amount to and how does it answer the questions posed early in Chapter One? Does it point to a future where organisations will be better able to compete because they are using human resources more effectively? And if the answer is 'yes', does that mean that employees themselves are better off or worse off in consequence? To respond to these kinds of questions, it is not enough to summarise the piecemeal evidence. For as Chapter One noted, HRM policies are likely to be fully effective only when they are brought together at workplace level and combined in a way that can be called strategic. So our task in describing the changing British workplace is not complete.

Unfortunately, there is little agreement on what are the key elements of an HRM strategy, or on how to recognise an HRM strategy when one bumps into it. Is a strategy any more than a collection of practices which an organisation happens to accumulate? What is the added value of a strategy, either from the viewpoint of the organisation trying to survive and prosper, or from an observer's viewpoint trying to understand changes at work?

In the absence of any wide consensus on these points, we have to take our own stand on strategy. The definition of strategy adopted in this chapter is: a combination of workplace practices which *has a unifying interpretation or meaning* that points to what an employer is aiming to achieve. A simple example, which will shortly be examined in more detail, is the combination of reduced employee numbers with a high and/or increasing use of outsourcing. A reduction in numbers on its own could just indicate hard times for the organisation, not any kind of strategy. But cuts in employee numbers *together with* increased outsourcing suggests something different – a coherent effort to reduce labour costs. Bringing together practices in this way can therefore provide more insight into what organisations are trying to do. Presumably, also, senior managements themselves see connections between the various people policies they use or might use, and this helps them to choose the direction they want to go.

The problem with this simple idea of HR strategy is that there are many workplace practices and an enormous number of potential combinations. As previous chapters have also indicated, a great many of these potential combinations exist in reality. For example, workplaces which offer career ladders also tend to have appraisal systems, to offer pensions and other benefits, to have active communications with employees, to be increasing their use of team organisation, to have a high level of ICT use ... Where and how are we to draw the line around groups of practices so as to call them strategies?

The approach adopted here is in essence to *pre-define* a limited number of combinations of practices to focus upon, without any claim to generate a comprehensive set. This selection is guided by debates that have recently been taking place in the HRM arena, and ideas which have been put forward about strategies that are important. Obviously, the selection of strategies is also limited by the coverage of questions in the CEPS-02 employer survey. For instance, the survey did not include questioning about quality practices and customer service practices, so we cannot examine 'total quality' strategies.[1] None the less, the discussion of strategies here is reasonably extensive. We look at *five main strategies* and, most importantly, consider how they are spread across workplaces with various characteristics. This gives a balanced perspective across a diversity of organisations. It also provides a way of condensing many of the findings from the previous chapters and looking at them from a different vantage point.

Readers who are familiar with the business strategy literature will realise that our idea of strategy is a moderate one. For example, we do not claim that a strategy involves an explicit analysis by management so as to link their practices with their business goals (after all, would the strategy work any less well if it evolved in a fluid, trial-and-error manner, rather than by armchair thinking?). Nor do we imagine that workplaces can be divided into distinctive types on the basis of their HRM strategies.[2] Nor do we insist that having one kind of strategy must involve the exclusion of another kind of strategy. Any one workplace, according to our way of thinking, can pick-and-mix its strategies.[3] Part of this chapter considers how the strategies under consideration are actually mixed together at workplace level.

Defining strategies

Defining any strategy involves a considerable element of interpretation and choice, and there is no one set of criteria that is manifestly the best. Here we reveal how our choices were made, and why we think each of the strategies is important. In defining strategies, we also bring another consideration to bear. Each type of strategy should say something distinctive about the organisations which have them. Presumably, too, when an organisation develops a strategy, it is trying to gain an advantage by pushing ahead of the pack in one direction. Our definitions try to pick out those organisations that are towards the front in each type of change strategy.

Downsizing

Downsizing has been described as 'corrosive' and a 'preoccupation' of management in recent years.[4] This type of comment, which reflects a common viewpoint, seems to assume not only that downsizing has damaging effects but that it is very widespread. Later in the chapter we will consider whether it is necessarily corrosive or damaging. How widespread it is, of course depends on how it is defined. If it is simply the occurrence of redundancies at the workplace, then it certainly is widespread – but probably too widespread to be regarded as a distinctive strategy. For example, in the single year of 1998, well over one-half (57%) of unionised workplaces conducted bargaining over redundancies.[5] A stricter view of downsizing is that the total employment at the workplace should have decreased, and Chapter One showed that this applied (over the period 2000–2) to nearly one in four workplaces. But even this is too broad if downsizing is to be regarded as a strategy, since many of these cases of contraction must simply reflect loss of market to stronger competitors, or other adverse circumstances which the organisation is powerless to resist. Downsizing becomes a strategy when it also involves the active *replacement* of previous employees with less costly forms of labour.

The two main possibilities that fit this description are flexible labour (such as temporary and casual workers), and the outsourcing of work to contractors. Details of both are given in Chapter Two. As explained there, flexible labour is not in fact specifically linked with reductions in the workforce – it is equally prevalent among growing establishments. But outsourcing in all its guises is linked to a shrinking total of employees. This suggests that, in many cases though doubtless not all, workplaces that have both shrunk their workforce and engaged in outsourcing have been actively seeking to cut labour costs rather than just succumbing to disaster.

Downsizing is therefore defined for present purposes as (a) a reduction in the workforce over the past three years, *plus* (b) at least one of the following three indications of outsourcing: former employees transferring to self-employed status but remaining on-site; current use of on-site contracted labour; or an increased use of outsourcing contracts to replace employees.

On this definition, a downsizing strategy is not extremely prevalent: it occurs in about one in six workplaces overall. The proportions are one in ten of small workplaces (less than 25 employees), one in eight of medium sized workplaces (25–99 employees), and one in five of large workplaces (with 100 or more employees).

Delayering

Delayering is another type of slimming-down strategy but one which involves movement towards a particular kind of flat organisation, which can be seen as more participative for employees, and especially for the middle managers – at least, for those who survive and get more responsibility.[6] Chapter Four presents findings that address this area. As shown there, more workplaces are *increasing* the number of job layers they recognise, than the reverse. However, there are sizeable minorities which have either cut out management grades or below-management grades. In addition, a minority of workplaces report that the proportion of managers within their total employment has been reduced.

Delayering is most often taken to refer to cuts at the middle management level. This is what is distinctive about it, since reductions below management level have always been common during business downturns or competitive setbacks. Accordingly, we define the delayering strategy as either a reduction in management grades, or a reduction in the proportion of managers employed (or both). We exclude non-management grade reductions from the definition.

Delayering might be pooled with downsizing, since they are both related to labour cost reductions. But whereas downsizing seems purely about labour costs, delayering also connects, potentially, with distinctive aims for flatter structures and more responsibility pushed down the hierarchy. Also, delayering more often occurs without downsizing than with it. Altogether, one in six (17%) of workplaces delayer, but only one in 16 (7%) *both* downsize *and* delayer (see Chart 9.1).

'High performance/high commitment' strategies

An enormous amount has been written about HRM strategy from the viewpoint of building a higher-performing workforce.[7] It is often argued or assumed that an essential part of such a strategy is to increase employees' commitment to or involvement with their organisation. Accordingly the

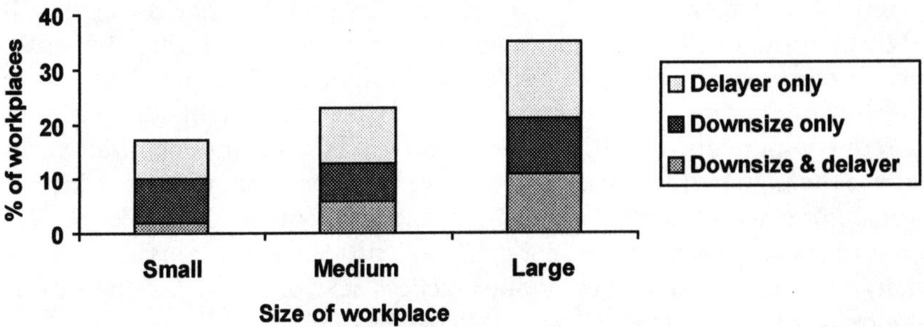

Chart 9.1 Downsizing and/or delayering, by size of workplace
Note: Column percentages, weighted by employment.

terms 'high commitment strategy' or 'high involvement strategy' are often used interchangeably with 'high performance strategy'. Furthermore, the specific management practices involved are highly similar across all these prescriptions. However, those writing from a high-performance perspective often stress that improved performance only arises when a full bundle of practices has been implemented, and when the composition of this bundle in some sense matches or fits the product-market strategy or mission of the organisation.[8] This is less of a key point in discussions of HRM strategy from the viewpoint of the employee's commitment, involvement or well-being. Indeed two of the main research studies in this area have shown that HRM practices can separately contribute to positive outcomes for employees, without any particular bundles being offered.[9]

We base our definition on four components: participation/communication, team organisation, skills/development, and incentives. These components are acknowledged as important in most prescriptions, although with varying emphasis. When they are brought together, they should be working roughly as follows.[10]

- Participating employees are able to offer their knowledge and expertise to improve performance and facilitate change,
- the development of their skills enhances their ability to make a contribution,
- and incentives give them the motivation to do so.
- Team organisation underpins all three processes, broadening participation and communication, providing for knowledge transfer between employees, and strengthening motivation through commitment.

Each of the components just outlined can of course be realised via different paths – for instance, there are many different ways in which communications can be developed. For each component, we specify three types of practice that are relevant (see Table 9.1). To qualify as having a particular component in place, the workplace must have at least two of the three practices implemented or being developed. To qualify as having an overall high performance/high commitment strategy, we specify that the workplace must have at least three of the four components in place.

By only requiring two out of three practices per component, and three out of four components overall, this definition leaves scope for organisations to pursue the high performance strategy in varied ways. A more rigid definition would not make allowance for organisations' different circumstances and the varying preferences of their senior managements. Smaller organisations, especially, may do better if they adopt practices selectively, rather than over-stretching their resources by chasing every idea in sight.[11]

Altogether, nearly three in ten workplaces (29%) have a high performance or high commitment strategy according to this definition.

This high figure is striking, in view of the tough criteria applied.[12] If our approach to defining strategy is reasonable, then it seems that a strategic approach to human resources is being quite widely extended in Britain, with the probable result of increasing the nation's competitive strength.

The descriptive results by size of workplace are summarised in Chart 9.2. Not surprisingly, large workplaces with their greater resources are twice as likely to follow a high performance strategy as are small workplaces.

High-benefits strategy

Employee benefits are sometimes regarded as part of 'old' personnel management rather than as part of the HRM change agenda. But any casual reading of the situations vacant columns will show that the benefits package features prominently in employers' attempts to attract staff. And, as noted in Chapter Seven, recruitment and retention have moved to the top of many managements' priority list. In addition, occupational pensions

Table 9.1 Elements of a high performance/high commitment strategy

Participation/ communications	*Group organisation*	*Skills/ development*	*Incentives*
– Briefing groups	– Increase in formal teams	– Increased task variety	– Career ladders
– Works council or staff committee	– Work improvement groups	– Training for job cover	– Pay for group performance
– Suggestion scheme	– Teams without supervisors	– ICT feedback for training	– Appraisal-based pay

Note: High performance or high commitment strategy requires at least two practices to be in use under at least three of the headings.

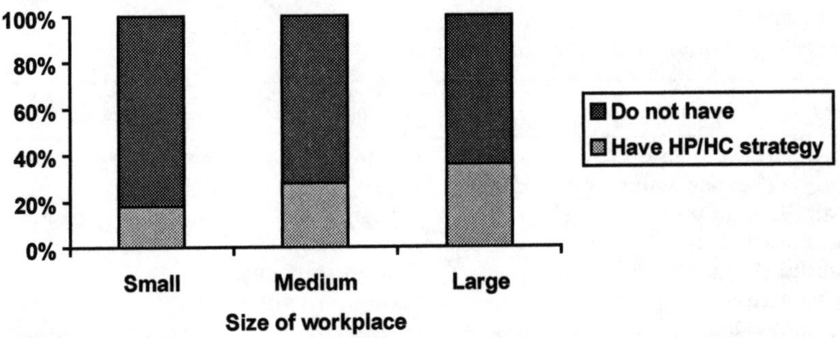

Chart 9.2 High performance (HP)/high commitment (HC) strategy, by size of workplace

Note: Column percentages, weighted by employment.

and family-friendly practices have been receiving the keenest attention in the British media, which suggests that the public is very interested in this kind of provision. From the employer's viewpoint, they could perhaps be considered as incentives and so become part of the definition of the high performance/high commitment strategy. Such an argument has recently been strongly advocated in the USA, where family-friendly practices in particular are increasingly being seen as a crucial element of enhanced employee performance.[13] But there is a strong case for keeping them separate, since their importance for the employer is primarily to support the distinct aims of recruitment and retention, rather than to stiffen the motivation of existing employees.[14]

Our definition of whether employers are using a benefits package as a recruitment and retention strategy has two parts. The first considers fringe benefits as traditionally understood, while the second considers the newer family-friendly practices. To have a high profile on traditional fringe benefits, a workplace must offer *all* its employees at least three out of a list of seven benefits, and at least one of these must be an occupational pension scheme or a sick pay scheme that is more generous than the statutory scheme.[15] The list of fringe benefits is shown in Table 9.2.

The second criterion in defining the benefits package as a strategy is whether the workplace offers at least three from a list of six family-friendly practices. These are also listed as part of Table 9.2.

A high-benefits strategy is then defined as having *both* a high level of traditional fringe benefits *and* a high level of family-friendly practices. This seems reasonable in view of the high profile of work-life balance issues currently. In addition, where fringe benefits are at a high level there is also, statistically, a considerably higher chance of a high level of family-friendly practices (and *vice versa*), so it is natural to treat the two kinds of policies as a group.

Overall, just over one in five workplaces (21%) follow a high-benefits strategy. In the larger establishments, the proportion rises to nearly one in

Table 9.2 Elements of a high-benefits strategy

High on fringe benefits	*High on family-friendly practices*
Occupational pension *	Employees choose own work-times *or* work flexi-time hours
Sick pay beyond statutory minimum *	Maternity pay beyond statutory basic
Staff discount purchases	Assistance with childcare costs
Subsidised meals	Career break scheme
Subsidised transport to work	Term-time working
Subsidised health scheme	Parental leave beyond statutory minimum
Subsidised loans for home purchase	

Note: 'high' level requires at least three items from each list.
* At least one of these items is required.

three, which is more than three times as high as in small workplaces and more than twice as high as in medium-sized workplaces. The results are summarised in Chart 9.3.

High-tech (ICT) strategy

Defining an employer high-tech strategy based on ICT usage is particularly difficult. As Chapter One showed, a high level of ICT usage by employees is widespread. It is not enough just to consider the proportion of employees using the technology. Equally important is the variety of ways in which ICT is used and how far it is becoming the framework for the whole organisation. This reflects aims, expressed by some of the leading thinkers on ICT, of making the technology into an 'infrastructure'[16] or using it to transform the administrative framework.[17] Our definition of a high-tech strategy, accordingly, takes account of ten items indicating breadth of usage. The full list is shown in Table 9.3.

Chart 9.3 High-benefits strategy, by size of workplace
Note: Column percentages, weighted by employment. High-benefits strategy includes family-friendly practices: see text.

Table 9.3 Elements of a high-tech strategy

- Proportion of employees using ICT is close to 100 per cent
- Workplace has increased its use of ICT very much in past three years
- Electronic point-of-sales systems are in use at the workplace
- Stock control/purchasing applications are in use at the workplace
- Engineering applications (CAD/CAM/CIM/CAE) are in use at the workplace
- There is a computer network facilitating e-mail use between staff
- There is a computer network providing information services to staff
- Work is continuously monitored by ICT *and* the information is used by line management
- The Internet is sometimes used for recruitment purposes
- Teleworking is being used.

Note: High-tech strategy is defined as any six of the above.

To qualify as having a high-tech strategy, an organisation must pass six or more of the ten tests. This is a fairly arbitrary cut-off, chosen largely on the basis of convenience rather than anything deeper. Drawing the line as low as four items would result in the majority of workplaces being classified as high-tech, thus saying nothing distinctive about them, while very few have as many as eight ICT items in being. But five or seven items, instead of six, would not give absurd results.

Overall, around one in five workplaces (22%) has a high-tech strategy according to this definition. Chart 9.4 shows the breakdown by size of workplace. The larger workplaces are twice as likely to have a high-tech strategy as the small workplaces, a result that is similar to the high-performance strategy.

How strategies mix

The way that the strategies have been defined does not preclude any one strategy occurring alongside any other. Yet in practice some strategies might sit uncomfortably with others, while conversely some might complement one another. So what are the actual tendencies – how far do workplaces adopt various *strategy mixes*?

In assessing this, the size factor must be taken into account. As Charts 9.1–9.4 have shown, every strategy is more likely to be adopted at larger workplaces than at smaller workplaces. Larger workplaces have more resources, and they also tend to have more complex problems, so it is not surprising that they develop more elaborate combinations of people practices. Small workplaces may well achieve equally good results by a more selective approach. Accordingly, the analysis is performed separately for small, medium and large workplaces.

In Table 9.4, findings are summarised for the pairwise combinations of strategies. The earlier Chart 9.1, concerning downsizing and delayering, illustrates the kind of analysis which produces the results in each element

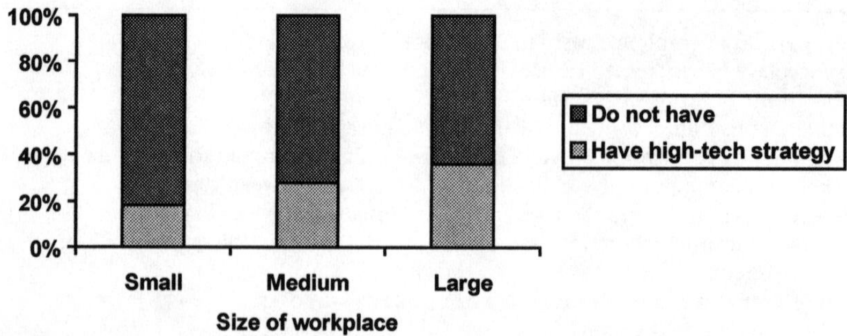

Chart 9.4 High-tech strategy, by size of workplace
Note: Column percentages, weighted by employment.

Table 9.4 Joint occurrence of pairs of strategies, by size of workplace

		Delayering	*High-commitment*	*High benefits*	*High-tech*
Downsizing	Small	+ **	0	0	0
	Medium	+ ***	0	0	0
	Large	+ ***	0	+ **	0
Delayering	Small		0	0	0
	Medium		0	0	0
	Large		+ ***	0	0
High-commit.	Small			+ ***	+ ***
	Medium			+ ***	+ ***
	Large			+ **	+ ***
High benefits	Small				+ *
	Medium				+ **
	Large				0

0 means that the two strategies occur independently.
+ means that each of the two strategies increases the chance of the other occurring as well.
* means that the association is significant at the 1 per cent level.
** means that the association is significant at the 0.1 per cent level.
*** means that the association is significant at the 0.01 per cent level.

of this table. The symbol '0' in a cell of Table 9.4 means that the two strategies occur independently for that particular size of workplace. In other words, the presence of one strategy in a workplace of that size makes it neither more likely nor less likely that the other strategy will occur in that workplace. The symbol '+' indicates that the presence of one strategy in the workplace makes it more likely that the other strategy will also be present there. The number of asterisks after the '+' symbol indicate the statistical strength of the link. If any strategy made the occurrence of another strategy *less likely*, that would be indicated by a minus-sign, but no such negative relationship actually occurred.

The absence of any negative links is a particularly important point. It means that none of these strategies acts as a barrier to the adoption of any of the other strategies. Most strikingly, downsizing is just as likely to be present alongside a high-commitment strategy or a high-benefits strategy as not. In large workplaces, delayering is actually *more likely* to be accompanied by a high-commitment strategy. The fact that the downsizing strategy frequently occurs along with other strategies that help to recruit, retain, involve and develop staff suggests that it is not necessarily a negative approach to human resources. The survey does not tell whether these combinations produce good results, but there are evidently plenty of managements who believe that they are compatible.

None the less, there is a clear division visible in Table 9.4. Downsizing and delayering have a positive tendency to occur together, but they are with two exceptions (which apply only to large workplaces) independent of the other three strategies. The other three strategies, however, are all strongly linked with one another. High-commitment, high-benefits, and high-tech are mutually supportive, and this applies across all sizes with just one exception (high-benefits and high-tech are independent of each other in large workplaces[18]).

So it does not appear that the 'new' high-commitment strategies involving combinations of HRM practices are displacing the 'old' personnel or welfare emphasis on benefits. On the contrary, both are more often working together than apart.

Most interestingly, the workplaces with an extensive adoption of ICT are apparently tending to complement this with strategies to recruit, retain, involve and develop a high-quality workforce. In fact, only eight per cent of workplaces have a high-tech strategy with neither a high-commitment nor a high-benefits strategy, while 14 per cent of workplaces have a high-tech strategy in combination with one or both of these. This is more consistent with a knowledge worker view of ICT than with a de-skilling interpretation. In the majority of cases, a high-tech strategy increases rather than reduces the HRM role.[19]

Lean and mean?

Downsizing and delayering can and do occur alongside high-commitment and high-benefits strategies, but there is a special interest in cases where they occur on their own. In these cases, without the compensating effect of the employee-friendly strategies, downsizing and delayering take on a character both lean and mean. How often does the lean-mean variant arise in practice?

To examine this, we first define a wider measure of 'lean strategy' based on the presence of *either* downsizing *or* delayering at the workplace. Just over one in four of workplaces (26%) are slimming-down by one or the other (or both) routes. This one-in-four can then be divided into those with and without the friendlier strategies. The findings are as follows, with the percentages relating to the proportion of all workplaces:

- Lean with neither 'high-commitment' nor 'high-benefits' strategy: 12 per cent
- Lean with 'high-commitment', but not 'high-benefits': six per cent
- Lean with 'high-benefits', but not 'high-commitment': four per cent
- Lean with both 'high-commitment' and 'high-benefits' strategy: four per cent.

So about one in eight workplaces has a fully 'lean-mean' strategy mix, focusing on downsizing and/or delayering to the exclusion of high-commitment and high-benefits approaches. Unlike the basic strategies considered earlier, the 'lean-mean' mix is equally distributed across workplaces of all size, with the smallest workplaces just as likely to adopt it as the largest.

What shapes strategy?

Where an organisation chooses a particular strategy or mix of strategies, the outlook and preferences of senior management are likely to be major influences. Indeed, a constant refrain of the management literature on workplace innovation is the need for top management commitment to change. Since the survey does not collect information on management's beliefs and goals, these important influences cannot be analysed here. However, management choices are themselves likely to be influenced by the circumstances of the organisation. What, then, are the circumstances or characteristics of workplaces which affect the strategies they adopt? How far do these circumstances or characteristics help to explain why any of the strategies are developed? The size of the workplace is clearly very important, but what other factors have a comparable impact?

In the case of *downsizing*, the strategy is much more prevalent in manufacturing industry than in services. This doubtless reflects the greater pressure from international competition and the greater scope for continual productivity increases. Manufacturing workplaces are also less likely to have a high-benefits strategy than service workplaces (see below), so they tend to be at the 'lean-mean' corner. None the less, manufacturing is now such a small part of employment that it only accounts for about one-third of downsizing, with the remainder widely spread across other industries.

A further factor which appears to influence the downsizing strategy is the presence of trade unions at the workplace. In fact, it has long been known that employment tends to contract over time at unionised workplaces.[20] But downsizing, as defined here, involves outsourcing as well as cutting employment: a union presence appears to increase outsourcing as well. This might reflect either the pressure which unions exert on wages, leading senior management to seek compensating savings in labour costs, or a more general, indirect pressure on management to operate efficiently.[21]

Delayering is another strategy which turns out to be stimulated by the presence of unions at the workplace. Since delayering is defined as a reduction in *management* grades or proportions, union pressure on wages and labour costs is unlikely to be the direct explanation here. More plausible is the indirect pressure on the organisation to adopt efficient practices. Notably, manufacturing workplaces are *not* more likely to have a delayering strategy than workplaces in other industries. Delayering is broadly distributed, though more prevalent in PLCs than in non-PLC private sector companies or in publicly-owned services.

The presence of trade unions on-site again proves to be an important factor linked to the *high-performance or high-commitment strategy*. Links between unionisation and HRM practices have been found in the past, so this is not a surprise. The explanation could on one hand be the general union pressure to adopt positive practices, and the capacity of unions to support management in bringing about change which they see as being in members' long-term interests. Alternatively, a high-commitment strategy could be developed because management wants to build strong direct relations with employees so as to balance or limit the role and influence of unions.[22]

Apart from trade unions, the high-commitment strategy is influenced particularly by the complexity of job structures. The greater the number of job levels, the more likely a workplace is to develop an extensive set of high-commitment practices. In addition, the high-commitment strategy is particularly prevalent in workplaces that are open seven days a week, which usually involves shift arrangements and other complications for control and management. What the high-commitment strategy represents, perhaps, is *formal or systematic* practices, needed in complex organisations. Possibly in smaller, simpler organisations the same goals are being pursued in more informal or personal ways, which lack an HRM label. If this is so, then we have underestimated the extent of the high-commitment strategy.

As already mentioned, the *high-benefits strategy* is found at a relatively high level throughout the service sector, and less in manufacturing. This fits the interpretation of the strategy as a support for recruitment and retention, which are particular problems of the growing and volatile service sector.

Another important factor favouring a high-benefits strategy is a high proportion of female employees. This is understandable since the high-benefits strategy is partly defined in terms of family-friendly practices. The sex composition of the workplace is also important for the *high-tech strategy*. Workplaces where most employees are male[23] are *less* likely to adopt a high-tech strategy. As noted in Chapter Seven, this is likely to be a factor of diminishing significance in future, because of the progressive desegregation of jobs which is taking place.

A more important long-term factor is the proportion of part-time employees at the workplace. Where there is a high proportion of part-time workers, the likelihood of a high-tech strategy being followed is *reduced*, even though most part-time employees are female and the influence of high female employment pushes in the opposite direction. The explanation may be that management becomes more likely to switch away from part-time to full-time staffing as ICT investment intensifies. The plausible reason is the heavy cost of ICT equipment and training, which will be aggravated by a part-time workforce.[24]

Complexity is another important factor influencing the high-tech strategy. Workplaces with very simple job structures (one to three levels only) are less likely to adopt a high-tech strategy. Above that level, however, the differences in take-up are negligible. In addition, seven-day opening favours the high-tech strategy. Visualising a large superstore, it is not hard to see why this is so: the control problems are formidable and ICT helps to solve them.

All these influences on strategies are summarised in Table 9.5, which makes it easier to look at how each type of influence is mapped across the five kinds of strategy. It is then apparent that there is not a great deal in common among the various strategies – rather, each of them tends to be influenced by distinctive factors. The factors which extend across several strategies in an influential way are (a) the presence of trade unions, (b) complexity – if tall job structures and seven-day opening are both regarded as aspects of complexity, and (c) the sex composition, including part-time employment as a mainly female issue. Beyond these few common influences, the tendency of strategies to cluster – downsizing with delayering, and high-commitment, high-benefits and high-tech all together – perhaps depends on management seeing them as mutually supportive.

Conclusions

This chapter has considered five types of human resource strategies, each defined as a combination of practices with a unifying meaning or

Table 9.5 Circumstances or characteristics influencing strategy choice

Downsizing	*Delayering*	*High-commitment*	*High-benefits*	*High-tech*
Manufacturing (+)				
	Public services (–)		Services (+)	
	Private non-PLC (–)		Private non-PLC (–)	
TU present (+)	TU present (+)	TU present (+)		
		Many job levels (+)		At least 4 job levels (+)
		Seven-day opening (+)		Seven-day opening (+)
			% female (+)	% female very low (–)
				% part-time (–)

+ means positive influence on strategy adoption; – means negative influence.

interpretation. The five in question, with their interpretations, can be briefly summarised as follows:

- Downsizing: a combination of workforce reductions with outsourcing, indicative of efforts to cut labour costs.
- Delayering: reductions in the number of management grades and/or the proportion of management jobs; indicative of efforts to cut labour costs, coupled with desire to achieve a flatter organisation and greater individual responsibility.
- High performance/high commitment strategy: various combinations of communications/participation, team-working, skills/development, and incentives practices; pursuing ideas of developing human resources to achieve greater employee commitment and organisational effectiveness.
- High-benefits strategy: various combinations of both traditional fringe benefits and of family-friendly practices, intending to facilitate recruitment and retention.
- High-tech strategy: a broad range of indicators of extensive ICT usage, indicative of using ICT as a means of progressively transforming administration and operations.

The criteria for each type of strategy were set in such a way as to select only a minority of workplaces. The proportions selected, across the five strategies, were in the range 15–30 per cent of workplaces. This should have increased the chances of the strategies being distinct from one another, whereas more inclusive criteria would have tended to reduce their distinctness and increase their overlap. Additionally, no workplace practice was used in the definition of more than one strategy.

Despite these efforts to separate the strategies, in practice they still form two groups. Downsizing and delayering have some tendency to occur together, but are independent of the other three strategies. High-commitment strategy, high-benefits strategy, and high-tech strategy tend to occur together, which suggests that management find them to be mutually supportive.

Notably, no one strategy blocks the adoption of any other strategy. Downsizing and delayering are about as likely to be adopted alongside other strategies, such as the high-commitment strategy, as without them. In many circumstances, management do not see these strategies as incompatible, despite their contrasting purposes. A 'lean and mean' combination – downsizing and/or delayering in the absence of both the high-commitment and high-benefits strategies – occurs in just one in eight workplaces and so does not amount to a major feature of British employers' strategies.

The finding that high-tech strategy occurs most frequently alongside either high-commitment strategy or high-benefits strategy (or both) is significant for the skills debate around ICT. In the great majority of cases, management when pursuing an extensive development of ICT also supports this with many actions to recruit, retain and develop employees. This strongly suggests a predominant high-skill development path for ICT, rather than one involving de-skilling of employees – although the latter of course does occur in some cases.

The overriding factor influencing the adoption of these strategies is the size of the workplace, with large workplaces around two or three times more likely to 'strategise' than small workplaces. But this does not prove that small workplaces are less effective or less orientated towards change and development. It may be that small workplaces have simpler and more informal ways of pursuing the same goals, which are difficult to detect in a survey.

Apart from size, a rather miscellaneous bunch of circumstances influences adoption of these strategies. The easiest to interpret concern industry sector. Downsizing is more prevalent in manufacturing (which faces severe competition and continually needs to cut labour costs), while high-benefits strategy is more prevalent in services (which needs to emphasise recruitment and retention in the face of growth and volatility).

A finding of crucial concern is that the high-tech strategy is less likely to be pursued where the proportion of part-time employees is high. A possible interpretation is in terms of the capital costs and training costs of ICT. The smaller the number of workers, and the longer their hours, the more these costs can be contained, making part-time working less desirable from a management viewpoint. The advance of the high-tech strategy therefore has potentially huge implications for working time and for work-life balance, and these implications are most immediate for women because they still constitute the great majority of part-time employees.

One of the most striking findings of the chapter concerns the role of unions in relation to employers' people strategies. Where trade unions are present, downsizing, delayering, but also the high-commitment strategy, all become more probable. This seems entirely contrary to the stereotype of unions as opponents of cost-efficiency and more generally of innovation. Rather, trade unions seem to be a favourable factor – but how? They certainly do not seem to be a spent force, but remain an enigma. This is a topic which will be further considered in the next chapter.

Finally, the findings of this chapter help to fill in answers to some more of the questions posed in Chapter One.

First, downsizing and delayering strategies remain a significant part of the British scene, but by no means a dominant part.

Second, the extent of the five strategies taken together is impressive, especially taking account of how they were defined. Contrary to one of the main doubts expressed in the Porter report (see Chapter One), British organisations do appear to be embracing 'modern management practices', and moreover in a more concerted way than has previously been identified.

Third, the balance of workforce strategies seems reasonably favourable to employees. High-commitment strategies and high-benefits strategies certainly tend to support one another, and these can be expected to improve employees' prospects in a variety of ways. Even the downsizing and delayering strategies are often combined with high-commitment or high-benefits strategies.

Finally, the message about ICT in this chapter is different from the rather worrying one that came out from Chapter Two. The difference is that here we are highlighting the top end of ICT use, where it becomes a high-tech strategy that potentially transforms the organisation. Once it gets to this more strategic level of use, ICT seems to link up with HRM policies of a positive type, implying higher skill demands and better prospects for employees. This is the kind of 'high road' which holds out particular promise for the future.

10
Management *versus* Regulation?

Not all is roses in British workplaces. The extent and pace of change, detailed across the preceding chapters, inevitably create growing pressures on employees in terms of continual adaptation and the quest for higher performance. Moreover, the change agenda is falling short of what employees – or society – aspires to in terms of work-life balance and family-friendly policies. What all this adds up to, for the great majority of employees, is a more 'stressed-out' working life. Research evidence shows that this is not just a fashionable phrase of the chattering classes, but a hard reality.[1]

Managers, of course, bear a large portion of this strain.[2] Already in Chapter One, we saw that of all the changes revealed by the employer survey, the most widespread was more time being spent by managers on people-related issues. Managers face added work-strain, not only because they have to take the lead in the change process, but also because they now face rising pressures *from outside*: from government, from the legal process, and from trade unions. From all these sources, management's scope for action is being *regulated* and it is often argued, by business leaders, that this hampers them in the competitive struggle. Certainly the halcyon days of the 1980s, when management could exert its prerogatives with little opposition and few questions asked, are far in the past.[3] The central question for this chapter is, How is management responding to the external pressures of regulation, and the additional uncertainties those create? When we have answered this question, we will have completed the review which was mapped out in Chapter One.

Among recent developments in government regulation of the workplace, the one most closely relevant to employees' current discontents is the Working Time Regulations 1998 (WTR). The WTR provide the initial focus of this chapter. They are the first major example of the new drive towards regulation on the part of the European Commission, and managers' responses should provide clues to their likely engagement with future regulation.

Alongside the resurgence of central regulation in recent years, there has been a notable increase in litigation by employees against their employers.

A recent CIPD survey revealed that nearly two in three HR managers spend more than 20 per cent of their time on legal issues.[4] Developments which encourage employees to try litigation include the emergence of USA-style 'no win, no fee' legal representation, and the increasing emphasis placed by trade unions on their legal services to individual members. In 2000/1, the number of Employment Tribunal (ET) cases reached a peak at just below 15,000 in the year.[5]

Apart from their involvement in litigation on behalf of members, unions have shown numerous signs of reviving in the 2000s, potentially adding to the pressure on management. In part this could be put down to the existence of a government that is more favourable to unionism than in the Conservative years. From June 2000, unions have had a statutory right to refer recognition claims to the Central Arbitration Committee (CAC) for adjudication, and between 2001 and 2002, the number of cases referred doubled.[6] This however is just the tip of the iceberg. A graphic picture of the galloping rate of change is given in an Incomes Data Services (IDS) Report.[7] Many new agreements cover large numbers of workplaces: for example, in 1998 Tesco signed an agreement with USDAW covering 150,000 retail staff in about 600 stores around the country, a lead which it appears has been copied by some of the company's main suppliers. The new agreements also often reverse marked trends towards union decline: in the printing industry, where unions experienced a collapse of their power in the 1980s, more than 40 new agreements are noted in the IDS report.

But it is by no means obvious that unions in themselves mean more work and more pressure for management. The partnership approach between management and unions, which has been so widely spoken of,[8] can in principle *help* managers to take forward the change agenda. Later in this chapter, we consider evidence from the survey of employers about whether, in 2002, the presence of unions in the workplace helps or hinders managers in carrying out their people-management tasks.

One of the functions of unions is to give employees 'voice', but that is not the only way that voice can be obtained. Another is the development of formal *non-union* channels such as consultative committees or Works Councils. Long established in a substantial minority of British workplaces, such consultative arrangements survived the years of union retreat with relatively little damage.[9] Yet the UK is one of only two EU countries[10] which gives no statutory rights to such committees. This is due to be remedied as a result of the EC's Information and Consultation Directive (ICON). From March 2005, most UK organisations with at least 150 employees will need to conform to the requirements of this Directive as it passes into national law, and this could be extended to organisations with 50 or more employees by 2008. The final section of this chapter considers the current and likely development of consultative committees in the run-up to this change.

Throughout this chapter, then, the focus is specifically on management, rather than upon employees as a whole. Accordingly, the findings in this chapter are presented in a different way from previous chapters. In the previous chapters, figures were weighted to reflect employee coverage, but here they are weighted to be representative of the total number of workplaces. In other words, we give as much weight to a workplace with 10 employees as to one with 1000, because each has a management and it is the pressures on that management in which we are interested.[11]

In time with WTR?

Issues about working time are at the root of the discontents over work-life balance, and this constitutes one of the chief developing problem-areas for management. Against this background, the Working Time Regulations (WTR) were introduced in 1998. Unlike most other EU countries, however, the British government interpreted the EC Directive in a way that would give employers the greatest scope for maintaining the practice of working long hours[12] without disturbance. Not surprisingly, the majority of managers initially thought that the WTR would not make much difference to them.[13] However, case study research shows that subsequently, in a minority of organisations, the WTR were used as a catalyst for change in work practices: two examples are summarised in the Box on page 152. The findings from our employer survey also show that the WTR are not quite the non-event that was at first assumed.

The WTR provisions

The feature of WTR which grabs attention is the limitation of the average working week to 48 hours.[14] At first glance, the WTR seem bound to have a major impact in limiting long hours. However, the 48-hour limit does not apply to employees who have personal choice over their hours. This potentially excludes, for instance, many managers and professional staff, who alone amount to nearly four in ten of all employees. In addition, the impact of WTR can be minimised through individual employee 'opt-outs' or collective agreements, although employees cannot be compelled to opt-out.

In addition to the 48-hour limit, the WTR include a number of other provisions intended to benefit employees. Rest breaks between working days, and rest days between working weeks, are regulated under the heading of 'time off'. During the working day, also, a rest-break of at least 20 minutes is now required for each six-hour period worked. There are new regulations concerning night work, and for juvenile employees. Moreover, the annual paid holiday entitlement has been increased from three weeks to four weeks. Importantly, this holiday entitlement – in common with the other requirements of WTR – applies to all workers, including those hired on a temporary or casual basis.

WTR: catalyst for strategic change

Case studies of WTR implementation, prepared by Fiona Neathey and James Arrowsmith, reveal a wide range of responses from the minimal to the strategic. Two examples are particularly striking because they illustrate a long-term decision to move towards shorter hours in situations where long hours have been endemic.

In an *NHS trust*, the process of change began with a review of working practices and a series of studies carried out by working parties including union representatives. The conclusion reached was that extensive change was needed, which would have to be phased in over several years, on a negotiated basis. Among the early changes were: holiday pay given to previously excluded 'bank' (i.e., casual) staff; increasing holiday pay to reflect shift premia; changes to rotas and working patterns. Fundamentally, it was decided that 'derogations' (exclusions from the 48-hour rule) did not apply to *any* staff and there would be no voluntary opt-outs. The staffing and cost implications of this decision were being addressed progressively.

In a *security service* company, management had already made a strategic decision to move away from the long-hours, low-pay culture of the industry and had increased pay by consolidating overtime into basic rates. An agreement was negotiated with the union to enforce the 48-hour maximum and to average it over a four-week period (the WTR permit averaging over much longer periods). Business managers were then given the responsibility for negotiating the new arrangements with customers, which they did on a contract-by-contract basis. In some cases, long individual shifts were replaced by a mixture of full-time and part-time cover. Typically, in about 80 per cent of cases, customers accepted a price increase to cover the costs of fully implementing the WTR.

Source: Neathey, F. and Arrowsmith, J. (2001) *Implementation of the Working Time Regulations*, Employment Relations Research Series No. 11, London: Department of Trade and Industry.

Management responses to WTR: the 48-hour week

The employer survey asked two main questions about WTR and the 48-hour limit to the average working week. The first was whether management made any changes in work arrangements to comply with the 48-hour limit. The other was whether management asked any staff to opt out of the regulations.[15] Combined information from the two questions provides an assessment of the management response to this most important aspect of the WTR.

The picture provided by the two questions is that the impact of the 48-hour provisions is wider than sometimes assumed, but that avoidance through the opt-out is more common than compliance through change in working practices. One in ten workplaces has changed its work arrangements to conform with WTR, but the proportion seeking opt-outs from employees is nearly twice as high, at 18 per cent (Chart 10.1). These figures

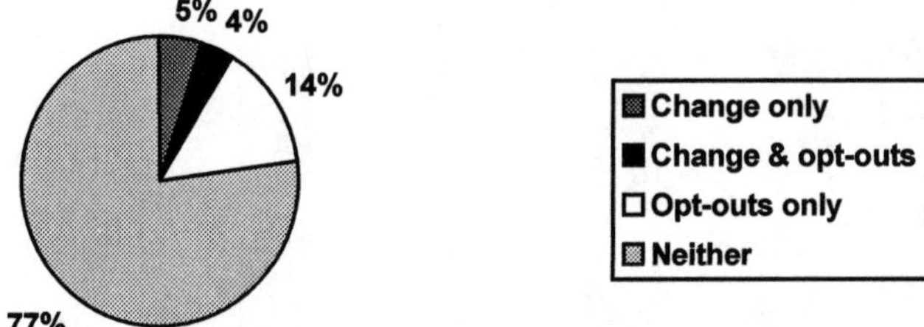

Chart 10.1 Responses to the 48-hour limit: changed work practices and opt-outs
Note: Total percentages, weighted by establishments. Legend reads clockwise beginning with 'Change only' (5%). 'Change' refers to changes in work practices to adapt to the WTR 48-hour limit. 'Opt-out' refers to obtaining employee opt-outs from the 48-hour limit.

vary sharply with size of workplace: those with 100 or more employees are about twice as likely to change their working arrangements, and/or to seek opt-outs.[16]

Seeking opt-outs does not always mean that no change in working practices occurs. In four per cent of employers they are combined with changes in working practices. But more frequently – in nearly one in seven workplaces – opt-outs are the sole response. There are just one in 20 workplaces where the employer has made a wholly positive response, with changes in working practices unaccompanied by opt-outs. Overall, nearly one in four workplaces made some practical response to the 48-hour limit (change in work practices, opt-outs, or both) while three-quarters made no response.

Additionally, 15 per cent of workplaces increased paid holidays for some employees as a result of the WTR, and two thirds of workplaces set up a system to monitor working hours so as to ensure compliance with the 48-hour limit. However, these are changes with few implications for management beyond the direct costs involved.

Management responses to WTR, and time pressures

Of the one-in-ten managements that have changed working practices to comply with the 48-hour limit, an above-average proportion are experiencing increased people-management pressure on their time (Chart 10.2). Changing and controlling working time practices is known to be a very difficult task for management,[17] so it is not surprising to find such a link. More surprisingly, managements that have obtained staff opt-outs from the 48-hour limit also experience people-management pressures on their time, to about the same extent (also shown in Chart 10.2).

On face value, obtaining opt-outs does not seem an onerous task for management. The apparent link with management time-pressures perhaps comes about because active responses to the WTR (whether changed practices or opt-outs) arise in organisations that are already busy with a change agenda. Alternatively, the decision to handle WTR through opt-outs may

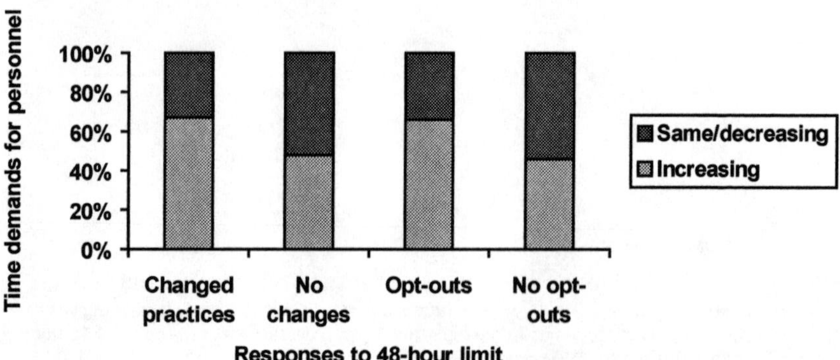

Chart 10.2 WTR changes, opt-outs, and changes in management time demands
Note: Column percentages, weighted by establishments. Time demands for personnel matters refer to changes experienced by management over the past three years.

not always be as simple as it looks. Having decided to use opt-outs for certain categories, there may need to be continuing care in managing the time of categories that have *not* opted-out. Links of these kinds are suggested by a CIPD survey of 2001, which followed-up people who were known to be working more than 48 hours a week during 1998.[18] Although few of these were now working less than 48 hours, nearly one in three reported that their organisation had revised work systems or made efficiency improvements to reduce hours, and about one in four said that their own manager had talked to them about ways to ease workload. Moreover, their actual working hours had on average decreased substantially (although part of this came from moving to less demanding jobs).

Overall, the response of management to WTR cannot be written off as negligible, even though it does not measure up to the national discontent on work-life balance. In one in four workplaces, either some working arrangements were changed, or opt-outs were sought, and both of these developments have tended to take place where the pressures of managing people are increasing. Management's response could have been much lower, since the Regulations were framed in such a way as to minimise compulsion. Managements that used WTR as a catalyst for change, in most cases chose to do so rather than having to do so. However, unions also played a part in the story, and their role will be considered later in the chapter.

In litigation's shadow

It may be easy for managers to duck government regulation of working hours, but it is less easy to escape the rising tide of employee litigation. The survey confirms the wide compass of this development, especially in larger workplaces. One in sixteen workplaces say they have been taken to ETs by employees in the preceding 12 months. As shown in Chart 10.3, the figure is nearly four times as high in the larger workplaces.[19]

The results also confirm that for those managers involved in ET proceedings over unfair dismissal, the perceived trend of litigation is upwards. Four in ten of this group of managers say that their recent experience is an increase on the past, with far fewer recording a decrease (Chart 10.4). Increasing experience of litigation is particularly spreading to smaller workplaces, where it may create particular havoc. But even among large workplaces the increases are more than twice as numerous as the decreases.

Litigation's costs: time and money

Faced with employee litigation, management can bring to bear two main kinds of resource: their own time, and the services of legal advisors (yet

Chart 10.3 Workplaces involved in unfair dismissal cases, by size
Note: Column percentages, weighted by establishments.

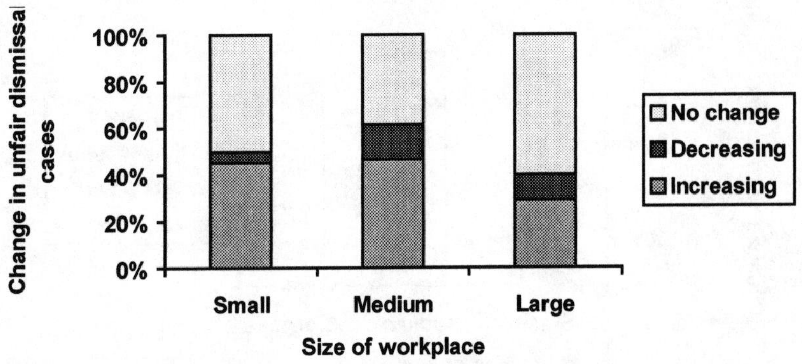

Chart 10.4 Workplaces' changing experience of unfair dismissal cases 2000–2, by size
Note: Column percentages, weighted by establishments. Excludes those with no unfair dismissal cases.

another kind of outsourcing). It is already known from the CIPD survey, cited earlier,[20] that HR managers have been spending a large and increasing part of their time on legal issues. The present survey confirms a strong connection between managers' recent experience of employee litigation and their sense of increasing time demands for personnel issues. This is shown in Chart 10.5.

The survey asked managers whether their legal fees for advice on all employment matters increased, decreased or remained the same over the preceding three years. About one in six workplaces overall have spent more on legal advice, but the proportion is almost twice as great in the larger workplaces. Much smaller proportions of workplaces have been able to cut their spending on legal advice (Chart 10.6).

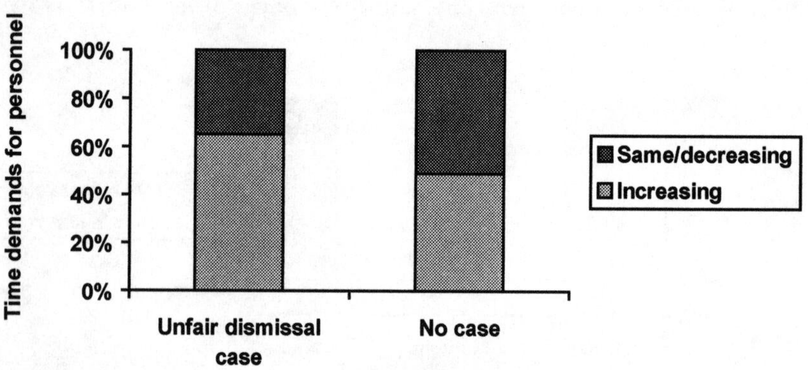

Chart 10.5 Employee litigation, and changes in management time
Note: Column percentages, weighted by establishments. Employee litigation refers to the past 12 months.

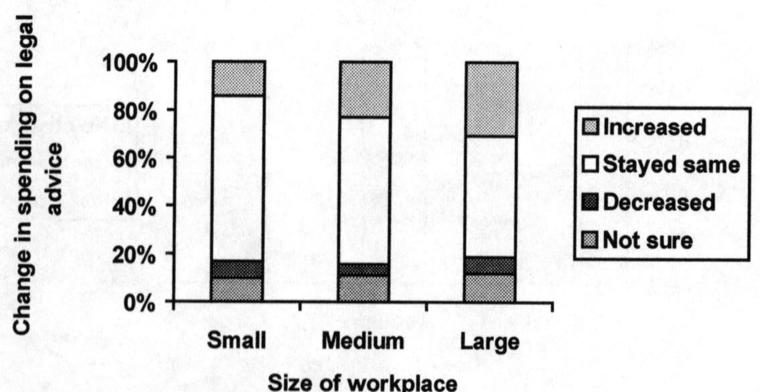

Chart 10.6 Change in spending on legal advice, 2000–2
Note: Column percentages, weighted by establishment.

Although the results in Chart 10.6 cover a wide range of employment issues, it is plain that unfair dismissal cases are a main influence on changes in legal costs. Nearly half the workplaces with unfair dismissal cases in the past 12 months report a rise in legal costs, whereas only one in seven do so if they have had no involvement in cases (Chart 10.7). The picture is of management needing to use both more of its own time and more external legal expertise to cope with employee litigation. The two kinds of resource are certainly not substitutes for one another. In fact, increased management time and more outside legal expertise are much more likely to be reported together than apart.

Employee voice grows louder

Employers face one further external pressure on their workforce policies: the pressure to give more voice to their employees. On one side is the re-emergence of trade unions as a force to be reckoned with. The most obvious sign of this is a recovery of union recognition, after many years of decline. On the other side is the invigoration of consultative committees by the forthcoming implementation of the EC Directive on Information and Consultation (ICON).[21]

This report does not go into the details of union recognition and representation at the workplace, since the Workplace Employee Relations Surveys provide authoritative information on this subject.[22] Instead, we focus on the part which unions are currently playing in relation to change at the workplace, so as to assess the implications of an extended union presence.

If as seems likely unions are making ground once more, should management attempt to resist or slow down the movement, or can they gain by

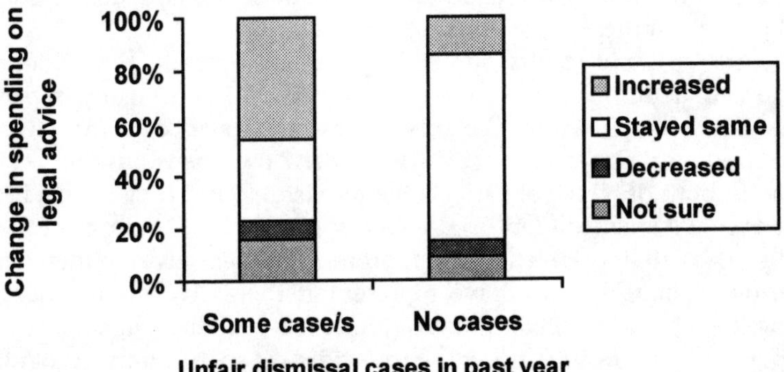

Chart 10.7 Unfair dismissal cases and changes in costs of legal advice
Note: Column percentages, weighted by establishments. Legal costs refer to employment and personnel matters. Change refers to the past three years.

going along with it? The rational argument for resistance is an economic one, backed by innumerable research studies: it is that unions push up wages, salaries and benefits. So the employer that can avoid these pressures has an immediate competitive advantage in terms of labour costs.

But the argument is not all on one side.[23] The higher earnings and benefits available in union workplaces can act as a magnet to recruit and retain more productive workers, a highly-ranked objective for many employers. Unions can also act as a conduit of information from employees to management, helping management to keep their finger on the organisation's pulse. Indeed the British industrial relations tradition is particularly strong in this respect, since union representatives are usually drawn from the employee ranks and know what is happening at the 'sharp edge'.

Through bargaining, moreover, unions create pressure for productivity, which can help to persuade employees to go along with change which they might otherwise resist. Where this argument falls down is if unions gain such power that they can add costs with one hand and obstruct productivity with the other. But this type of excessive dominance appears to have receded. There is said to be a new climate of union moderation, and growing cooperation between management and unions, illustrated by the existence of partnership agreements.[24] In that case, employers who block or evade employees' desire to have union representation are potentially missing out on something positive.

The present survey, with its emphasis on change at workplace level, is in a position to shed light on this often heated issue. Across all the areas of workforce policy discussed in previous chapters, we have made comparisons between the workplaces with recognised trade unions and those that are not unionised. In doing so, we have taken account of industry, size, ownership and many other background characteristics of the workplaces (further details can be found in Annex 2). From this review, we have found 11 important differences between unionised and non-unionised workplaces and these are summarised in Table 10.1.

The first group of results, shown in panel (a), confirms that unions are linked with additional costs for employers, even apart from any impact on wages and salaries, which the survey was not designed to investigate.[25] Unionised workplaces more often have their own pension and sick pay schemes, both of which are expensive provisions, and they have a higher level of involvement in family-friendly policies. These findings fit in well with the way that unions have been promoting themselves to members or potential members. They have represented themselves as defenders of welfare benefits and as champions of improved work-life balance.

However, the results provide no evidence that union recognition obstructs *any* aspect of employers' flexibility practices or human resource policies. On the contrary, unionised workplaces are *more likely* to use temporary workers and *more likely* to engage in outsourcing. Traditionally

Table 10.1 Differences between unionised and non-unionised workplaces

(a) Differences affecting employers' costs

Unionised workplaces more often:
- Provide occupational pensions
- Provide sick-pay above the statutory minimum
- Have family-friendly policies

(b) Differences affecting employers' flexibility

Unionised workplaces more often:
- Employ workers on temporary contracts
- Outsource activities that were formerly done by own employees

(c) Differences affecting employers' human resource development

Unionised workplaces more often:
- Are increasing the training of employees to cover additional jobs
- Have career ladders
- Are increasing the use of work improvement groups
- Have suggestion schemes
- Have briefing groups
- Are making increasing use of IT by employees

See also Table 9.5 for union influences on 'strategies'.

unions have been thought to oppose practices of this type, but that now seems to apply no longer. Furthermore, a union presence is *positively linked* with a series of human resource and staff development policies. Indeed, as shown in Chapter Nine, union recognition is more commonly found *both* in organisations with a downsizing strategy, *and* in organisations with a high-performance HRM strategy, than in those without. So union recognition appears capable of co-existing with patterns of management practice of widely varying types.

It would be going too far to claim that unions in any direct way bring about adoption of the flexibility practices or human resource practices concerned. It may well be, though, that the pressure on labour costs exerted by unions at the workplace has stimulated management towards higher levels of organisational change and innovation. What these results show, at any rate, is that unions do not now generally stand in the way of such policies, even though at a past time they may have been a significant obstacle to change.

The findings of Table 10.1 refer to internal management policies or practices, and do not cover the types of external pressure discussed earlier in this chapter. To complete the picture, we need to consider whether a union presence modifies management's response to the Working Time Regulation or management's experience of employee litigation.

What unions do for the *implementation of the WTR* depends critically on the size of the workplace. Changes in work arrangements to comply with the WTR's 48-hour rule have taken place more often in large workplaces with recognised unions, but there is no clear pattern across small and medium workplaces (Chart 10.8). The larger workplaces with recognised unions are also clearly *less likely* than the large non-unionised workplaces to ask employees to opt-out of the 48-hour limit (Chart 10.9), whereas in small workplaces, if anything the influence of unions has gone in the opposite direction, with medium-sized workplaces intermediate.[26] Overall, in the larger workplaces, the presence of recognised unions is helping to implement the WTR in the spirit of improving work-life balance. This is consistent with the national stance of the TUC and of many unions. However in small workplaces, union representatives may be less influenced by national policy and may see their role as to prevent earnings losses which could come about from a reduction in overtime.

Turning to *employee litigation*, there is once again a crucial difference in the role of unionisation that depends on the size of the workplace. Here, however, it is in *small* workplaces that the presence of a recognised union

Chart 10.8 Union recognition and change in work practices for the WTR 48-hour limit

Note: Cell percentages (each bar is a separate percentage), weighted by establishments.

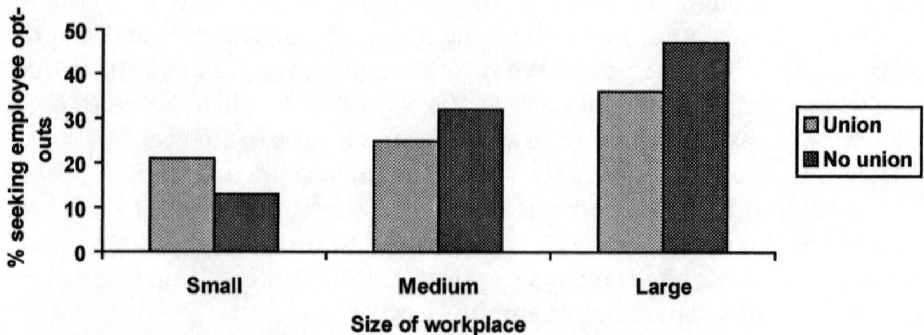

Chart 10.9 Union recognition and opt-outs from the WTR 48-hour limit

Note: Cell percentages (each bar is a separate percentage), weighted by establishments.

has an impact (a sizeable one), whereas in medium and larger workplaces employee litigation is about as likely in the non-unionised as in the unionised (Chart 10.10). In small workplaces the risk of employee litigation that management faces is extremely low in the absence of a union. In these workplaces, employees may be particularly dependent on a union for the information and support they need to start a complaint. Case study research has also suggested that small firms tend to fare badly in unfair dismissal proceedings because of their lack of formal procedures and documentation,[27] and this may make them particularly exposed to unions' expertise in this field.

Unions, then, are involved in the external pressures on management in a variety of ways, alongside their overall supportive role in the change agenda. Does this mean that unions contribute to the growing time requirements for managing people? In fact, the survey revealed no link between union recognition and managers' increasing time requirements: this applied to workplaces of all sizes. This may seem surprising, since unions are linked in so many ways to management having to do more. However, an answer that has been given in the past is that unions provide resources that management can use, as well as demanding resources from management.[28] For example, unions can help with communications in an efficient, organised way. Whatever the explanation, it seems that the mere presence of unions does not in itself exacerbate the time-pressures on management. But of course unions may be involved in other developments which do put pressure on management time, such as employee litigation.

Channels of consultation

Works Councils and Staff Committees – in general terms, consultative committees – are representative bodies which speak for employees but lack bargaining 'clout'. Currently these non-union forms of representation

Chart 10.10 Employee litigation and union recognition in the workplace
Note: Cell percentages (each bar is a separate percentage), weighted by establishments.

slightly outnumber union recognition, since they cover one in four workplaces in the survey whereas unions cover one in five. Between 1990 and 1998, when union recognition declined steeply, consultative committees actually increased a little in the private sector although they declined in the public sector.[29]

Like union recognition, consultative committees are much more common in large workplaces. Even so, more small workplaces have consultative committees than have recognised unions: one in five as against one in seven. There are also more consultative committees on their own (16 per cent of workplaces) than alongside unions (10 per cent of workplaces). Furthermore, one in five workplaces without unions has a consultative committee. None the less, where a union is recognised, the chances are higher that a consultative committee is also in being.

Putting these basic points together, one can see two different situations for consultative committees, and two different purposes. Where they coexist with unions, they complement them both in providing a channel for the non-unionised employees and in covering issues which are outside the remit of bargaining. Where they exist on their own, they provide an alternative to unions, until now one which gives employees less power.[30] With the implementation of the EC Directive on Information and Consultation (ICON) in 2005, however, their status and influence is potentially much increased.

The survey reveals that one in seven workplaces is planning extension or introduction of consultative committees over the next year. This planned growth, if it comes to pass, will outstrip any recent increases in union recognition. Five per cent of all workplaces intend to introduce a consultative committee for the first time – pointing to the formation of about 35,000 new consultative committees in workplaces with five or more employees. A further nine per cent of workplaces already have some consultative arrangements but plan to extend them. This means that nearly one in three of the workplaces with consultative committees is extending their use.

A key question is how far the consultative developments planned by managements tend to be located alongside union recognition arrangements. In fact, just one in four of the planned developments of consultative committees is at unionised workplaces. Even though in the past union recognition has been positively linked with consultative committees, the planned growth of consultation is essentially independent of whether or not unions are present at the workplace.

Obviously, then, the planned development of consultative committees is very different from the existing pattern, which has been much influenced by the presence of recognised unions. If these plans are sustained and continued, there will be a major extension of non-union voice into areas where no union representation exists now. Notably, too, much of the extension of consultative committees will take place in smaller workplaces. As Chart 10.11 shows, even in the smallest (5–24 employees), one in eight is planning some development. For workplaces with 50 or more employees, the proportion is one in four. Consultation with employees seems set to become a larger feature of managers' responsibilities in the near future, irrespective of the forthcoming ICON legislation.

Finally, there is the usual question about the implications of consultative committees for pressures on management time. For large workplaces, there is no relationship between the presence of consultative committees and management's reports of time-pressures. But such a link does emerge for workplaces with less than 100 employees (Chart 10.12). Surprisingly, consultation appears to be more burdensome for management than working with a union, for all but the largest workplaces.

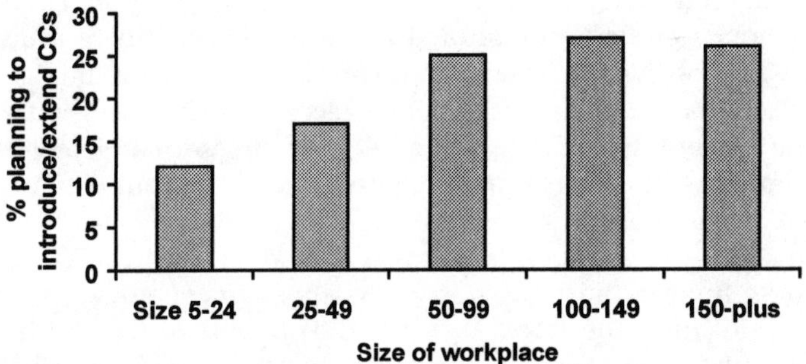

Chart 10.11 Planned extensions or introductions of consultative committees
Note: Column percentages (those with no plans not shown), weighted by establishments. Planning refers to the following 12 months.

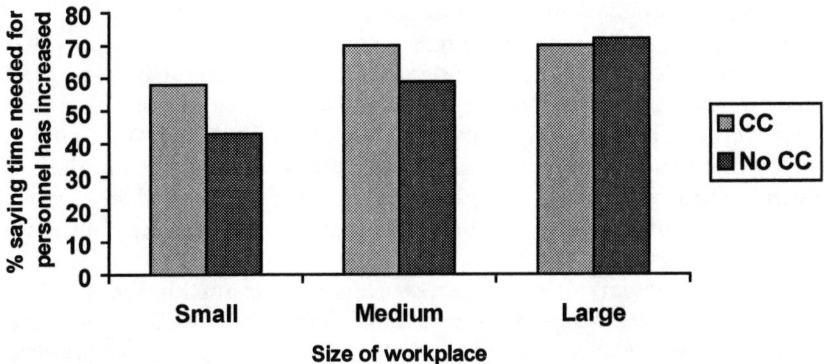

Chart 10.12 Consultative committees and changes in management time
Note: Cell percentages (each bar is a separate percentage), weighted by establishments.

Conclusions

This chapter has examined the fourth and final type of pressure for change that was outlined in Chapter One: regulation. Regulation has been looked at largely as a source of pressures on management, and four aspects of pressure have been covered: government regulation of the workplace, employee litigation against unfair dismissal, trade unions, and the impending requirement to consult with employees. The extent of change in all these areas helps to explain why so many managers report that managing people takes up an increasing proportion of their time.

The Working Time Regulations illustrate government regulation in an area of live concern for employees. On first sight, many more managements are evading or ignoring the Regulations than are changing their policies because of them. But this may be a superficial, or hasty, judgement. Even if the Regulations have not produced rapid change in most employers' working time practices, they have got managers' attention. Employees' working hours are being monitored as never before. Where a union is recognised, a positive response becomes more likely, at least in large workplaces. The WTR can also work with managers' own change agenda, being used as a catalyst for change. Whether changing working practices or seeking opt-outs, managers responding to the 48-hour limit tend to report increased pressures on their time.

Another point to think on is that it is early days for the WTR, and the longer-term implications may not yet be apparent. The development of employee litigation illustrates this point. Tribunals to deal with unfair dismissal claims and other grievances originated in the early 1970s, but the impacts on employers and managers are still growing. Experience of unfair dismissal proceedings is widespread, even penetrating to very small workplaces if unions are present there. Where there have been recent cases, managers report pressure on their time and more money being spent on legal advice. Employment law has become a management preoccupation.

Trade unions are the third kind of external pressure on management that this chapter has assessed. After a long period of decline, there is evidence of union resurgence from various sources. As already noted in these conclusions, unions appear to sharpen the teeth of both the WTR and of employment law, with obvious implications for management. But there is much in the results of the survey to support claims of a more cooperative type of relationship between unions and management. Where unions are present, labour flexibility is higher in important respects and lower in none. Unionised workplaces are also developing their human resources in a greater variety of positive ways, by comparison with the non-unionised. And unionised workplaces are more likely to have a recognisable workforce strategy of some kind. Of course, unions put pressure on labour costs via pay and conditions, but their cooperation can also enhance progress towards management's own change objectives. Moreover, the survey found no indication that unions in themselves increased the time-pressures on management.

Along with the apparent revival of unions, there is a marked surge in establishing or extending consultative committees. In the past these non-union bodies have tended to exist alongside recognised unions, but the majority of the new growth is taking place in previously non-union territory, and independent of union recognition. There may be several reasons for this development.[31] One possibility is that management is adapting and preparing for the regulation of this field that is coming from the ICON Directive. But while this will be true in some cases, the majority of the workplaces engaging in these developments will not be affected by the new regulations until 2007 or 2008, if ever.[32] Another possibility is that, when facing the possible spread of union recognition, some managements see in consultative arrangements a way of preventing, delaying or weakening recognition in their own workplaces.

However, another less cynical interpretation is that consultation is becoming recognised as an important part of HRM and of the change process. Indeed, in the previous chapter the presence of a consultative committee formed part of the definition of a high-performance or high-commitment strategy. This interpretation is the most consistent with the apparent link between consultation and pressures on management time. The pressures on management do not just come from external sources, but through management's own choices for change. Management is developing a wider repertoire of communication and involvement practices to bring about change, and they can gain by incorporating consultative committees into this process.

We can now sum up our answers to the main questions about regulation that were posed in Chapter One. Managements' responses to regulation vary widely. Many employers, for example, appear untouched by the WTR, one of the major regulatory changes of recent years. Employee litigation on the other hand emerges as an area where employers and management are on the defensive, and putting in increased resources to contain the problem. In some other respects, however, the response to regulation has a distinctly positive side. Some employers have been using the WTR to promote their own change agenda, and the current upsurge in the formation of consultative committees is running well ahead of government's regulatory timetable. Most remarkably, a union presence at the workplace appears to have helped rather than hindered the key people policies and strategies of management. Regulation therefore emerges as less of a negative force than generally supposed. Like competition or changing technology, it places pressures upon management, but these can lead to innovative developments, of a constructive and sometimes surprising kind.

11
Interpreting the Trends

In this concluding chapter, the detailed findings presented in the previous chapters are drawn together and interpreted. We will look at change both from the viewpoint of organisations, and from the viewpoint of employees – not forgetting that managers are themselves employees. The broad pressures for change that were sketched in Chapter One will provide the main framework for the interpretation. But the somewhat simple picture of the introductory chapter will need to be adjusted and modified to fit the more complex reality of current workplace developments identified along the way.

At the end of our explanations, will we also be able to forecast the future developments which lead on from here? There are three main complications that stand in the way. One is that the course of development at a particular time depends in part on the changes they have produced in the past. To use the economic jargon, development is *path-dependent.* We only have to be wrong about what happens at one branch-point for all the subsequent predictions depending on that branch-point to be wrong, as well.

A second complication is that the trends do not operate in a uniform way. Circumstances vary between organisations or between industries (and, of course, between countries), for a host of reasons. One reason for the seeming absurdity of so many of the interpretations about trends in management, is their tendency to over-simplify and over-generalise. One size does *not* fit all. Yet many of these interpretations make sense if limited to particular types of organisation in specific circumstances.

Thirdly, and probably most importantly, organisations consist of people and people have choice and imagination. The background pressures for change place some limits on what people are likely to do, but the scope remaining is wide. Indeed, as people get a clearer idea of what the trends are, they may make different choices which change the direction of future trends. As problems become clearer, hopefully they will act to counter the problems.

Despite these cautionary words, the evidence of the survey, with its emphasis on current directions of change, does we believe make clearer the choices and opportunities that face both management and employees, and indicates, if not *the* future, then at least some of the possible futures ahead.

A summary of trends

First let us briefly recap on the main findings of the previous chapters. Of course, in summarising, it is necessary to bypass many of the details which those chapters provide. It is also necessary to express the trends, sometimes, in a simplified way which rides roughshod over some of the uncertainties indicated earlier on. Interpretation is kept to a minimum within this summary so as to give an unobstructed view of the trends.

- The use of flexible labour – such as agency, temporary, casual or freelance – has already spread to every type of employer.
- But the further use of flexible labour is approaching a limit and is slowing down.
- The outsourcing of work, which employees could do internally, is also very extensive and is becoming prominent in many managerial or professional activities, such as recruitment, training and ICT.
- Outsourcing is often linked to internal workforce reductions. The combination of the two into a downsizing strategy covers about one in seven workplaces and is particularly concentrated in manufacturing.
- Increases in 'intelligent' flexibility, through more versatile and interchangeable employees, are extremely widespread.
- This is accompanied by increasingly wide use of team-based organisation and an increased use of team performance rewards.
- Career opportunities are enjoying a revival. The majority of workplaces are attempting to offer internal career paths to employees, and not just at management level. This is being supported by the creation of extra grades in the job structure, and by expansion of management jobs, in a substantial minority of workplaces.
- Delayering – the cutting-out of management grades and reduction of management numbers – is also continuing but in a smaller minority of workplaces.
- The use of HRM practices such as appraisal systems, performance based pay, and involvement through communications, is diffusing widely and tends to accompany internal flexibility, team organisation, and internal career structures.
- An extensive use of HRM practices, amounting to a high performance 'strategy', can be identified in about one in three workplaces.

- Management is seeking to use work-space more efficiently and flexibly, with widespread reorganisation of facilities, increased use of open-plan layouts, and a high rate of relocation.
- Increasingly, management is also developing hot-desking, teleworking, and flexible working between home and office. The finance and business services industry is playing a leading role in these developments.
- ICT continues to spread rapidly in the workplace. Most workplaces are making substantial use of ICT, and in one in three workplaces, all or nearly all employees use it to some extent in their jobs.
- Extensive and pervasive use of ICT, amounting to a 'high-tech strategy', can so far be attributed to about one in five workplaces. Where this occurs, it also tends to link up with a high performance HRM strategy.
- Where ICT usage is at a high level, or is progressing rapidly, many of the other changes described here are intensified or accelerated.
- ICT now provides direct monitoring of work in about one-half of workplaces. As yet ICT monitoring is mainly used by senior and line management, and is used to give feedback to employees in only a minority of cases.
- With recruitment and retention becoming a high priority, many workplaces are recruiting women into jobs formerly held only by men and *vice versa*.
- Part-time jobs continue to be the main opportunity in Britain for reconciling work and family.
- Flexi-time working is *not* spreading rapidly from its existing small base, and few workplaces are planning to extend or introduce family-friendly practices. However, the development of working from home (see earlier) provides some additional possibilities for work-life balance.
- Most workplaces have recently been recruiting from groups that often face employment barriers. Those recruiting through the Internet, a practice which has spread rapidly, are more likely to recruit from these groups.
- A 'high benefits strategy' to strengthen recruitment and retention, incorporating both significant fringe benefits and family-friendly practices, can be identified in about one in five workplaces.
- In the majority of workplaces, managers face increasing demands on their time to manage people. In part this is linked with external pressures from regulation. These include changes in response to the Working Time Regulations, effects of employee litigation, and development of new or extended consultative arrangements.
- Trade unions continue to make a difference. For example, workplaces with a union presence are more likely to have family-friendly practices. Unionised workplaces also make *more* use of flexible labour, outsourcing, and a wide range of HRM practices.

Competition's iron hand

We can now turn to the main explanations for change that are presented in Chapter One, and see how well they account for the findings just summarised. The first source of change described in Chapter One is the emergence of a more competitive world in which organisations must learn to survive. The days of large, safe companies and nationalised industries, cushioned against competitive pressures, have all but receded beyond memory. Management is much more exposed than in the past to the economic and financial consequences of every decision.

Yet in the latter 1990s, general business conditions improved, and from 2001 there has also been an increase in the funding of many public services. As a result, the majority of organisations have been able to invest more in people, taking a more long-term view. In these conditions, the development of external flexible labour is easing off, and downsizing applies to only a fairly small minority. Moreover, good business conditions lead to increasingly tight job markets, and this helps to widen the recruitment base, producing more desegregation and more diversity in the workforce.

Yet at the same time, the underlying force of the competitive pressures and uncertainties remains clear. Nothing shows this so well as the near-universal emphasis on *flexibility*. Although the use of external flexible labour is flattening off, it is not in absolute decline and it is ensconced in every part of industry, commerce and the public services. This is accompanied by a growth of outsourcing, and by the development of flexibility within the regular workforce in a variety of ways.

The cutting edge of competition is also still highly visible in the manufacturing sector, which is internationally exposed and suffers more from a high exchange rate. In manufacturing, workforce contraction, outsourcing, and the combination of the two into a downsizing strategy, remain widespread. Investment in a variety of HRM and family-friendly practices is also relatively low. Career opportunities are restricted and recruitment is subdued. In many manufacturing workplaces, the insecure and bleak environment of the early 1990s appears to linger on.

- The example of manufacturing, and the retention of cost-cutting flexibilities in most workplaces, suggests that a general reversion toward survival-first tactics would take place if the economy once more entered a prolonged down-turn.

Another indication of the continuing competitive pressures on management, even in relatively good times, is the vigorous way in which cost-saving innovations are being pursued *alongside* a more long-term view of human resources. Most obviously, this applies to the widespread efforts to cut overhead costs by using work-space more effectively, and to the extension of outsourcing into a wider range of technical, professional and managerial services.

- There is every reason to expect that both innovative reductions in work-space and tendencies to outsource professional activities will go further, although there will also be practical limits.

Sensitivity to costs also helps to explain what is otherwise a puzzling feature of the findings, namely the low priority being attached by management to work-life balance, despite widespread employee depression on this topic. Any real reduction in hours represents a direct cost to an employer unless there is a corresponding reduction in wages or increase in productivity. Introducing and operating a flexible hours system can be an expensive process. So too are some family-friendly provisions, such as employer-run day-centres, or financial support for childcare.

- The business case for family-friendly policies has so far relied chiefly on non-quantified or intangible savings or benefits, and these are unlikely to persuade management in an era when cost competition remains at the forefront of attention.

Another strong indication of the continuing primacy of competitive pressure concerns career development. The next section of these conclusions will argue that the resurgence of careers reflects the deep-seated requirements of, especially, large service organisations. Yet it is also crystal-clear that growth or contraction of the workplace has a massive impact on organisations' career policies. Whatever the long-term logic of employee development, it remains conditioned by short-term economic circumstances. Competition rules with an iron hand, even when it wears a velvet glove.

Varieties of knowledge work

The second type of background pressure for change suggested in Chapter One was the growth of what is often called 'knowledge work'. The growth of knowledge work is, supposedly, largely bound up with the growth of professional occupations and the advance of ICT, which provides new ways in which organisations can provide services, change cost structures, and compete. Many findings that have been presented indicate that ICT is indeed a vital factor. But the findings also suggest that the idea of knowledge work needs to be modified. Organisations are developing wider strategies to meet their needs for know-how, which extend beyond the technical and professional domains and beyond the new technology.

The picture of the knowledge worker presented in a great deal of recent management writing is of a highly mobile professional who carts technical knowledge from one organisation to the next. For this to be possible, the knowledge must itself be equally valid, and valuable, across organisational boundaries.[1] Portable knowledge breaks down the walls of the organisation, or renders them futile: no longer can talent be guarded within, since the job market prevails inside as well as outside. If this is generally the situation, then in-house training and career development become wasteful activities.

Yet, our survey finds that the development of adaptable employees and the revival of careers are now at the centre of what a large proportion of employers are trying to do. After declaring only a decade earlier that long-term career promises were cancelled, organisations are now pursuing a whole range of policies to reinstate internal careers and make them attractive to managers and employees.

This type of development, or re-development, makes most sense when employees who stay for long periods become specially valuable to their employers – more valuable than those they can hire on the job market. That happens if the employees learn useful things within the organisation which they would not learn in other organisations. The resurgence of internal development and career policies supports the idea of knowledge workers being of increasing importance to many organisations, but it also points to a particular kind of knowledge worker. The knowledge in question must be specific to the business or organisation.

- The resurgence of careers, and the primacy of internal adaptability over flexible labour brought-in from outside, both point to the continuing and growing need for *in-house* knowledge.[2]

The development of ICT helps to explain *in part* what is taking place, but does not provide anything near the full explanation. Certainly ICT in many cases involves special in-house systems which create a need for corresponding in-house knowledge, not only on the part of the technical staff but on the part of the much more numerous using staff. Moreover ICT, when used to innovate in service delivery and administrative organisation, leads to a need for adaptability, and for enhanced capacities in managing change. It is easy to see why career development is emphasised where the pace of ICT is *rapid* and new organisational learning has to be retained. But when all this is said, there is still a gap between what ICT can explain and the full picture. In particular, there has been a large growth of career development and associated HRM systems in distribution, hotels and catering, and leisure/personal services, none of which are usually classified as knowledge-based industries of the technical/professional type. Nor is their use of ICT of a particularly intensive kind.

These kinds of services have grown, alongside financial and business services, to be the main providers of employment growth in the economy, and they are also increasingly dominated by large organisations operating chains of local businesses. These large organisations are sophisticated in many branches of management, including purchasing, logistics, marketing, control, finance, and site investment and development.[3] While some of these functions may be staffed with mobile professionals, others will demand experience of a specific kind relating to internal business systems, suppliers, and so on. With their complex branch and support structures, these organisations also need large numbers of competent and reliable managers and supervisors. It is not hard to imagine, therefore, why service industries are facing an increasing need to develop staff internally and to build up in-house knowledge. They do indeed compete on knowledge, namely the know-how in providing their own services and in managing dispersed organisations. Retention and development provide them with an economical route to providing the specific types of know-how they require.

- The need to retain and develop staff to meet in-house requirements for know-how is very likely to persist, especially in the larger service businesses (and the many new entrants that emulate them). Interruptions, resulting from business downturns, are likely to be of a temporary nature.

Where organisations need a particular kind of knowledge or skill which does not have a large in-house dimension, then they will often do better to avoid the costs of career development and the liabilities of deferred rewards and benefits. This helps to explain the advance of outsourcing, and especially the penetration of outsourcing into technical, professional and even managerial areas. ICT specialists themselves have some highly portable kinds of knowledge. Where they combine these with detailed knowledge of internal systems and procedures, employers want to retain them and incorporate them in career development. Where their general technical knowledge is what is needed, without much in-house component, employers prefer to outsource. In addition, the use of ICT itself lowers administrative costs involved in external contracting (e.g., costs of records and of communications), and for this reason makes outsourcing more attractive.

Overall, then, what we see is a wide development of internal career structures *alongside* a growing use of outsourcing for business services. It is perfectly possible for organisations to develop both in tandem, and this may well happen more in the future. At present, though, there are some contrasts between the two paths. The more intensive use of outsourcing, connected with cuts in internal staff numbers, is more concentrated in manufacturing industry and seems in part to reflect competitive pressures rather than solely a desire to focus on core business competences.

Conversely, the buoyant service businesses are mainly concentrating on internal development while outsourcing, at least in its more intensive forms, is less prominent there.

- Service industries could move further down the path to outsourcing if competition grows more severe. It is easy to see outsourcing grow further, and hard to see it contracting.

Assuming more growth of outsourcing for knowledge-based services, does this mean less settled careers for knowledge workers in this category, and more footloose, freelance working lives? This does not follow at all. Many such knowledge workers are already employed by substantial organisations providing the knowledge-based services (e.g., accounting or law firms, or ICT contractors), and there seems no reason to suppose that this will decline.

- As the markets for outsourced services grow, there will be more incentive to develop substantial businesses to meet the demand, and these businesses will in many cases be large enough to offer careers to their employees.

Making change and managing change

The third source of change discussed in Chapter One was the shift in the managerial culture towards an active pursuit of change, and towards creating a resilient and committed workforce by adopting human resource management (HRM) practices and strategies. Much of the change which workplaces undergo now seems to come from inside rather than outside the organisation, or through an active grasping of outside opportunities. Continuous change has become the order of the day. This, if true, is a fundamental shift, since only a generation ago most British workplaces, and their managements, appeared to change only when forced to do so.

The sheer extent of change at the workplace speaks loudly of active managements. Well over one-half of workplaces have introduced or extended HRM practices within the past three years *on a substantial scale.*[4] Each of these practices is of a type which probably involves significant management activity either in bringing about the change or managing it. Moreover, management is *not* for the most part correspondingly cutting back or discontinuing other types of practice at the same time.[5]

A clear example of management initiative and innovation is the development of 'intelligent flexibility', involving multi-skilling, cross-job training, job rotation, and team organisation: this is the most widespread of all HRM changes. Another area of extensive innovation is the organisation of workspace, with one in four workplaces developing hot-desking as well as others extending teleworking or encouraging flexibility of working between office and home. The pressures of overhead costs are a factor here, but the extent and radical nature of the recent changes also suggest active innovation.

The overall picture is one where the great majority of workplaces has adopted a raft of basic HRM practices and is building on these with further initiatives. Personal appraisals and briefing groups are approaching universal adoption (recall that the survey included workplaces down to five employees). A variety of reward and control practices bolt-on to appraisals, while other forms of communication, such as suggestion schemes, intranets, and consultative committees, go well beyond briefing groups. The development of 'intelligent flexibility' has just been highlighted, but outsourcing and the use of external flexible labour are equally widespread. Admittedly, more cohesive bundles of practice, deserving to be called strategies, are far from universal. Even so, nearly three in ten workplaces satisfy a fairly tough definition of high-performance HRM strategy, involving 6–12 practices across 3–4 aims.

On top of this, there is the extensive growth of ICT both in terms of the proportion of employees involved as users and in terms of the range of uses. While ICT is less central to staff development and career issues than we initially supposed, this does not mean to say that it is of minor significance overall. ICT in the first place involves continuing effort in the management of change, with one-half of workplaces extending system coverage. Furthermore, ICT is involved in several of the changes in HRM already referred to, acting as either catalyst or facilitator. Where ICT usage is high, management is more likely to be developing task variety, self-organising teams, and flexible working-from-home arrangements. But it is also more likely to be adopting external flexible labour contracting and/or outsourcing.

What emerges from all this is that ICT is an enabling technology which supports management choices *without* determining what they should choose. It can be used as a low-level de-skilling technology which supports a cost-cutting flexible labour approach. Conversely it is when ICT is applied in a wide range of ways, so as to become a kind of transforming infrastructure for the organisation, that the link with high-performance HRM strategies emerges most clearly. ICT is not in itself the high road to the future: rather it is involved in both a low road and a high road, between which organisations must eventually choose.

One area where ICT is rapidly expanding management choices is in monitoring and control systems. With the great majority of employees now using computer systems in their work, and many others involved in customer communications, ICT-based continuous monitoring is already in place for about one-half of the workforce. ICT monitoring information could connect up with other parts of the HRM agenda, if it is made accessible and entrusted to employees for personal feedback and learning. This has certainly not happened widely as yet and the trend towards *control without participation* is deeply disquieting.

- If ICT-based control continues to be seen as a management prerogative and the monitoring information is not shared with employees, then this is likely to become a divisive and damaging issue. There is also a substantial risk that the low cost of automatically generated control information will lead management to over-emphasise 'control by numbers' of a particularly narrow type.

Overall, the picture from the survey is of active managements not merely managing change but making it happen. It is true that this activity is still often patchy, and much influenced by short-term pressures rather than, or as well as, by long-term aims. Yet it seems that management of the workforce is progressively being influenced by a recognisable if incomplete HRM agenda.

- Where there remain major gaps in management's response to employee needs, as in the case of monitoring and control systems, or in the failure to develop impressive work-life balance policies, the best chance of further advances seems to rest in the HRM agenda becoming more developed and more consistent.

Regulation's deep waters

The fourth and last of the pressures for change, which we pointed to in Chapter One, is the regulation imposed on organisations by government, law and the trade unions. In the Thatcher era, this kind of regulation was rolled back, but recent years have witnessed numerous signs of resurgence. The survey examined four aspects of regulation: the Working Time Regulations 1998, unfair dismissal cases, trade union activities and influences, and consultative committees.

The survey's findings on regulation are in a number of ways surprising, and hard to fathom. The simplest and least surprising finding is that, from a management viewpoint, regulation is indeed burdensome. Managers responding positively to the WTR's 48-hour limit seem to experience added pressures on their own time – a result which has a certain irony about it. The experience of unfair dismissal claims is another significant pressure on management time, and HR budgets for legal services are expanding. Even consultative committees, which might be thought a low-key activity, are associated with rising time-pressures for management. Strangely, of the four regulatory pressures reviewed in the survey, the only one which does *not* appear to add directly to management time-pressures is the presence of recognised trade unions.

Apart from this last point, however, trade unions still seem to have the greatest implications of any regulatory pressure on management. Unionised workplaces tend to offer occupational pensions, sick pay above the basic, and family-friendly practices, to a greater extent than the non-unionised.[6] We also know, from other research, that unionised workplaces tend to have greater equality of pay.[7] Large unionised workplaces are more likely to have responded positively to the WTR and small unionised workplaces are more likely to have been hit by a recent unfair dismissal claim.

- Unions do therefore continue to make a difference to what employees get, and to create cost pressures on employers. With clear signs of recent revival in union recognition, the union influence appears set to increase in the immediate future.

But not all the effects of unions are troublesome from a management viewpoint. Local unions do *not* in general prevent the use of external flexible labour. Temporary employees are *more often* found at unionised than non-unionised workplaces, and much more significantly, there is a *positive* link between a union presence and the use of outsourcing. Moreover, recent talk of partnership between management and unions seems broadly supported by a number of other findings. The use of half-a-dozen HRM practices is more common at unionised than at non-union workplaces. The additional support for management which unions, when in partnership, provide, may explain why on average they do not add to the time-pressures on management. Perhaps, also, unions prod management into being more strategic. At any rate, where unions are recognised, management is much more likely to have some recognisable strategy, whether at the downsizing end or the empowering end.

The findings about unions illustrate how hard it is to fathom the effects of regulation, which can be various and contrary, at different times or even at the same time. Set up as supposedly permanent institutions, regulatory bodies or laws change their purpose or their meaning as employers, individuals or other institutions adapt to their existence, and as background conditions change. Trade unions, like businesses, have had to adapt to a very different world from that of a generation ago, and it is still hard to understand how that has affected and is going to affect their impact on organisations. Still less can we foresee the long-term implications of the 1999 Employment Act and the subsequent rise in new union recognition. Unions themselves will be faced with a difficult balancing act as they seek to champion employees' rights and interests while engaging as partners in the workplace change agenda.

Nowhere is there a harder task for unions than with issues of work-life balance, which are so important to employees yet – as appears from this survey – so low among management priorities. Where managements have preferred to ignore or contain the Working Time Regulations they have found it easy to do so (as the authors of the legislation presumably intended). Yet it is already clear, from case studies, that the WTR are being interpreted very differently in different workplaces, and in some at least they are being used by organisations (often in partnership with unions) as a catalyst for change. The success or failure of these initiatives is likely to influence how other employers and unions eventually respond. Both management and unions stand to gain if work-life balance can be brought inside a partnership for innovation. Alternatively, it could develop into an area of conflict that undermines the existing basis of cooperation.

- What can be said is that the WTR have entered management awareness and that some process of change is taking place. How this turns out will depend on the choices of all the main actors, including employees and unions, but so far the most important role has been that of management itself.

Much the same can also be said of the next main regulatory change around the corner, on employee information and consultation. The British government is believed to be lukewarm on this development, and introduction has been spread out over the years 2005–8. Yet already in 2002 there has been a notable surge in the forming of consultative committees and the extension of existing consultative activities. It is far-fetched to suppose that this activity, much of it in small workplaces, is inspired by regulation which is years away. Some of it is probably a defensive reflex generated by anxiety around growing levels of union recognition. But much of it can reasonably be seen as an aspect of the HRM agenda which so many organisations are actively adopting or pursuing. In other words, consultation is currently growing because management sees it as consistent with its broader aims of developing employee relations and performance.

- The management agenda, rather than impending EC and government regulation, is most likely to guarantee the continuing development of employee consultation in the coming years.

Conclusion

The Change in Employer Practices Survey of 2002 has provided a unique picture of change at the British workplace. To interpret that picture, we have placed it against the background of four main long-term background trends:

- intensifying competition
- knowledge as an increasingly vital organisational resource

- the rise of an active agenda for continuous change, shaped by concepts from the HRM movement
- the growth of external regulation.

The picture from the survey is one of tumultuous change. The great majority of workplaces have engaged in new forms of recruitment, have added to flexibility, have made a multiplicity of advances in their human resource development or people practices, and have extended their use of ICT through much of their workforce, including new and rapidly growing applications to communication and control. The restructuring of work-space has become yet another major area of management initiatives.

The four long-term background trends, bulleted above, help to structure and interpret this plethora of findings:

1. *Competitive and financial pressures* remain in the forefront, even in the favourable economic conditions of the early 2000s where growth or stability prevails for most. This is signalled by the way that flexibility remains a part of every organisation's concerns, and by the pursuit of new sources of cost reduction – extended outsourcing, reduction of work-space, ICT-based controls. Where conditions are less favourable, as in manufacturing, the downsizing strategy remains a salient feature. Some of the favourable developments of recent years could soon be thrown into reverse by recession. Nothing but competitive strength provides much reassurance against these uncertainties.
2. *Knowledge work and knowledge workers* – and organisations' appreciation of their importance – are playing a crucial part in current trends. This is evident in the strong re-emergence of career opportunities within the organisation, and in the widespread use of HRM practices which develop and support intelligent flexibility. These developments are not simply accounted for by the growth of professional occupations or of ICT. Major new players are the consumer service industries. Overall, it is in-house knowledge, or know-how specific to the organisation, that is most in demand. As employers are torn between short-term competitive and cost pressures, and the longer-term need to develop the in-house knowledge base, careers may well take on a stop-go form.
3. *A cultural revolution in management*, favouring internally-driven change and a more intensive development of human resources, is under way but far from complete. The extent of change is obvious, and so is the emergence of a clear HRM agenda, which a sizeable minority of organisations has taken to a strategic level. Yet there are also important shortcomings and weaknesses. These include the low priority being given to work-life balance policies, and the failure to apply new control systems in a way that involves employees. Another troubling feature is the linking of ICT with increased use of external, flexible labour. In

these respects, management appears to be dominated by short-term cost pressures and lacking the foresight or imagination to move to the next level.

4. *External regulation* is a real pressure experienced by management in the majority of organisations. This is shown most simply by the increasing demands on their time. Yet it is wrong to assume that regulation's effects are largely negative from a management viewpoint. Some organisations are using the Working Time Regulations as a catalyst for change, and many are installing or extending employee consultation of their own choice. Regulation in these cases acts as a short-term catalyst for change that conveniently fits the management agenda. In addition, the trade union presence at the workplace appears more to help than hinder management's policies, be they in the area of flexibility or of HRM development.

This book opened by pointing to two basic questions about change in the workplace. One concerns employees: what do all the changes add up to in terms of an improving or a deteriorating prospect for the near future? The other concerns the competitiveness of British organisations, and hence the longer-term welfare of its citizens: is current change making the nation stronger or weaker?

Employees and managers have come through troubling years of insecurity in the early 90s. Relative to that experience, the current trends are much improved. Flexibility is turning intelligent, careers are back, knowledge and know-how are valued, recruitment barriers are lowered. But there are newer issues for employees that have not yet been effectively addressed. Chief among these are the problems of long hours and work-life balance. And ICT has not emerged as an unmixed blessing – the implications depend too much on whether you are in a high-end or a low-end application, whether it enhances your capabilities or controls your eye-blinks.

On the competition front, there is a similar mix. The pace of change is brisk and there is a discernible movement towards those high-end HRM practices and strategies, which are widely regarded as crucial for a nation's competitive capacities. ICT adoption is also rapid and extensive. We judge that perhaps three in ten workplaces are strategic users of HRM and one in five of ICT. The proportions are appreciably higher in the large workplaces. At this strategic level, HRM and ICT tend to come together. This, surely, is an important signpost to that sought-after 'high road' to the future. But weaknesses remain, as we have just now stressed. The HRM agenda remains patchy in its implementation and management remains slow to innovate in response to unfamiliar issues.

Yet the overall picture from the research gives more grounds for encouragement about the eventual solution of these problems than we would have felt a decade ago. Of course, by the time they are solved there will be other problems and other anxieties. No process of change can be either perfect or complete. The important point is that Britain's managers and employees are facing up to the pressures. Despite all the uncertainties and shortcomings, British workplaces *are* managing to change.

Appendix 1
The Change in Employer Practices Survey 2002 (CEPS-02)

This appendix describes the sample, survey procedures and response to the employer survey. It is based on a technical report on the survey provided, in September 2002, by IFF Research Ltd., the survey organisation which was responsible for carrying out the survey on behalf of the research team.

Scope

The survey consisted of a total of 2000 telephone interviews with employers in Great Britain.

The survey was establishment based, whereby information was collected on an individual site basis irrespective of whether or not the site formed part of a larger organisation. (In the main body of the report, the term 'workplace' is normally used in place of 'establishment'.)

Only those establishments employing five or more staff were included within the scope of the survey.

Sampling

The sample of establishments was drawn from BT's Business Database (now known as Yell Data), a regularly up-dated comprehensive list of establishments in Britain with a business telephone line.

Sample was drawn, and target number of interviews set, on an interlocking size by sector basis. This sampling process used four size bands (5–24 employees, 25–99, 100–499, 500 plus) and five sectors (manufacturing and construction (SICs 01–45); wholesale and retail (SICs 50–55); transport, storage and distribution (SICs 60–64); finance and business services (SICs 65–74); public sector (SICs 75–99)).

The target number of interviews in each cell was set so as to be approximately representative of the share of employment in that cell. (Truly proportional sampling is not generally possible with employer sampling, because of the extreme size of the largest establishments or organisations.) This means that larger establishments are over-sampled relative to their frequency of occurrence while smaller establishments are under-sampled.

For the analysis stage, weights were computed to gross up the sample to the universe of establishments with five or more employees, on a size by sector basis. The figures for grossing were derived from the Interdepartmental Business Register (IDBR). This was done on an employer and then an employee basis. Overall results have been grossed up to a total of 770,425 establishments in Great Britain with five or more employees, which employ 22,036,398 employees.

Piloting and briefing

Prior to the main stage, a small-scale pilot exercise, consisting of 23 interviews, was undertaken. This led to a number of changes in the questionnaire.

The interviewers were briefed concerning the purpose and nature of the survey, and the interpretation of the questions, by IFF's project director, Mark Winterbotham, and by the research team, both prior to piloting and prior to the main stage of interviewing.

Interviewing

The main stage of interviewing was carried out between 23rd July–2nd September 2002. Data collection was carried out using Computer Assisted Telephone Interviewing (CATI) from IFF's call centre in London. The interviewers were members of IFF's telephone interviewing staff who specialise in conducting surveys of management respondents.

The principal respondent was the senior person responsible for human resource or personnel issues. Generally, in establishments with 100 or more employees this was the human resource/personnel director or manager. In establishments with fewer than 100 employees it was typically the owner, proprietor or the site or office manager.

The approximate average length of the interview was 30 minutes.

Response

The following table provides details of the response:

Sample drawn	**5417**
Fax number	331
Number unobtainable	513
Valid sample issued	**4573**
Less than 5 employees	32
Out of quota (in a size and or sector category already filled)	219
Eligible sample issued	**4322**
Withdrawn (no interview after 7+ calls)	136
Still live (called but no definite outcome)	555
Refusals	1631
Complete interviews	2000

Calculation of the effective response rate depends on the assumptions regarding incomplete sample processing that arises because of termination of the fieldwork upon attainment of the target number of interviews.

On the extreme assumption that none of the 'withdrawn' or 'still live' categories would yield interviews, the response rate is the number of complete interviews divided by the eligible sample size, namely 46 per cent.

An assumption more usually made is that 'withdrawn' or 'still live' categories would yield the same proportion of interviews as in cases brought to a conclusion (i.e., completed or refused). In that case, a reasonable estimate of the effective response rate is the proportion of complete interviews to those brought to a conclusion, namely 55 per cent.

Appendix 2
Methods of Analysis

In the main text, results are usually shown in a simplified form for presentational reasons. This appendix explains the analysis methods and conventions which underlie the charts and tables in the text.

Weighting

As explained in Appendix 1, the survey was derived from a sample of employers defined by the business telephone database now known as Yell Data. This identifies units that are often referred to as establishments. The obtained sample was then weighted by national figures to make it more representative. These figures were derived from the government database, known as IDBR, which also identifies establishments but does so in a different way. Because of the different ways in which establishments are identified, and because of differences in the coverage and maintenance of the databases (e.g., IDBR is less frequently updated), there is a degree of error in the weighting process. IFF Research Ltd., which is a continual user of these databases, carried out the computation of the weights. Any error involved in the weighting process is likely to be small by comparison with the errors of using unweighted data.

Two kinds of weighting are used: throughout Chapters 1–9, employment weighting, and in Chapter 10 only, establishment weighting. When employment weighting is used, the weighted results reflect the distribution of national employment across the cells of the industry-group by size-band matrix used for sampling. The full interpretation of a percentage derived in this way is that of the employment coverage in the sub-population of establishments concerned, as a proportion of the employment coverage of the population from which the total sample is drawn. When establishment weighting is used, the weighted results reflect the distribution of numbers of establishments across cells of the sampling matrix, and the interpretation of any percentage is that of the number of establishments in the sub-population concerned, as a proportion of all establishments in the population from which the total sample is drawn.

All descriptive results in the text, as well as in tables and charts, are weighted as above.

Chart and table conventions

The figures shown in the tables or charts have often been simplified for presentational purposes. The following notes explain what has been done in moving from an underlying complete table to the simplified table/chart that is presented.

Nearly all charts and tables are in the form of percentage distributions. At the foot of each chart or table there is a note, indicating the type of weighting that has been applied, as explained above. The chart or table note also indicates what type of percentage is being used: 'column', 'total', or 'cell'.

Column percentages refer to tables where each column adds to 100 per cent. In the case of charts, the convention is adopted that the X-axis or horizontal axis represents the column or break variable in the original table, while the Y-axis or vertical axis represents the response variable. Usually values from the 'total' column are omitted from the chart. Occasionally, one of the values of the break variable is also omitted; in this case, the omission is noted at the foot of the chart or table.

Total percentages refer to cases where the cells of the underlying table are all in one dimension and add to 100 per cent. In this case, the form of chart used is *always a pie-chart*, so this is easily identifiable and interpretable.

In cell percentages, each percentage presented (e.g., a cell in a table, or a bar in a chart) represents a cell taken from a *separate* column-percentaged table. This type of table is widely used in the text, since it provides a compact means of presenting a large amount of information. Implicitly, responses which are not of interest in the chart are omitted, e.g. the chart typically describes the presence of several workplace practices while ignoring their absence (which can easily be inferred).

Explanatory analysis

Many of the results presented in chart or table form in the text concern the relationship of a workplace practice (e.g., whether any temporary workers are employed at a workplace) with a characteristic of the workplace which is assumed to explain, in part, the presence/absence or increase/decrease of workplace practices.

By characteristics, is meant such relatively persistent attributes as industry, size, type of ownership (PLC, other private, public, voluntary), gender composition, and so on. These are particularly valuable because generally (although not in every case) the workplace has acquired these characteristics independently of the changing workplace practices that are to be explained. If there is a statistical association between such a variable and a workplace practice, then it is implausible (in most cases) that the workplace practice has brought about the workplace attribute. It is however possible (though not certain) that the workplace attribute has influenced the adoption of the workplace practice.

The above can be illustrated by a simple example. The use of electronic point-of-sale technology (EPOS) tends to be particularly high in workplaces in the retail industry. This statistical relationship can be explained in terms of the retail industry having certain operational features which make EPOS cost-effective. An explanation which runs in the opposite direction is, in this case, nonsensical.

We usually want to examine the association between each workplace practice and, not just one attribute of workplaces, but several of these practices. The simple association between a workplace practice and any one attribute could be misleading, however, because the attributes themselves tend to be associated with one another. For example, public-sector workplaces are more concentrated in some industries than in others. These associations between the attributes can be removed statistically, so that the remaining relationship between any attribute and a workplace practice is independent of the other attributes. This is usually done by means of regression analysis. The main practical difficulties with this method are presentational. The results consume a great deal of space and are difficult to follow for those who do not have statistical training.

To resolve this difficulty, we have in most cases used regression analysis (linear or non-linear) as a preliminary stage to assess the significance of the relationship between each attribute and a given workplace practice, after controlling for all the other available attributes. Only those relationships which are statistically significant, at the five per cent significance level (that is, an association of the observed size would occur by chance only one in 20 times, or less frequently), in the regression analysis are then considered for inclusion in the published charts or tables. The charts or tables present the statistically unadjusted figures, not the regression results, but they are underwritten by the regression analyses. The attributes included in the regression analyses are shown in the Table at the end of this appendix.

In many cases, we wish to examine the associations between workplace practices: for example, does the use of temporary workers tend to be accompanied by the practice of outsourcing services? If there is a statistically significant association, then it too could reflect a shared association of each practice with some workplace attribute or attributes. However, in general we do not regard the association between two workplace practices as any the less real because they are both concentrated in workplaces with certain kinds of attribute. Accordingly, with one exception to be considered in the next paragraph, we make no attempt to control for workplace attributes when examining these associations between workplace practices. However, we usually report such simple associations only if they are statistically significant at the one per cent level (that is, an association of the observed size would occur by chance only 1 in 100 times, or less frequently).

In some cases, workplace practices are of a kind which is likely to be much affected by size of workplace, in a way which is artefactual rather than having a real interpretation. For example, questions about the occurrence of recruitment of a certain type are, other things being equal, more likely to be answered positively in large workplaces, because large workplaces recruit on more occasions than small ones. Associations involving practices of this type are therefore best conducted controlling for size of workplace. We have usually done so by preparing cross-tabulations separately for workplaces with 5–24 employees, 25–99 employees, and 100 or more employees.

Survey design

The survey has a complex design involving stratification and unequal selection probability across strata. Both these factors affect the computation of statistical significance. Adjustment methods to obtain correct test statistics in the presence of complex survey design have been used in all analyses.

Table of workplace attributes used in regression analyses

Industry group (based on Standard Industrial Classification 1992)

- Agriculture, extraction, utilities (not shown in tables and charts because of small number of workplaces)
- Engineering and metal manufacturing industries
- Other manufacturing industries
- Construction
- Hotels and catering
- Distribution and repair services
- Postal, telecommunications and transport services
- Financial and business services
- Public services (health, education, welfare, etc.)
- Other services (leisure, personal services, etc.)

Ownership

- Private PLC
- Private non-PLC
- Public sector
- Other non-profit

Size of workplace (natural logarithm of number of employees)

Trade union recognised at workplace (yes or no)

Number of job levels

- 1–3
- 4
- 5
- 6
- 7
- 8 or more

Proportion of female employees

- five quintile groups

Part-time employees as percentage of total (continuous measure)

Number of days open per week

- 5 or less
- 6
- 7

24-hour opening (yes or no)

Estimated level of staff coverage by ICT (nearest value)

- None, 25%
- 50%
- 75%, All

Alternative to above used in a few analyses (as reported in text):

Perceived change in ICT usage in past three years:

- Large increase
- Some increase
- No increase, reduction

Notes

1 Profiling Change at Work

1. The importance of astrology in English society, and the widespread respect accorded to it, are described in Keith Thomas, 1971, Chapters 10–12. Thomas points out that the high-point of astrology, in terms of the publication of books and manuals which had a wide readership, was in the latter half of the seventeenth century when Isaac Newton and others were transforming the understanding of the natural world.
2. This book does not directly review this literature but at various points reference is made to particular ideas or interpretations from writers such as Ulrich Beck, Michael Dertouzos, Peter Drucker, Charles Handy, Charles Leadbeater, Robert Reich and Jeremy Rifkin, who have contributed to the debates about the future of work.
3. The role of cartels, lobbies, unions and other special-interest associations in impeding innovation and economic renewal has been analysed by the economist Mancur Olson, 1982, who saw Great Britain as a good illustration of this idea.
4. This has frequently been advanced, especially by S.J. Prais in a series of publications by the National Institute for Economic and Social Research, and in a 1988 article by David Finegold and David Soskice. The historian Corelli Barnett, 1986, also blamed the inadequacies of the British educational system for many of the failings of the war effort in the Second World War.
5. This was put forward by the historian M.J. Wiener in 1981. The early 1980s saw a spate of books analysing Britain's economic decline, a little in advance of the resurgence of the British economy.
6. Michael Porter and Christian Ketels, 2003.
7. Imitation of competitors' products or services was identified as a major form of business strategy by organisation theorists R.E. Miles and C.C. Snow, 1978. Robert Reich, 2002, argues that the advance of the information age greatly reduces the advantage of product innovation and provides some vivid illustrations.
8. According to the 1951 Census of Population, 39 per cent worked in manufacturing, but in 2001 according to National Statistics the figure was only 14 per cent.
9. Duncan Gallie and colleagues, 1998: Chapter 2.
10. Anthony Heath, 1981.
11. W.W. Daniel, 1980, provides results from a 1979 survey; Claire Callender and colleagues, 1997, provide comparable results from a 1996 survey. The 1979 figure was based on resuming employment within nine months of the birth while the 1996 figure was based on a period of ten months.
12. Neil Millward and colleagues, 2000.
13. For the classic exposition of the way in which the market system was 'organised', see Karl Polanyi, 1957.
14. More precisely, Britain's spending on imports rose by 104 per cent and receipts from exports grew by 105 per cent, at current prices. Excluding services, the growth was still well over 80 per cent in both directions. See GDP and trade statistics time series available on the National Statistics website.

15. J.P. Womack and D.T. Jones, 1994, explain the ideas of lean production and how they can be extended to the whole organisation.
16. Figures reported by Philip Morgan and colleagues, 2000: Table 5.1, derived from the government's Economic Trends Annual Supplement of 1997.
17. See Richard Walton's article 'International Comparisons of Profitability', available on the National Statistics website. (This information is annually updated by the Office for National Statistics.) The article shows British companies in fifth position overall at the turn of the century, with British services in third position.
18. Representative of this pessimistic school of thought in the European context is Ulrich Beck with his *Brave New World of Work*, 2000. In the USA, a similar view was expressed by Jeremy Rifkin in *The End of Work*, 1995. However Rifkin subsequently developed a different interpretation, pointing to the potential for radically new types of services especially for high-income customers and clients, in *The Age of Access*, 2000.
19. For an imaginative view of the services which ICT will make possible in the future, see Michael Dertouzos, 1997. Dertouzos led a research group at MIT which has had a major influence on the development of the technology, including the Internet.
20. Peter Drucker, 2002: 253.
21. The story is told in D.B. Yoffie and M.A. Cusumano, 1999.
22. See for example E. Geisler, 1999 or N. Tichy, 1999. A related issue, about which a great deal has been written, is the 'learning organisation': this subject is described in Joseph Boyett and Jimmie Boyett, 1998, Chapter 3.
23. The optimistic contributions include Robert Reich, 1993 and Charles Leadbeater, 2000. For a short critique, see Peter Nolan and Stephen Wood, 2003.
24. Reich, 2002: Chapter 3 and footnote to page 69.
25. See Timothy Bresnahan, 1999.
26. This is the viewpoint put forward by Rifkin, 1995 and Beck, 2000.
27. See Bresnahan, 1999.
28. See Charles Handy, 1984, 1989. An overview of Handy's ideas is provided in Boyett and Boyett, 1998.
29. M.L. Tushman and E. Romanelli, 1985, argued that in order to survive, organisations needed to master both small-scale incremental change and major discontinuous change to stave off disaster.
30. This argument has been put forward by many writers on management, and particularly clearly by R.E. Walton, 1985 and 1987.
31. See Eileen Appelbaum and colleagues, 2000, who also review earlier US research.
32. For a review of the British evidence, see Peter Nolan and Kathy O'Donnell, 2003. The Centre for Organisation and Innovation, at Sheffield University, has called for a national study to test the effectiveness of HRM practices in terms of organisational performance. See: ESRC Centre for Organisation and Innovation, Annual Report 2002 (Web document).
33. The Advisory Conciliation and Arbitration Service. See Annual Reports for statistics of mediation and of cases reaching Employment Tribunals.
34. 'Arriva il lavoro superflessibile', *La Repubblica*, 7 June 2003 pages 2–3.
35. Over the years from 1999 to 2002, an additional 625,000 employee jobs were created in the British economy. Source: Labour Force Surveys.
36. The survey's results in this respect are inevitably biased towards optimism, since they only cover going concerns and not those which have recently closed or become insolvent.

37. 17 per cent of large workplaces relocated part of their business within Britain, and nine per cent did so overseas. For small workplaces, the corresponding figures were seven per cent and five per cent, for medium-sized workplaces, 11 per cent and seven per cent.
38. To make this estimate, the answers to the question are first replaced by the mid-point for the band expressed as a proportion. The resulting numbers are 0.06, 0.25, 0.50, 0.75, and 0.94. These are then multiplied by the actual number of employees per establishment, with the establishment weights applied.

2 Flexible Labour at its Limit?

1. See for example, Mark Beatson, 1995; Neil Millward and colleagues, 1992.
2. 'Lavoro usa e getta'.
3. Even in the late 1980s, when part-time employees had less job protection than full-time employees, in practice they were less likely to experience redundancy and had low feelings of insecurity: see Michael White and Duncan Gallie, 1994.
4. See Catherine Hakim, 1996 and 2000.
5. See Michael White and John Forth, 1998.
6. Peter Robinson, 1994, describes trends towards involuntary part-time and temporary working. White and Forth, 1998, argue that many women enter part-time jobs reluctantly following a period of unemployment.
7. TUC, 2003: the report says that the number of people forced to take temporary jobs unwillingly, fell by nearly 40 per cent between 1999 and 2002, while the corresponding fall for unwilling part-time workers was 29 per cent.
8. Ulrich Beck 2000, Charles Handy 1984 and 1989.
9. See for example A. McGregor and A. Sproull, 1991; A. Pollert, 1991; D. Gallie and M. White, 1994; B. Casey and colleagues, 1997; D. Gallie and colleagues, 1998: Chapter 6.
10. For further details see Kate Purcell and John Purcell, 1998.
11. See Craig Littler and Peter Innes, 2003.
12. These figures, and subsequent figures in the chapter, are on an employment-weighted basis, as explained in Chapter One.
13. Purcell and Purcell, 1998: pages 49–50. For their discussion of outsourcing, these authors drew largely on case study evidence and it is possible that this led them to underestimate the extent of outsourcing at that time.
14. 'Firms resist HR outsourcing', *People Management,* 13 June 2002. The article stresses that the success of BP's outsourcing experiment is not yet known.
15. See Chapter One and Chart 1.3 for further details about ICT definition and usage.
16. Some earlier information on the replacement of employees by contractors comes from Mark Cully and colleagues, 1999 (page 36). They reported such replacement at 28 per cent of workplaces, which is very close to our figure, but they considered a five-year period whereas we use a three-year period, and they covered only workplaces with 25 or more employees. Taking these points into account, it is likely that there has been an increase in this kind of employee substitution.
17. Cully and colleagues, 1999, reported that nearly one-half (48%) of workplaces using contractors to replace employees gave cost savings at their primary reason.
18. Part-time employees are included among the peripheral workers in the core-periphery model of the firm's labour force, put forward by John Atkinson, 1984

and 1987, and used as the starting-point of most subsequent discussions. Arne Kalleberg, 2003, continues to combine part-time employees with temporary and other flexible types of labour.

19. In October 2002, the Fixed-term Employees (Prevention of Less Favourable Treatment) Regulations were introduced. These give employees on fixed-term contracts a general right to the same conditions and benefits as apply to employees of the same job or skill level who have permanent contracts with the same employer. There are also numerous other more specific provisions, which tend to reduce the scope for employers to use fixed-term contracts as a way of cutting labour costs. Similar Regulations were introduced for part-time employees in 2000.

3 Intelligent Flexibility

1. The thinking which connects business performance with adaptable, committed employees is expounded in Michael Beer and colleagues, 1984, or R.E. Walton, 1987. For a more recent application, see Eileen Appelbaum and colleagues, 2000. For review and critique from a UK perspective, see John Storey, 2001, or Peter Nolan and Kathy O'Donnell, 2003. There have been numerous studies in Britain attempting to link employee commitment or involvement with measures of performance: see for example Harvey Ramsay and colleagues, 2000.
2. The importance of firm-specific knowledge and skills provides the economic rationale for training within the firm. Timothy Bresnahan, 1999, argues that the development of ICT increases the requirement for knowledge and skills specific to the firm. For a review of skill and training issues in Britain, see David Ashton and Alan Felstead, 2001.
3. Pin manufacture was the example of specialisation used by the founder of economics, Adam Smith, in his masterpiece, *The Wealth of Nations*.
4. A key text on flexible specialisation is the book by Michael Piore and Charles Sabel, 1984. Another term used to describe this approach is 'mass customisation'. Some of the early influential ideas on team production systems came from the Tavistock Institute's work on the British coal-mining industry: see E.L. Trist and K.L. Bamforth, 1951.
5. May Tam Yeuk-Mui, 2001 describes the social skills of call centre staff in Australia, which the majority of these staff regard as the most important skills they need. Staff must be 'sensitive and empathetic' towards customers, so as to interpret their needs rapidly and correctly. They also need to pick up subtle cues which help them to detect fraudulent callers, and be able to adapt their approach to dealing with angry or abusive calls.
6. Union roles are discussed further in Chapter Ten.
7. These figures and subsequent figures in the chapter are weighted by employment, as explained in Chapter One.
8. A great deal has been written about these changes. See for example Rosabeth Moss Kanter, 1989 and 1991; Christopher Hendry, 1990; Stephen Hill, 1991a, 1991b, and 1995; John Kay, 1993; and Stephen Hill and colleagues, 1997 and 2000.
9. These findings echo some research from past years, although comparisons involving very different business conditions and technologies may be hazardous. The British sociologist Joan Woodward showed in her 1965 book that tall, vertically integrated organisations made the greatest demands on management.

In the USA, social psychologists M.L. Kohn and C. Schooler, 1983, showed that employees in large bureaucracies had particularly complex jobs and developed more complex skills. This complexity may explain why, as Manuel Castells, 1996, demonstrated, many large and vertically extended bureaucracies have been shifted by their senior managements towards flatter corporations, as part of their response to unpredictable conditions.

10. For case studies describing the importance of team developments in several industries in the USA, see Eileen Appelbaum and colleagues, 2000.
11. There have been several revealing pieces of case study research focusing on team pressures: see for example J.R. Barker, 1993 and A. Danford,1998.
12. For the role of incentives in high-performance work systems, see Appelbaum and colleagues, 2000. Incentives have a central place in economists' ideas about business organisation: see for example Paul Milgrom and John Roberts, 1994.
13. See Michael Porter and Christian Ketels, 2003. For ideas of 'performance management' involving pay for performance, which came to the fore in the late 1980s, see I. Smith, 1992.
14. See Castells, 1996.
15. As emphasised by, for example, Soshana Zuboff , 1988 or Timothy Bresnahan, 1999.
16. See Richard Sennett, 1998 for the decline of trust: he regards team-working as part of the problem rather than as a potential solution.

4 Resuscitating Careers

1. For further explanation and case study of the employability concept in the USA, see R.H. Waterman Jr. and colleagues, 1994, who see it as a positive development.
2. See Peter Cappelli, 1999a and 1999b for detailed evidence. There is still widespread pessimism among British managers about career prospects: in a recent CIPD survey, many HR professionals felt that employees' career opportunities would plateau earlier through a reduced number of higher-level jobs, and that people would have to change employers to get up their career ladder (CIPD, 2003).
3. The report, *The Future of Careers*, was edited on behalf of CIPD by Imogen Daniels and Jennifer Schramm, who also published a summary in *People Management*, 30 May 2002, entitled 'Evolution at Work'.
4. Cappelli, 1999b.
5. See, for example, S. Crainer and D. Dearlove, 1999, or D.B. Yoffie and M.A. Cusumano, 1999.
6. See James Johnston, 2002, who analyses data from 220 of Britain's largest companies.
7. These figures, and subsequent figures throughout the chapter, are weighted by employment, as explained in Chapter One.
8. Examples from the US retail sector are cited by Sanford Jacoby, 1999, and include Dayton-Hudson, Home Depot, Lowe's (a DIY chain), and Wal-Mart.
9. See, for example, Heather Rolfe, 1994.
10. The 1992 survey is reported in Duncan Gallie and colleagues, 1998.
11. Sickness pay can be considered a deferred benefit in the sense that, although it is available to young employees, it is more likely to be used when older. In addition, company schemes sometimes increase the period of sickness pay for employees with longer periods of service.

12. The OPRA report of 2000/1 states that 11.5 per cent of live schemes were on a deferred benefit basis, while the 2001/2 report indicates that the figure by then was 11.1 per cent (own calculations from published table).
13. See Jacoby, 1999.
14. Since appraisal systems vary greatly in their details, including how formally or informally they are conducted, surveys can give widely different figures depending on how they ask questions on this topic. The present employer survey asks about appraisals that are formal, regular and concerned with performance. A similar approach is adopted in the companion employee survey. The slow but steady spread of appraisals is visible through data using comparable questions asked of employees in 1986, 1992 and 2000.
15. There have been numerous research studies in recent years applying the concept of employee involvement. For review, see Mick Marchington, 2001.
16. Duncan Gallie and colleagues, 1998: Chapter 9 showed that 'open communications' was one of the factors most clearly linked to organisational commitment. Alex Bryson, 1999, showed the importance of communications for the financial performance of smaller organisations.
17. In his 1999 article, Jacoby points out that similar swings in employer commitments and policies have occurred in previous economic recessions, notably in the 1930s.
18. These requirements have been analysed in detail by Timothy Bresnahan , 1999: see also case research referred to there.
19. Jonathan Michie and Maura Sheehan-Quinn, 2001, show that innovation is positively linked to internal and functional flexibility and to positive HRM policies, but is at a lower level in companies which rely on external labour flexibility.

5 Shrinking the Workspace

1. Source: *www.commercial-sense.uk*, Market Commentary, July 2001. This review found above-inflation increases in 16 of 20 city centres surveyed, with the other four remaining in line with inflation.
2. A particularly good comparison for London is with Frankfurt, the other main financial centre in Europe. According to Jacco Hakfoort and Robert Lie, 2001, employees in banking and insurance in London had just one-half the office space per employee of their counterparts in Frankfurt.
3. For conflict between work and family life, see Michael White and colleagues, 2003.
4. 'Top-flight ground control', *Sunday Times*, 21 June 1998.
5. For further details about call centres in India, see Incomes Data Services Report 881, May 2003. This source refers to the insurance group Norwich Union opening a 750-strong call centre at Norwich while at the same time developing a 1000-strong centre in Bangalore, India. The report also notes Axa, British Airways, and British Telecoms among other companies with overseas call centres.
6. Efforts to use space more efficiently are doubtless continuing in other kinds of workspace including manufacturing plants. However, it seems likely that the majority of work activity in advanced economies now takes place in an office context: Michael Dertouzos, 1997: 192 estimated that 58 per cent of the US workforce were engaged in office work.
7. Manufacturing workplaces often have extensive offices attached. The companion survey of employees showed that managerial, professional, administrative and

clerical support staff comprised 41 per cent of employees across the engineering and metal industries, and 32 per cent of employees across the remaining manufacturing industries.

8. There have been numerous earlier studies of outworking, teleworking and split working between home and employer's workplace. The experience of this earlier research is that results are very sensitive to the definitions used for each type of work arrangement. See especially Alan Felstead and colleagues, 2001a and 2001b.
9. Felstead and colleagues, 2001b, report that in 1998 one in ten workplaces had some employees working from home during normal working hours, and that nine per cent of workplaces (one in eleven) had more than five per cent of employees doing so.
10. Felstead and colleagues, 2001b, also find that working from home is more common in establishments where team-working has been developed.

6 Extending Management Control

1. See for example Duncan Gallie and colleagues, 1998: Chapter 3. This shows how forms of control including tight supervision, incentive payment systems, target-setting and appraisals all increased during a period in the late 1980s and early 1990s when there was a particularly rapid development of multi-skilled workers enjoying considerable discretion in how they carried out their jobs.
2. See Peter Bain and colleagues, 2002, for an extended case study of call centre management.
3. For case study evidence, see May Tam Yeuk-Mui, 2001.
4. Amitai Etzioni, 1975, coined the phrase 'remunerative power' to describe the typical control method of complex, commercial organisations.
5. The information here and in Table 6.1 is derived from the *New Earnings Survey 2002: United Kingdom – Streamlined and Summary Analyses*, National Statistics (available from the National Statistics website).
6. This figure comes from the companion survey of employees (WIB-00).
7. The companion survey of employees shows that one in three (34%) of those who take part in appraisals believe that they are used to determine aspects of their pay. Other uses of appraisals include to plan training and development, and to assess people for promotion.
8. According to Gallie and colleagues, 1998: Chapter 3, target setting was perceived as an important influence on personal effort by about one half of employees. By 2000, according to our companion survey of employees, two-thirds of employees were set targets although a lower proportion (around one third) felt they were an important influence on effort.
9. See Gallie and colleagues, 1998, for survey evidence. Michelle Brown and John Benson, 2003 provide recent case study data from a large public sector organisation.
10. See Edward Lazear, 1995.
11. The extent to which different groups seek the more protected kinds of careers is discussed by W.P. Bridges and W.J. Villemez, 1994, but their data relate to 1981 and may not be relevant to current conditions. The subject has not received much attention in HRM sources more recently.
12. For a recent analysis of the links between various performance practices at work and employees' views of work-life balance, see Michael White and colleagues,

2003. This shows that team membership, group-based incentives, and membership of work improvement groups (quality circles) are linked with feelings that work is at conflict with family life.

13. This information comes from the companion survey, WIB-00.
14. For numerous examples of the possibilities offered by ICT, see Michael Dertouzos, 1997: Chapter 9.
15. The companion survey of employees shows that just over three in five employees in 2000 used the Internet and/or emails in their job. It is not known what proportion of these are in a network system.
16. About one in four of senior managers and professionals, the same proportion as for all employees, believed that ICT records of their work were used to assess their performance.
17. The companion survey, WIB-00, shows that the proportion whose hours were checked by a time-clock or similar device in 2000 was 19 per cent, while in 1992 it was 17 per cent (see also Gallie and colleagues, 1998). About twice the proportion of men as of women are subject to 'clocking'.
18. This type of Victorian prison design, called the Panopticon, was based on ideas from the social philosopher and reformer Jeremy Bentham; the significance of the Panopticon for modern society was revived by the French philosopher Michel Foucault. Peter Bain and Philip Taylor, 2000 argued that the Panopticon principle was applicable to call centre management.
19. See Norbert Wiener, 1954.
20. The variety of ways in which employees relate to control systems is considered by Paul Edwards, 1986 and 1993.
21. A short case study of the 'virtual call centre' at the AA (in which members calling in for help are answered by employees located at home but connected by a central ICT system) is described by Andy Bibby, 2002.
22. This positive finding about call centres is reported by Vicki Belt, 2002, though she also provides evidence of a continuing lack of representation of women (who comprise the majority of call centre staff) at senior management level.
23. Alan Felstead and colleagues, 2003.
24. The importance and value of feedback of performance and progress data has also been learned in production lines, and has been a feature of Japanese manufacturing management systems. See, for example, G. Sewell and B. Wilkinson, 1992.
25. See May Tam Yeuk-Mui, 2001, page 190.
26. In October 2003, wildcat strikes broke out in the British postal service. Media interviews with strikers indicated that employees' grievances included the growth of monitoring at work, and management was also criticised for using video surveillance of strikers away from the workplace.

7 Lowering the Sexual Barriers

1. CIPD, 2002b. To put the quoted results in perspective, the next-highest vote for the number one spot was 'improving productivity and efficiency', put forward by 15 per cent of managers.
2. The two main academic explanations for segregation of occupations and for inequality of pay between men and women are patriarchy theory and preference theory. While patriarchy theory attributes women's disadvantages to men's deliberate use of their dominant power, preference theory argues that women

themselves make varied personal choices between home, work and career and that these play an independent part in the outcomes. For recent expositions of patriarchy, see Sylvia Walby, 1986 and 1990, and for preference theory, see Catherine Hakim, 1996 and 2000. A critical analysis of both these theories has been offered by Robert Blackburn and colleagues, 2002.

3. This point was made in the CBI's evidence to the Equal Pay Task Force: CBI, August 2000.
4. See Claire Callender and colleagues, 1997.
5. See the government publication, *Social Trends 2001*.
6. Mounted by the Department of Trade and Industry: see DTI website for details and case studies.
7. See 'Changing Times News' on the TUC website, which is largely devoted to work-life balance issues and developments.
8. See Neil Millward and Stephen Woodland, 1995.
9. A detailed analysis for the pharmacy profession has been provided by Karen Hassell and colleagues, 2002.
10. See 'Sectoral Employment Prospects', Chapter 3 from the 2002 Employment Projections of the Institute for Employment Research, available from the Skillsbase website of the Department for Education and Skills. This shows that women in the business services sector increased from 42 per cent of jobs in 1971 to 48 per cent in 1999, a period during which the sector grew from 12 per cent of all employment to 24 per cent (Table 3.6 therein).
11. See Michael White and Duncan Gallie, 1994.
12. There is generally close agreement between these figures and figures from the companion survey of employees. This suggests that the managers gave reasonably reliable break-downs of their workplaces' employment by sex and full-time/part-time status.
13. This and subsequent figures are weighted by the numbers employed at each workplace, as explained in Chapter One and Appendix Two.
14. In addition to the DTI's website referred to in note 6, information and guidance about flexible hours and related issues can be found on Employers for Work-Life Balance, part of the website of The Work Foundation.
15. The same result was obtained by the Work-Life Balance Survey 2000: see Terence Hogarth and colleagues, 2001: Fig. 4.7.
16. Hogarth and colleagues, 2001: Table 4.9 states that six per cent of women and seven per cent of men actually took a career break in the previous 12 months. This figure is quite high, but it is possible that some of these career breaks were for educational rather than family reasons, since the Work-Life Balance Survey did not ask a separate question about educational leave. Also, the question did not exclude short breaks and so did not accord with the normal understanding of career breaks as involving substantial periods, of at least several months.
17. Economists consider that experience is an important influence on earnings, and so explain the lower earnings and progression of women who take career breaks through the reduction in work experience which results. But direct prejudice against those who take career break undoubtedly exists. Taking career breaks is cited as one of the main obstacles to career progress by HR managers in a CIPD survey, 2003.
18. Results concerning this relationship can be found, for the USA, in Paul Osterman, 1995, and for Britain in Stephen Wood, 1999a, and in Sue Fernie and Helen Gray, 2002. In the present survey, the number of family-friendly practices is positively and significantly associated with the number of communications

practices, the number of skill development practices, the number of team-working practices, and the number of performance related pay practices.

19. The analysis by Blackburn and colleagues, 2002, suggests that change in the distribution of jobs and pay between men and women involves many factors and is inevitably a gradual process.
20. See Michael White and colleagues, 2003.
21. See Helen Gray, 2002.

8 Developing Diversity

1. For a review which covers recent evidence about both women and minority groups in the context of employee relations, see Sonia Liff, 2003. For older workers and ageism, see Colin Duncan, 2003.
2. See B. Reskin and P. Roos, 1990.
3. For an exposition of diversity management from a practitioner viewpoint, see Rajvinder Kandola and Johanna Fullerton, 1998.
4. The case study, presented in Louisa Wah's 1999 article, is also of interest in describing the steps taken by the company to develop team-work and effective communications and involvement in an organisation with a diverse staff composition.
5. The Cabinet Office project, which involved a 15-month programme of management and staff workshops to embed diversity policy, starting in 2001, is outlined in a document available from the Schneider-Ross website (*www.schneider-ross.com*) entitled *Building Diversity Awareness at the Cabinet Office.*
6. See for example A. Lorbieki and G. Jack, 2000.
7. Chartered Institute of Personnel and Development, 2002b.
8. There have been many studies of discrimination in the recruitment and careers of ethnic minorities. For discussion, see Tariq Modood and colleagues, 1994.
9. The existence of widespread recruitment difficulties in 2001/2 is documented in the CIPD's recruitment and retention report, 2002b.
10. It is possible that unions influenced the amount of diverse recruitment per workplace, which was not investigated by the survey.
11. See J. Bone and S. Mercer, 2000.
12. The differences persist when size and other factors are taken into account.
13. See A. Gray, 2002: page 658.
14. The importance of overseas recruitment for these industries is of course not new. There is a long tradition for hotels to employ overseas staff, often on a seasonal basis, and the National Health Service's recruitment of overseas doctors and nurses is of long standing.

9 Which Strategies?

1. For an earlier review of the total quality strategy, see Stephen Hill, 1995.
2. For an attempt to classify workplaces by their HRM practices without any prior views about how they should be grouped, see Stephen Wood and Lilian de Menezes, 1998.
3. The name of 'organisational adaptation' has been given to the common-sense idea that organisations choose their strategies in a highly flexible way that depends partly on their circumstances and preferences. For further explanation, see Stephen Wood and colleagues, 2003: 223–226. For evidence of mixed people strategies in the USA, see Arne Kalleberg, 2003.

4. Peter Turnbull and Victoria Wass, 2000: 59.
5. See Neil Millward and colleagues, 2000: Table 5.10.
6. For an exposition of delayering from the management viewpoint, see Colin Coulson-Thomas and Trudy Coe, 1991.
7. Much of this literature is from the USA. For a wide ranging review, which points out some of the limitations, see Stephen Wood, 1999b.
8. There is by no means complete agreement on this score. Some writers seem to suggest there is 'one best way' of achieving high performance through a combination of HRM policies. For further discussion, see Wood, 1999b, John Storey, 2001, and Peter Nolan and Kathy O'Donnell, 2003.
9. See Eileen Appelbaum and colleagues, 2000, who conducted research in three industries in the USA, and John Godard, 2001, who used a national survey of employees in Canada.
10. This account draws particularly on the formulation by Appelbaum and colleagues, 2000.
11. Evidence indicating that small or medium sized workplaces do best with small, tightly focused sets of practices is provided by Alex Bryson, 1999.
12. Having a flexible definition of HRM strategy is probably a crucial factor in getting a higher estimate than most previous reviews. If the entry-ticket required all four components of the strategy to be present, the proportion qualifying as having an HRM strategy would drop to only ten per cent.
13. See, for example, Susan Eaton, 2003.
14. Previous research treating benefits as related to commitment includes that by Duncan Gallie and colleagues, 1998: Chapter 9, and that by Appelbaum and colleagues, 2000: Chapter 7.
15. In practice, nine in ten workplaces that offer staff an occupational pension also offer them enhanced sick pay. So there is little difference between the adopted definition and one which specified that both occupational pension and sick pay must be among the three or more fringe benefits available.
16. For ICT as an infrastructure for society, see Michael Dertouzos, 1997: Chapters 1 and 9.
17. See Soshana Zuboff, 1988 and Timothy Bresnahan, 1999.
18. The association is in the positive direction but falls just short of statistical significance at the 1 per cent significance level.
19. Bresnahan, 1999, has provided a review of the reasons why ICT developments add to employers' needs for a wide range of skills, most of which are concerned with the management of change, adaptability, team-working and social and customer relations, rather than being technical in nature.
20. For earlier evidence, drawn from the Workplace Industrial Relations Survey, see David Blanchflower and colleagues, 1991.
21. When asked whether 'unions help find ways to improve performance', 43 per cent of managers in the 1998 Workplace Employee Relations Survey expressed their agreement (Mark Cully and colleagues, 2000: Table 5.2).
22. The development of human resource management in the USA was initially linked with non-union or anti-union management. See for example the set of case studies in F. Foulkes, 1980.
23. More precisely, those workplaces which are in the lowest one-fifth of the distribution by percentage of women employed.
24. The companion survey of employees showed that over the 1990s, working with ICT was an important factor that substantially pushed up the average hours worked by women.

10 Management *versus* Regulation?

1. The Bristol Stress and Health at Work study provides the most authoritative analysis: for a short account, see Andrew Smith, 2001, who also gives references to more detailed reports. The Bristol study established connections between employees' reports of experiencing stress on one hand and objective tests of mental and physical health on the other. Smith concludes that around five million people in the UK may have 'very high levels of stress at work'.
2. Smith, 2001, Table 7 shows that stress is most often reported by teachers, nurses and managers. Terence Hogarth and colleagues, 2001 (Figure 4.2) report that in 75 per cent of establishments, senior managers and professionals regularly work longer than their contractual hours. For a detailed analysis of pressures on management, see Les Worrall and Cary Cooper, 2001.
3. For a discussion of the managerial freedom of the 1980s, see John Purcell, 1991.
4. Chartered Institute of Personnel and Development, 2002a.
5. For statistics of unfair dismissal and other ET cases, see Advisory Conciliation and Arbitration Service (ACAS), annual reports. The 1999 Employment Act attempted to staunch the flood by instituting new procedures aimed at averting litigation, to be followed by employees, employers and ACAS, and in 2001/2 the number of ET cases fell to 10,852. This was still 12 per cent higher than in 1999/00.
6. In its annual report for 2001, the CAC recorded that 59 new recognition cases were received in the preceding 12 months, while in its 2002 report the corresponding figure was 119.
7. In *IDS Report 836*, July 2001. For some other reviews of the growth of trade union recognition, see TUC, 2002; Stephen Wood and Sian Moore, 2002.
8. See, for example, John Knell's report, 2001, for the Department of Trade and Industry.
9. For the position of consultative committees up to 1998, see Mark Cully and colleagues, 1999: 98–102, and Neil Millward and colleagues, 2000: 108–113.
10. The other country without a statutory framework for employee consultation is Ireland.
11. However, all findings in Chapter 10 have also been prepared separately for each size-group (5–24 employees, 25–99 employees, 100-plus employees). Where the picture differs by size-group, this is mentioned in the text.
12. For further details concerning this difference in UK implementation from other EU countries, see David Goss and Derek Adam-Smith, 2001. The most significant feature of the UK implementation is individual opt-outs from the 48-hour rule.
13. See Institute of Personnel and Development, 1999.
14. To put this in perspective, three in ten of male employees worked 48 or more hours per week in 2000, and four in ten men believed that all or most of their colleagues regularly worked overtime (paid or unpaid). The source for these figures is the companion survey of employees, WIB-00 (see Chapter One). Goss and Adam-Smith, 2001, show that full-time workers in the UK worked the longest average hours of any EU country shortly before the WTR were introduced.
15. The survey did not establish whether staff agreed to opt-out. Under the legislation, opting-out is voluntary, but case studies suggest that the initiative is taken by management and that staff almost always agree: see Fiona Neathey and James Arrowsmith, 2001.
16. The full breakdown is as follows: of workplaces with 5–24 employees, six per cent changed working practices and 14 per cent sought opt-outs; 25–99 employees,

13 per cent changed working practices and 30 per cent sought opt-outs; 100-plus employees, 20 per cent changed working practices and 40 per cent sought opt-outs.

17. As noted in Neathey and Arrowsmith, 2001.
18. CIPD, 2001.
19. Comparison of the figures with national statistics suggests that they must include cases which are resolved before reaching Tribunal hearings, since otherwise they would be too high. Figures published in the annual ACAS reports show that the majority of unfair dismissal cases are resolved before reaching a Tribunal.
20. Chartered Institute of Personnel and Development, 2002a.
21. For further details of the Information and Consultation Directive, see Department of Trade and Industry, 2002.
22. See Mark Cully and colleagues, 1999, for the results of the 1998 WERS. Neil Millward and colleagues, 2000, provide information on changes in many aspects of workplace representation and voice across the 1990s. A new survey in the WERS series is taking place in 2003/4 and this is expected to provide important information about union recognition in the early 2000s.
23. For a full analysis of the economic and organisational role of trade unions, see R.B. Freeman and J.L. Medoff, 1984.
24. The Department of Trade and Industry has operated its Partnership at Work Fund since March 2000 and it is ongoing in 2003. Numerous workplace projects to develop management-employee cooperative working have been supported by the DTI, with funding up to £50,000. For details of the scheme, and brief notes on supported projects, see the DTI's 'Partnership at Work' website document, 2003, not to be confused with Knell, 2001, which has the same title.
25. Wages and salaries are not covered by the present survey, but detailed information at individual level has been collected in the companion survey of employees and permits comparisons between union members and non-members and between those working at unionised and non-unionised workplaces.
26. The results were statistically significant in the case of large workplaces (100-plus employees), but not in the case of smaller workplaces.
27. See Jill Earnshaw and colleagues, 2000.
28. See Freeman and Medoff, 1984.
29. See Millward and colleagues, 2000: Table 4.10.
30. Millward and colleagues, 2000, note that because consultative committees are formed and dissolved at the discretion of management, they have a rather high rate of turnover.
31. Case study evidence concerning consultative committees in the 1999–2000 period is presented by Sarah Oxenbridge and colleagues, 2003: 328–330. Management was using consultative committees in all the ways suggested in the conclusions to Chapter 10.
32. The survey information does not identify the workplaces which will be inside the scope of the coming regulations, since these are based on the number of employees in an organisation rather than the number at a workplace.

11 Interpreting the Trends

1. Another way in which professionals could be mobile between organisations is if they know how to acquire the knowledge that is special to each organisation

in a short time. Presumably, this is an uncommon capacity which attracts high rewards.

2. There have been numerous discussions in economics and in organisation theory concerning the distinction between generic knowledge (which is inherently portable) and knowledge which is specific to a firm or organisation, such as knowledge about its customers or its business systems. See for example Paul Milgrom and John Roberts, 1992: Part V.
3. Although consumer services have often been regarded as low-level or simple businesses, leading organisations from this sector have played a conspicuous part in business innovation (for example, Marks & Spencer with supply chain management). Ideas from manufacturing, such as automation, standardisation, and just-in-time, have also been taken to a high level in services.
4. By 'substantial', we mean that change has taken place in at least one in five of the HRM practices covered by the survey. For details relating to this point, see Table 1.1 in Chapter One.
5. The sole exception is in regard to external flexible labour practices, where decreases in use almost but not quite balances increases.
6. This association is significant after taking account also of size, industry and other background factors: this applies to other links or associations discussed in this section. See Annex Two for explanation.
7. See David Metcalf and colleagues, 2001, who present these findings about greater equality of pay as evidence that the unions' 'sword of justice' remains an effective one.

Bibliography

Appelbaum, E., Bailey, T., Berg, P. and Kalleberg, A.L. (2000) *Manufacturing Advantage: Why High-Performance Work Systems Pay Off*, Ithaca NY: Cornell University Press.

Ashton, D. and Felstead, A. (2001) 'From Training to Lifelong Learning: the Birth of the Knowledge Society?' in Storey, J. (ed.) *Human Resource Management: A Critical Text*, 2nd ed., London: Thomson Learning.

Atkinson, J. (1984) Manpower strategies for flexible organizations, *Personnel Management*, 16(8), 28–31.

Atkinson, J. (1987) Flexibility or fragmentation? The United Kingdom labour market in the eighties. *Labour and Society*, 12, 87–105.

Bain, P. and Taylor, P. (2000) Entrapped by the 'electronic panopticon'? Worker resistance in the call centre, *New Technology, Work and Employment*, 15(1), 2–18.

Bain, P., Watson, A., Mulvey, G., Taylor, P. and Gall, G. (2002) Taylorism, targets and the pursuit of quantity and quality by call centre management, *New Technology, Work and Employment*, 17(3), 170–185.

Barker, J.R. (1993) Tightening the iron cage: concertive control in self-managing teams, *Administrative Science Quarterly*, 38, 408–437.

Barnett, C. (1986) *The Audit of War: The Illusion and Reality of Britain as a Great Nation*, London: Macmillan.

Beatson, M. (1995) Progress towards a flexible labour market, *Employment Gazette*, 103(2), 56–66.

Beck, U. (2000) *The Brave New World of Work* Cambridge: Polity Press.

Beer, M., Spector, B., Lawrence, P.R., Mill, Q.D., and Walton, R.E. (1984) *Managing Human Assets*, New York: Free Press.

Belt, V. (2002) A Female Ghetto? Women's careers in call centres, *Human Resource Management Journal*, 12(4), 51–67.

Bibby, A. (2002) Home Start, *People Management*, 1 October 2002.

Blackburn, R.M., Browne, J., Brooks, B. and Jarman, J. (2002) Explaining gender segregation, *British Journal of Sociology*, 53(4), 513–536.

Blanchflower, D., Oswald, A. and Millward, N. (1991) Unionism and employment behaviour, *Economic Journal*, 101, Issue 407, 815–834.

Bone, J. and Mercer, S. (2000) *Flexible Retirement*, London: EFA.

Boyett, J.H. and Boyett, J.T. (1998) *The Guru Guide: The Best Ideas of the Top Management Thinkers*, New York: Wiley.

Breen, R. (1997) Inequality, economic growth and social mobility, *British Journal of Sociology*, 48(3), 429–449.

Bresnahan, T.F. (1999) Computerisation and wage dispersion: An analytical reinterpretation, *Economic Journal*, 109, F390–415.

Bridges, W.P. and Villemez, W.J. (1994) *The Employment Relationship: Causes and Consequences of Modern Personnel Administration*, New York: Plenum Press.

Brown, M. and Benson, J. (2003) Rated to exhaustion? Reactions to performance appraisal processes. *Industrial Relations Journal*, 34(1), 67–81.

Bryson, A. (1999) The impact of employee involvement on small firms' financial performance, *National Institute Economic Review*, No. 169, 78–95.

Callender, C., Millward, N., Lissenburgh, S. and Forth, J. (1997) *Maternity Rights and Benefits in Britain 1996*, DSS Research Report No. 67, London: Stationery Office.

Cappelli, P. (1995) Rethinking the 'Skills Gap', *California Management Review*, 37(4), 108–124.

Cappelli, P. (1999a) Career Jobs Are Dead, *California Management Review*, 42(1), 146–166.

Cappelli, P. (1999b) *The New Deal at Work: Managing the Market-Driven Workforce*, Boston, MA: Harvard University Press.

Casey, B., Metcalf, H. and Millward, N. (1997) *Employers' Use of Flexible Labour*, Report No. 837, London: Policy Studies Institute.

Castells, M. (1996) *The Rise of the Network Society*, Oxford: Blackwell.

Chartered Institute of Personnel and Development (2001), *Working Time Regulations: Have they made a difference?* Survey report, London: CIPD.

Chartered Institute of Personnel and Development (2002a) *Employment Law*, Survey report, London: CIPD.

Chartered Institute of Personnel and Development (2002b) *Recruitment and Retention 2002*, Survey report, London: CIPD.

Chartered Institute of Personnel and Development (2002c) *Casing it out: Why it can make sense to employ ex-offenders*, London: CIPD.

Chartered Institute of Personnel and Development (2003) *Managing employee careers: Issues, trends and prospects*, Survey report, London: CIPD.

Confederation of British Industry (CBI) (2000) *Tackling the pay gap between men and women – CBI evidence to the Equal Pay Task Force*, London: CBI.

Conger, J.A. (1998) How 'Gen X' managers manage, *Business and Strategy*, 10, 21–31.

Coulson-Thomas, C. and Coe, T. (1991) *The Flat Organisation: Philosophy and Practice*, Corby: British Institute of Management.

Crainer, S. and Dearlove, D. (1999) Death of executive talent, *Management Review*, July/August, 17–23.

Cully, M., Woodland, S., O'Reilly, A. and Dix, G. (1999) *Britain at Work: As depicted by the 1998 Workplace Employee Relations Survey*, London: Routledge.

Danford, A. (1998) Teamworking and labour regulation in the autocomponents industry, *Work Employment and Society*, 12, 409–431.

Daniel, W.W. (1980) *Maternity Rights: The experience of women*, PSI Report No. 588, London: Policy Studies Institute.

Daniels, I. and Schramm, J. (2002a) Evolution at Work, *People Management*, 30 May 2002.

Daniels, I. and Schramm, J. (eds) (2002b) *The Future of Careers*, London: Chartered Institute of Personnel and Development (CIPD).

Department of Trade and Industry (2002) *High Performance Workplaces: The role of employee involvement in a modern economy*, Discussion paper, July 2002, DTI website document.

Department of Trade and Industry (2003) *Partnership at Work*, DTI website document.

Dertouzos, M. (1997) *What Will Be: How the new world of information will change our lives*, London: Piatkus.

Drucker, P.F. (2002) *Managing in the Next Society*, Oxford: Butterworth-Heinemann.

Duncan, C. (2003) Assessing anti-ageism routes to older worker re-engagement, *Work Employment and Society*, 17(1), 101–120.

Earnshaw, J., Marchington, M. and Goodman, J. (2000) Unfair to whom? Discipline and dismissal in small establishments, *Industrial Relations Journal*, 31(1), 62–73.

Eaton, S.C. (2003) If You Can Use Them: Flexibility Policies, Organizational Commitment, and Perceived Performance, *Industrial Relations*, 42(2), 145–167.

Edwards, P.K. (1986) *Conflict at Work: A Materialist Analysis of Workplace Relations*, Oxford: Blackwell.

Edwards, P.K. (1993) *Attending to Work: The Management of Attendance and Shopfloor Order*, Oxford: Blackwell.

Etzioni, A. (1975) *A Comparative Analysis of Complex Organizations*, revised and enlarged edition, New York: Free Press.

Felstead, A., Jewson, N., Phizaklea, A. and Walters, S. (2001a) Working at home: statistical evidence for seven key hypotheses, *Work Employment and Society*, 15(2), 215–231.

Felstead, A., Jewson, N., Phizaklea, A. and Walters, S. (2001b) *Blurring the Home/Work Boundary: Profiling Employers Who Allow Working at Home*, Working Paper No. 15, ESRC Future of Work Programme, Centre for Labour Market Studies, University of Leicester.

Felstead, A., Jewson, N. and Walters, S. (2003) Managerial Control of Employees Working at Home, *British Journal of Industrial Relations*, 41(2), 241–264.

Fernie, S. and Gray, H. (2002) *It's a Family Affair: The Effect of Union Recognition and Human Resource Management on the Provision of Equal Opportunities in the UK*, Working Paper, Centre for Economic Performance, London School of Economics.

Finegold, D. and Soskice, D. (1988) The Failure of Training in Britain: Analysis and Prescription, *Oxford Review of Economic Policy*, 4(3), 21–53.

Foulkes, F. (1980) *Personnel Policies in Large Non-Union Companies*, Englewood Cliffs NJ: Prentice Hall.

Freeman, R.B. and Medoff, J.L. (1984) *What Do Unions Do?* New York: Basic Books.

Gallie, D. and White, M. (1993) *Employee Commitment and the Skills Revolution*, London: PSI Publishing.

Gallie, D. and White, M. (1994) 'Employer Policies, Employee Contracts and Labour Market Structure', in Rubery, J. and Wilkinson, F. (eds) *Employer Strategy and the Labour Market*, Oxford: Oxford University Press.

Gallie, D., White, M., Cheng, Y. and Tomlinson, M. (1998) *Restructuring the Employment Relationship*, Oxford: Oxford University Press.

Geisler, E. (1999) Harnessing the Value of Experience in the Knowledge-Driven Firm, *Business Horizons*, Vol. 42, No. 3, 18–26.

Gibson, V.A. and Lizieri, C.M. (1999) New business practices and the corporate property portfolio: how responsive is the UK property market? *Journal of Property Research*, 16(3), 201–218.

Glover, C. (2002) Room with a View, *People Management*, 8 August 2002.

Godard, J. (2001) High-performance and the transformation of work? The implications of alternative work practices for the experience and outcomes of work, *Industrial and Labor Relations Review*, 54, 776–805.

Goss, D. and Adam-Smith, D. (2001) Pragmatism and compliance: Employer responses to the Working Time Regulations, *Industrial Relations Journal*, 32(3), 195–208.

Gray, A. (2002) Jobseekers and gatekeepers: the role of the private employment agency in the placement of the unemployed, *Work Employment and Society*, 16(4), 655–674.

Gray, H. (2002) *Family-Friendly Working: What A Performance!* Working Paper, Centre for Economic Performance, London School of Economics.

Hakfoort, J. and Lie, R. (2001) Office Space per Worker: Evidence from Four European Markets, *The Journal of Real Estate Research*, 11(2), 183–196.

Hakim, C. (1996) *Key Issues in Women's Work: Female Heterogeneity and the Polarisation of Women's Employment*, London: Athlone.

Hakim, C. (2000) *Work-Lifestyle Choices in the 21st Century: Preference Theory*, Oxford: Oxford University Press.

Handy, C.B. (1984) *The Future of Work: A Guide to A Changing Society*, Oxford: Blackwell.

Handy, C. (1989) *The Age of Unreason*, Oxford: Blackwell.

Hassell, K., Fisher, R., Nichols, L. and Shann, P. (2002) Contemporary workforce patterns and historical trends: The pharmacy labour market over the past 40 years, *The Pharmaceutical Journal*, 269, August, 291–296.

Heath, A. (1981) *Social Mobility*, London: Fontana.

Heery, E. (2002) Partnership versus organising: alternative futures for British trade unionism, *Industrial Relations Journal*, 33(1), 20–35.

Hendry, C. (1990) The corporate management of human resources under conditions of decentralization, *Journal of Management*, 1(2), 1990, 91–103.

Hill, S. (1991a) How do you manage a flexible firm? The total quality model, *Work, Employment and Society*, 5(3), 1991, 397–415.

Hill, S. (1991b) Why quality circles failed but total quality might succeed, *British Journal of Industrial Relations*, 29(4), 1991, 541–568.

Hill, S. (1995) 'From quality circles to total quality management', in Wilkinson, A. and Willmott, H. (eds), *Making Quality Critical* London: Routledge.

Hill, S., Harris, M. and Martin, R. (1997) 'Flexible technologies, markets and the firm: strategic choices and FMS', in McLoughlin, I. and Harris, M. (eds), *Innovation, Organizational Change and Technology*, London: International Thomson Business Press.

Hill, S., Martin, R. and Harris, M. (2000) Decentralization, Integration and the Post-bureaucratic Organization: The Case of R&D, *Journal of Management Studies*, 37(4), 2000, 563–585.

Hogarth, T., Hasluck, C., and Pierre, G. with Winterbotham, M. and Vivian, D. (2001) *Work-Life Balance 2000: Results from the Baseline Study*, Research Report RR249, London: Department for Education and Employment.

Incomes Data Services (2001) Union recognition widens, *IDS Report 836*, July, London: IDS.

Institute of Personnel and Development (1999) *The Impact of the Working Time Regulations on UK plc*, IPD Survey Report 7, London: IPD.

The Industrial Society (1997) *Speaking Up, Speaking Out! The 2020 Vision Programme Research Report*. London: Industrial Society.

Jacoby, S.M. (1999) Are Career Jobs Headed for Extinction? *California Management Review*, 42(1), 123–145.

Johnston, J. (2002) Tenure, promotion and executive remuneration, *Applied Economics*, 34, 993–997.

Kalleberg, A. (2003) Flexible Firms and Labour Market Segmentation: Effect of Workplace Restructuring on Jobs and Workers, *Work and Occupations*, 30(2), 154–175.

Kandola, R. and Fullerton, J. (1998) *Managing the Mosaic: Diversity in Action* (2nd. ed.), London: Institute of Personnel and Development.

Kay, J. (1993) *Foundations of Corporate Success*, Oxford: Oxford University Press.

Kanter, R.M. (1989) *When Giants Learn to Dance* New York: Simon and Schuster.

Kanter, R.M. (1991) 'The future of bureaucracy and hierarchy in organizational theory: a report from the field', in Bourdieu, P. and Coleman, J.S. (eds), *Social Theory for a Changing Society*. Boulder, Colorado: Westview Press.

Knell, J. (2001) *Partnership at Work*, Employment Relations Research Series No. 7, London: Department of Trade and Industry.

Kohn, M.L. and Schooler, C. (1983) *Work and Personality*, New York: Houghton Mifflin.

Lane, N. (2000) The Low Status of Female Part-Time Nurses: A Bed-Pan Ceiling? *Gender Work and Organization*, 7(4), 269–281.

Lazear, E. (1995) *Personnel Economics*, London: MIT Press.

Leadbeater, C. (2000) *Living on Thin Air: The New Economy*, London: Viking.

Liff, S. (2003) 'The Industrial Relations of a Diverse Workforce', in Edwards, P. (ed.) *Industrial Relations: Theory and Practice* (2nd ed.), Oxford: Blackwell.

Littler, C.R. and Innes, P. (2003) Downsizing and deknowledging the firm, *Work Employment and Society*, 17(1), 73–100.

Lorbieki, A. and Jack, G. (2000) Critical Turns in the Evolution of Diversity Management, *British Journal of Management*, 11, S17–S31.

McGregor, A. and Sproull, A. (1991) *Employer Labour Use Strategies: Analysis of a National Survey*, Research Paper 83, Sheffield: Department for Employment.

Marchington, M. (2001) 'Employee Involvement at Work', in Storey, J. (ed.) *Human Resource Management: A Critical Text*, 2nd ed., London: Thomson Learning.

Marx, G. (1999) 'Measuring Everything That Moves: The New Surveillance at Work', in Simpson, I. and Simpson, R. (eds) *The Workplace and Deviance*, Greenwich, Connecticut: JAI Press.

Metcalf, D., Hansen, K. and Charlwood, A. (2001) Unions and the sword of justice: unions and pay systems, pay inequality, pay discrimination and low pay. *National Institute Economic Review*, No. 176, 61–75.

Michie, J. and Sheehan-Quinn, M. (2001) Labour Market Flexibility, Human Resource Management and Corporate Performance, *British Journal of Management*, 12, 287–306.

Miles, R.E. and Snow, C.C. (1978) *Organizational Strategy, Structure and Process*, New York: McGraw-Hill.

Milgrom, P. and Roberts, J. (1992) *Economics, Organization and Management*, New Jersey: Prentice-Hall.

Millward, N., Bryson, A. and Forth, J. (2000) *All Change at Work? British employment relations 1980–1998, as portrayed by the Workplace Industrial Relations Survey series*, London: Routledge.

Millward, N., Stevens, M., Smart, D., and Hawes, W. (1992) *Workplace Industrial Relations in Transition*, Aldershot: Dartmouth.

Millward, N. and Woodland, S. (1995) Gender segregation and male/female wage differences, *Gender Work and Organization*, 2(3), 125–139.

Modood, T., Lakey, J., Nazroo, J., Virdee, S. and Beishon, S. (1997) *Ethnic Minorities in Britain: Diversity and Disadvantage*, London: Policy Studies Institute.

Morgan, P., Allington, N. and Heery, E. (2000) 'Employment insecurity in the public services', in Heery, E. and Salmon, J. (eds) *The Insecure Workforce*, London: Routledge.

Neathey, F. and Arrowsmith, J. (2001) *Implementation of the Working Time Regulations*, Employment Relations Research Series No. 11, London: Department for Trade and Industry.

Nolan, P. and O'Donnell, K. (2003) 'Industrial Relations, HRM and Performance', in Edwards, P. (ed.) *Industrial Relations: Theory and Practice (Second Edition)*, Oxford: Blackwell.

Nolan, P. and Wood, S. (2003) Mapping the Future of Work, *British Journal of Industrial Relations*, 41(2), 165–174.

Olson, M. (1982) *The Rise and Decline of Nations*, New Haven: Yale University Press.

Osterman, P. (1995) Work/family programs and the employment relationship, *Administrative Science Quarterly*, 40, 681–700.

Oxenbridge, S., Brown, W., Deakin, S. and Pratten, C. (2003) Initial Responses to the Statutory Recognition Provisions of the Employment Relations Act 1999, *British Journal of Industrial Relations*, 41(2), 315–334.

Pearman, H. (1998) Top-flight ground control, *Sunday Times*, 21 June 1998.

Piore, M.J. and Sabel, C.F. (1984) *The Second Industrial Divide: Possibilities for Prosperity*, New York: Basic Books.

Polanyi, K. (1957) *The Great Transformation*, Boston: Beacon Press.

Pollert, A. (1991) 'The Orthodoxy of Flexibility', in: Pollert, A. (ed.) *Farewell to Flexibility?* Oxford: Basil Blackwell.

Porter, M.E. and Ketels, C.H.M. (2003) *UK Competitiveness: Moving to the Next Stage*, DTI Economics Paper No. 3, London: Department of Trade and Industry.

Prais, S.J. (1989a) Qualified Manpower in Engineering, *National Institute Economic Review*, No. 127.

Prais, S.J. (1989b) How Europe Would See the New British Initiative for Standardizing Vocational Qualificiations, *National Institute Economic Review*, No. 129.

Purcell, J. (1991) The rediscovery of the management prerogative: the management of labour relations in the 1980s, *Oxford Review of Economic Policy*, 7(1), 33–43.

Purcell, J. (2001) 'The Meaning of Strategy in Human Resource Management', in Storey, J. (ed.) *Human Resource Management: A Critical Text*, 2nd ed., London: Thomson Learning.

Purcell, K. and Purcell, J. (1998) In-sourcing, Outsourcing, and Growth of Contingent Labour as Evidence of Flexible Employment Strategies, *European Journal of Work and Organizational Psychology*, 7(1), 39–59.

Ramsey, H., Scholarios, D. and Harley, B. (2000) Employees and high-performance work systems: testing inside the Black Box, *British Journal of Industrial Relations*, 38, 501–532.

Reich, R. (1993) *The Wealth of Nations*, London: Simon & Schuster.

Reich, R. (2002) *The Future of Success*, London: Vintage. (First published in 2001 by Heinemann.)

Reskin, B. and Roos, P. (1990) *Job Queues, Gender Queues: explaining women's inroads into male occupations*, Philadelphia: Temple University Press.

Rice-Birchall, H. (2001) *Stress and employee burn-out*, paper presented at the ACAS Conference on the Future of Work, Harrogate, July 2001.

Rifkin, J. (1995) *The End of Work: The Decline of the Global Labour Force and the Dawn of the Post-Market Era*, New York: G.P. Putnam.

Rifkin, J. (2000) *The Age of Access*, New York: G.P. Putnam.

Robinson, P. (1994) *The British Labour Market in Historical Perspective: Changes in the Structure of Employment and Unemployment*, Discussion Paper No. 202, London: Centre for Economic Performance, London School of Economics.

Rolfe, H. (1994) *Employers' Role in the Supply of Intermediate Skills*, London: Policy Studies Institute.

Sabel, C. (1991), 'Moebius-strip organizations and open labor markets: some consequences of the reintegration of conception and execution in a volatile economy', in Bourdieu, P. and Coleman, J.S. (eds), *Social Theory for a Changing Society*, Boulder, Colorado: Westview Press.

Schor, J. (1991) *The Overworked American: The Unexpected Decline of Leisure*, New York: Basic Books.

Sennett, R. (1998) *The Corrosion of Character: The Personal Consequences of Work in the New Capitalism*, New York: W.W. Norton & Company.

Sewell, G. and Wilkinson, B. (1992) 'Empowerment or Emasculation? Shopfloor Surveillance in a Total Quality Organization', in Blyton, P. and Turnbull, P. (eds) *Reassessing Human Resource Management*, London: Sage Publications.

Smith, A. (2001) Perceptions of stress at work, *Human Resource Management Journal*, 11(4), 74–86.

Smith, I. (1992) 'Reward Management and HRM', in Blyton, P. and Turnbull, P. (eds) *Reassessing Human Resource Management*, London: Sage Publications.

Storey, J. (2001) 'Human Resource Management Today: An Assessment', in Storey, J. (ed.) *Human Resource Management: A Critical Text*, 2nd ed., London: Thomson Learning.

Syrett, M. and Lammiman, J. (2000a) Happily Landed, *People Management*, 28 September 2000.

Syrett, M. and Lammiman, J. (2000b) *Entering Tiger Country: Tracking Innovation Inside Organisations*, Roffey Park Management Institute.

Thomas, K. (1971) *Religion and the Decline of Magic: Studies in Popular Beliefs in Sixteenth and Seventeenth Century England*, Weidenfeld & Nicholson (reprinted by Penguin Books 1991).

Tichy, N. (1999) The Teachable Point of View: A Primer, *Harvard Business Review*, March-April, 82–83.

Trades Union Congress (2002) *Focus on recognition: trade union trends survey 02/1*, London: TUC.

Trades Union Congress (2003) *Things have got better – labour market performance 1992–2002,* London: TUC.

Trist, E.L. and Bamforth, K.W. (1951) Some social psychological consequences of the longwall method of coal getting, *Human Relations*, 4, 3–38.

Turnbull, P. and Wass, V. (2000) 'Redundancy and the paradox of Job Insecurity', in Heery, E. and Salmon, J. (eds) *The Insecure Workforce*, London: Routledge.

Tushman, M.L. and Romanelli, E. (1985) Organizational evolution: A metamorphosis model of convergence and reorientation, *Research in Organizational Behavior*, 7, 171–222.

Wah, L. (1999) Diversity at Allstate, *Management Review*, July–August, 24–30.

Walby, S. (1986) *Patriarchy at Work*, Cambridge: Polity Press.

Walby, S. (1990) *Theorizing Patriarchy*, Oxford: Blackwell.

Walton, R.E. (1985) From Control to Commitment in the Workplace, *Harvard Business Review*, 85(2), 77–84.

Walton, R.E. (1987) *Innovating to Compete*, London: Jossey-Bass.

Watad, M.M. and DiSenzo, F.J. (2000) The Synergism of Telecommuting and Office Automation, *Sloan Management Review*, Winter, 85–96.

Waterman, R.H. Jr., Waterman, J.A. and Collard, B.A. (1994) Toward a Career-Resilient Workforce, *Harvard Business Review*, July–August, 87–95.

White, M. and Forth, J. (1998) *Pathways through unemployment: The effects of a flexible labour market*, York: Joseph Rowntree Foundation.

White, M. and Gallie, D. (1994) 'Employer Policies and Individual Life Chances', in Rubery, J. and Wilkinson, F. (eds) *Employer Strategy and the Labour Market*, Oxford: Oxford University Press.

White, M., Hill, S., McGovern, P., Mills, C. and Smeaton, D. (2003) 'High Performance' Management Practices, Working Hours and Work-Life Balance, *British Journal of Industrial Relations*, 41(2), 175–196.

Wiener, M.J. (1981) *English Culture and the Decline of the Industrial Spirit, 1850–1980*, Cambridge: Cambridge University Press.

Wiener, N. (1954) *The Human Use of Human Beings*, New York: Doubleday.

Womack, J.P. and Jones, D.T. (1994) From lean production to the lean enterprise, *Harvard Business Review*, 72, March–April, 93–105.

Wood, S. (1999a) Family-Friendly Management: Testing the Various Perspectives, *National Institute Economic Review*, No. 168, 99–116.

Wood, S. (1999b) Human resource management and performance, *International Journal of Management Reviews*, 1, 367–413.

Wood, S. and de Menezes, L. (1998) High commitment management in the UK: evidence from the Workplace Industrial Relations Survey and Employers' Manpower and Skills Practices Survey, *Human Relations*, 51, 485–515.

Wood, S., de Menezes, L.M. and Lasaosa, A. (2003) Family-Friendly Management in Great Britain: Testing Various Perspectives, *Industrial Relations*, 42(2), 221–250.

Wood, S. and Moore, S. (2002) In the line of fire, *People Management*, 27 June, 36–39.

Woodward, J. (1965) *Industrial Organization: Theory and Practice*, London: Oxford University Press.

Worrall, L. and Cooper, C. (2001) *The Quality of Working Life: 2000 survey of managers' changing experiences*, London: The Institute of Management.

Yeuk-Mui, M.T. (2001) Information technology in frontline service work organization, *Journal of Sociology*, 37(2), 177–206.

Yoffie, D.B. and Cusumano, M.A. (1999) Building a Company on Internet Time: Lessons from Netscape, *California Management Review*, 41(3), 8–28.

Zuboff, S. (1988) *In the Age of the Smart Machine: The Future of Work and Power*, New York: Basic Books.

Index

UNIVERSITIES AT MEDWAY LIBRARY